THE
WINE & FOOD
OF
BULGARIA

DON PHILPOTT

To the memory of Tim Bleach, a good friend
of Bulgarian wine, and one of the pioneers
largely responsible for its success in Britain.

THE
WINE & FOOD
OF
BULGARIA

DON PHILPOTT

The Wine and Food of Bulgaria

Edited and designed by
Mitchell Beazley International Ltd
Artists House, 14/15 Manette Street, London W1V 5LB

ISBN 0–85533–753–2

A CIP catalogue record for this book is available from the
British Library

Art Editor Kelly Flynn
Editor Alison Franks
Illustrations Madeleine David
Maps Diana Durant
Photographs David Harrison
Managing Editor Chris Foulkes

Typeset in Bembo by Litho Link Limited, Welshpool,
Powys, Wales
Origination by Scantrans Pte Ltd, Singapore
Produced by Mandarin Offset
Printed and bound in Hong Kong

The author and publishers are grateful for the assistance of
the Bulgarian Vintners Company which made possible the
publication of this book.

For further information on the wines of Bulgaria contact
the Bulgarian Vintners Company Limited, Nazdrave
House, 154 Caledonian Road, London N1 9RD
Telephone: 01 278 8047

CONTENTS

INTRODUCTION

To most people in the West Bulgaria is a mystery. Few know just where it is, what language is spoken, or even the currency used. Bulgaria is, however, one of the oldest countries in Europe with a history stretching back through many great civilizations. It is situated in the southeastern corner of the Balkan Peninsula. To the north it has a border with Romania, to the west with Yugoslavia, to the south with Greece and Turkey and to the east lies the Black Sea. The country has a population of nine million and is about four-fifths the size of England. Every

year it attracts a growing number of tourists and holiday makers. It is not just the white sandy beaches, clear seas and more than 300 days of sunshine a year that attracts the visitors, the interior of the country is breathtaking – with mountains and rugged gorges, valleys filled with roses and spectacular waterfalls. There is even superb skiing, at a fraction of the price of Alpine resorts. Although over two-thirds of the country is mountainous there are fertile plains, a flourishing agriculture and certainly some of the finest and most modern vineyards in the world.

While few people may have sampled the hot and spicy Bulgarian cuisine, an increasing number are getting to know a little about the country by drinking its wine. The red wines, using the classic Cabernet Sauvignon and Merlot grapes, challenge the classic names of France. Quality whites, especially the Chardonnays, are a match for many wines with a French, Californian or Australian label which command double the price. There are the quality wines made from local varieties such as Mavrud, Gamza, Dimiat and Melnik, the latter for many years a favourite of Sir Winston Churchill.

The success of Bulgarian wine exports has been phenomenal. In 1980, in their first year of trading with Britain, they sold a respectable 50,000 cases. By the end of 1988 exports to the UK had topped 1,600,000 cases and the spectacular growth shows no sign of slowing down.

Bulgarian Vintners have started their first television advertising in the UK. They have launched a range of impressive Reserve wines and started to expand their market into mainland Europe. This success is matched by growing sales in the United States, Canada, Scandinavia and the Far East as well as an enormous presence in the USSR, Poland and other East European countries. Bulgaria is one of the success stories of the modern wine world. This book sets out to explain how this has happened, and to provide the background on the wines, the regions and the cuisine which will enable wine-lovers to know Bulgaria better.

HISTORY AT A GLANCE

For thousands of years the territory that is now Bulgaria has been attacked, annexed or absorbed into some of the greatest civilizations of Central and Southern Europe. There are reminders of Bulgaria's earliest history throughout the country, including examples of relics, early settlements and cave drawings. During the Copper Age, communities were established in fortified settlements, gold and copper was used for jewellery and a culture developed similar to those of the proud civilizations of Ancient Egypt and Mesopotamia. Because the country stands at the crossroads of Europe and Asia it attracted settlers from scores of nations, as well as the less welcome incursions from the armies of neighbouring states.

Sofia, which was part of the ancient Kingdom of Thrace, was the site of one of the most prosperous settlements. The Thracians introduced agriculture on a large scale and this included development of the vineyards and wineries. In fact, grapes could have been grown in Bulgaria as long ago as 6,000 BC. The Greeks developed colonies along the Black Sea Coast and the Celtic tribe the Gaelatae established a kingdom in the second century BC which was destroyed when the country was overrun by the armies of the Roman Empire. The Romans introduced new cultures, crafts, roads and administration, but as the fortunes of Rome ebbed, the power of Constantinople increased and Bulgaria became absorbed into the Eastern Roman Empire, later to become Byzantium. Many famous names occur in Bulgarian history during classical times, including Spartacus the slave, Pericles of Athens, and even Homer, who mentioned the wines of ancient Thrace in his Iliad and Odyssey.

After Rome, Slavonic tribes started to establish themselves and the first seeds of the nation were sown. Despite oppression and domination, the Bulgarian people kindled a national spirit and this was to lead to the formation of the First Bulgarian State in AD 681. The state prospered for more than 200 years but continual warring with neighbouring countries, especially Byzantium, weakened and divided the nation and in 1018 the whole country fell under Byzantine rule. This domination lasted for 169 years until the Byzantines were beaten in battle and the Second Bulgarian State was established between 1187 and 1396. This time of independence, which saw the birth of the golden age of Bulgaria, was short lived, however, and the country fell under the yoke of the Turkish Ottoman Empire – an occupation that was to last for five centuries.

Although throughout its history Bulgaria has been the battleground for other nations' power struggles, the fierce independent spirit of the Bulgarian people has never been crushed. Many parts of the country were not united until this century and it was not until September 10 1944 that the Socialist State of Bulgaria came into being.

VISITING MODERN BULGARIA

Today Bulgaria is a prosperous country attracting more than six million visitors a year, a third of whom come to enjoy the famous beaches, spas and mountain resorts. The Black Sea has miles of unpolluted beaches and some of the safest bathing in Europe as it is very shallow. In many places is still only shoulder height 137 metres (150 yards) offshore. Many of the beaches are six to eight kilometres (four to five miles) long, there are no tides and the water has only half the salt content of the Mediterranean. Some of the most famous beaches include Albena, Golden Sands, Drouzhba and Sunny Beach.

Albena was named after a famous Bulgarian beauty and is the country's youngest resort. It boasts some striking modern architecture and the spectacular beach is bordered by forests. The summer temperature averages 26°C (80°F). Golden Sands, 15 kilometres (nine miles) north of Varna, is the country's second largest resort. It is a careful blend of modern architecture and natural scenery with a breathtaking beach almost five kilometres (three miles) long and up to 92 metres (100 yards) wide. Sports vary from scuba diving to parascending, from basketball to horse riding. Drouzhba, known as the oasis of peace and quiet, is set in parkland and surrounded on one side by oak, beech and pines and on the other by small sandy coves and rock pools to explore. It is in striking contrast to Sunny Beach, the country's largest resort and a purpose built holiday city on a nine kilometres (six miles) long beach. You can relax on the sands all day, play sports or enjoy one of the many international music festivals Sunny Beach is famous for. And, at night you can dine out at a traditional restaurant and watch a floor show of local folk music and folk-lore.

Temperatures around the country can vary enormously and the Balkan Mountains which divide the country into the north and south have a major impact on the climate. Sunshine is high, averaging more than 300 days a year, but humidity is low. Between May and October air temperatures on the Black Sea Coast hardly ever fall below 21°C (70°F), while the sea temperature rises from 16°C (60°F) in May to 23°C (75°F) in August. Maximum temperatures along the Black Sea coast average 28°C (83°F) during July and August, but it can get very much hotter. During the summer of 1988 temperatures over 38°C (100°F) were recorded on many successive days, and in Sofia temperatures soared to more than 46°C (115°F). While the sea air is invigorating and healthy, you can really relax and become fit again by visiting one of the country's many spas. There are 600 natural springs around Bulgaria, many of them on the Black Sea Coast or high in the mountains.

FOOD AND DRINK

Bulgarian cuisine is built around natural, healthy foods but can be hot and spicy like the people. There is a flourishing agriculture in Bulgaria providing all the country's major needs, with vineyards and wineries to cater for the home market and fast growing export demand. Because of its climate, Bulgaria is able to produce a wide range of foodstuffs, with plenty of fresh vegetables, grain, fruit, milk and dairy products, as well as meat, poultry and game. The cuisine, which is based on home cooking, has been refined to high standards in some restaurants and hotels. It has evolved over the centuries and changes with the seasons as supplies of fresh produce vary. Spring dishes feature lamb and young chickens, spinach and young vegetables but as the seasons move through to autumn, the ingredients change accordingly, using fruits, root crops and game.

The most characteristic dishes of the Bulgarian national cuisine are soups, stews, various types of roast and grilled meats, kebapches (rissoles), and banitsa (a sort of cheese pastry). Much of this meat is stuffed and there is a great reliance on aubergines and peppers. Kepapcheta (strongly spiced meat balls) is a national favourite. The local sort of yoghurt is excellent, and was actually invented in Bulgaria. There are marvellous rich desserts in syrup, stewed dried fruit and a special version of Bulgarian rice pudding. There is also a delicious white Bulgarian cheese which is one of the main ingredients of the Shopska salad, one of the most popular starters on the local menus.

The wines of Bulgaria are now exported to more than 70 countries worldwide. Vine growing has always figured in the country's history and excavations near the town of Nova Zagora have unearthed grape seeds and berries which establish that wine was being produced by Thracian settlements in the area during the sixth to third millenia BC. Even when under the domination of Turkey, Bulgaria's wine production continued although many of the vineyards were destroyed. Today Bulgaria produces more than 400 million litres of wine a year with 55 per cent of production white and 45 per cent red. It is one of the world's leading exporters of wine and is the world's sixteenth largest producer.

The climate is ideal for vine growing and throughout the country there are more than 130 wineries in five major wine growing regions. The special characteristics of each region help produce distinctive and distinguished wines. In the northern regions for example, between the Danube and the Balkan Mountains, grey forest soils produce rich vineyards where Cabernet Sauvignon and Gamza reign supreme among the reds, and Riesling, Chardonnay and Sauvignon Blanc produce delicious whites. All the wines are characterized by their fruitiness, pronounced bouquet and strength of character. To the south, in the valleys between the mountains, the fertile dark black soils produce enticing Mavrud and Merlot wines, full bodied but soft and velvety.

Viticulture and viniculture have been transformed in the last 40 years and enormous strides in the last decade have been putting Bulgaria fairly and squarely alongside the world's best producers. Bulgarian spirits, especially brandies, have also made tremendous progress in the last few years. Many of the finer brandies are now matured for 12 or even 17 years in casks. Spirits include the famous Rose liqueur, distilled from the petals of roses which for more than 300 years have been one of the country's most important assets. Apart from the liqueur, the oil yielding varieties of rose are grown for the perfume industry. Liqueurs are also made from peaches and cherries that are grown in the orchards that flourish almost everywhere, and soft fruits, such as strawberries, are also used to make delicious liqueurs.

TOURIST TIPS The currency of the country is the Lev. Western visitors get a special currency bonus which effectively increases their spending money by around 50 per cent. Check with a Bulgarian travel office or your travel agent. In large hotels and restaurants most of the staff speak English but away from the cities it is advisable to carry a Bulgarian phrase book. Bulgarian Tourist Offices will supply one free. Remember, however, that in Bulgaria a shake of the head means "yes", while a nod means "no". There are duty free shops in most towns and resorts called Corecom stores and they carry a wide range of imported goods, perfumes, leather, wines and Bulgarian handicrafts. There are also souvenir shops selling local crafts such as pottery, leather and carved wood.

For those who want a rather less formal holiday than a resort hotel, there are more than 120 camp sites throughout the country, or a range of villas, apartments and even the chance to stay with a Bulgarian family in their own home to sample the real feel of the country and its people. Hiring a car is simple and gives you the freedom to see those parts of the country that the tourist on an organized tour never visits. Split the visit to take in the beach and the cities. Sofia has more than 7,000 years of history and more than 250 officially designated places of special historic and architectural interest. Plovdiv, Bulgaria's second city, can trace its history back 8,000 years, and is a remarkable blend of ancient and modern. There are many specialist holidays for those interested in such activities as angling, birdwatching, walking and art.

GEOGRAPHY

Bulgaria covers 110,912 square kilometres (42,823 square miles) and occupies a position in the eastern part of the Balkan Peninsula, covering the northwest approaches to the meeting point of Europe and Asia Minor. The country has land frontiers with four European states – Romania in the north, Yugoslavia in the west, and Greece and Turkey in the south. The Balkan Mountains (formerly called the Hemus Mountain range) run east to west and split the country in half. The plain to the

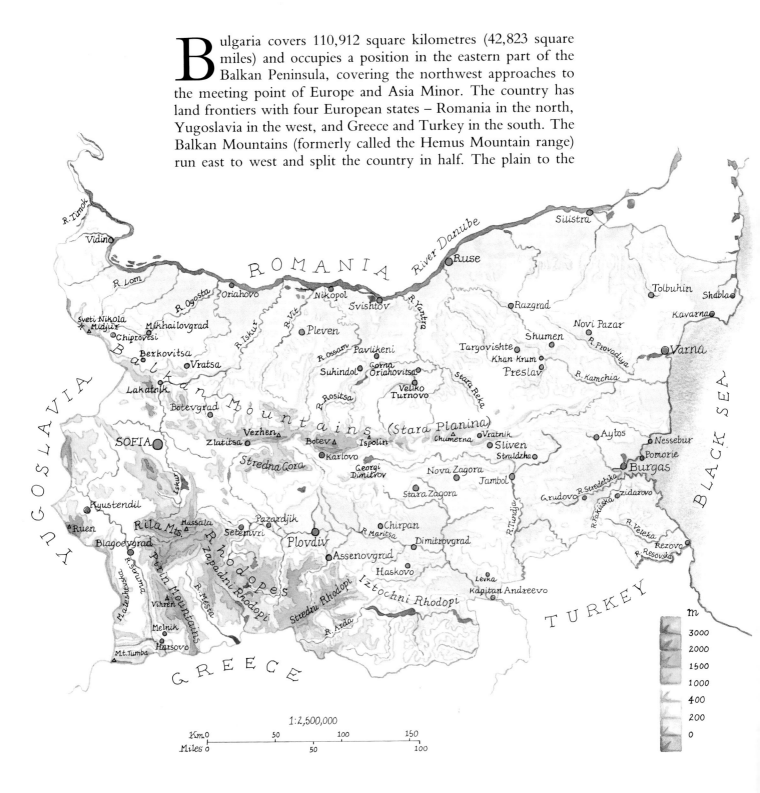

1:2,500,000

| Km 0 | 50 | 100 | 150 |
| Miles 0 | 50 | 100 | |

m
3000
2000
1500
1000
400
200
0

north stretches to the River Danube, while the southern half of the country is more mountainous although it contains many fertile areas, including the Thracian Plain and the beautiful Valley of Roses.

The country is 330 kilometres (205 miles) from north to south and 520 kilometres (323 miles) from east to west. The northern border with Romania runs for 609 kilometres (377 miles) and follows the River Danube from the mouth of the River Timok to the town of Silistra in the east, before crossing the Dobrudja lowlands to the Black Sea at the Romanian town of Vama Veke. The 378 kilometre (233 mile) Black Sea coast runs from Vama Veke in the north to the mouth of the River Rezovska in the south. In the south the border with Turkey and then Greece runs for 752 kilometres (467 miles) from the River Rezovska to Mount Tumba in the Belassitsa Mountains where the frontiers of Bulgaria, Greece and Yugoslavia meet. The western border with Yugoslavia runs for 306 kilometres (189 miles), at first through mountainous country, before crossing the western Balkan range and then following the River Timok to the Danube.

More than two-thirds of the country is less than 600 metres (1,920 feet) above sea level, but the altitude increases to the west and southwest. The lowlands occupy about 32 per cent of the total area, the plains and hilly uplands about 41 per cent and the mountains about 28 per cent. The country can be divided into four regions, each one corresponding with a period in the geology construction of the eastern Balkans. These regions are: the Danubian Hilly Plain, the Balkan Range, the Transition-Mountain-Depression Region and the Rila-Rhodope Massif.

The Danubian Hilly Plain is the most northerly region, an area covered by almost horizontal Mesozoic and Tertiary sediments. In the south the plain is bordered by mountains in the Balkan Range and runs for about 500 kilometres (310 miles) from the Black Sea to the River Timok in the west. The plain widens from about 20 kilometres (12 miles) in the west to 120 kilometres (74 miles) east of the Dobrudja, covers an area of 31,522 square kilometres (12,170 square miles) and has an average altitude of 178 metres (569 feet). The western part of the plain, between the Timok and Vit rivers, rarely rises above 200 metres (640 feet). These fertile lowlands are crossed by many rivers flowing into the Danube. In the eastern part of the plain, the hills rise to 500 metres (1,600 feet) and the rivers have cut deep canyons in the plateau which falls gently as it approaches the Black Sea. There is a narrow strip of land along the Danube which for centuries was a marshy floodplain. Most of this area between the River Timok and Silistra has been drained and is a very fertile agricultural region, including vineyards.

The Balkan Range, or Stara Planina, is the longest mountain range in Bulgaria. It was known to the Greeks as Hemus and got its Turkish name in the nineteenth century with the Balkan Peninsula named after it. Again, rivers criss-cross the region running through deep and narrow gorges, although the tributaries coming in at right angles tend to have wide, sloping valleys. There are many caves and chasms which have been carved into the limestone and cold springs bubble from the rocks. The western part of the Balkan Range is dominated by peaks such as Sveti Nikola (1,721 metres/5,507 feet) and Chiprovtsi-Berkovitsa, with its Midjur Peak towering to 2,168 metres (6,937 feet). The Iskur Gorge at Lakatnik is a beautiful natural phenomenon, and north of it is the deep and fertile valley of Botevgrad. The northern slopes of the western Balkan Range are very steep, while the southern slopes are more gentle, descending in steps to the Sofia Plain.

The middle Balkan Range contains the highest peaks between the Zlatitsa and Vratnik Passes – Vezhen (2,198 metres/7,033 feet), Botev (2,376 metres/7,603 feet), Ispolin (1,524 metres/4,876 feet) and Chumerna (1,536 metres/4,915 feet). The southern slopes of the mountains are very steep while the northern slopes are gentler and cut into deep depressions by the many rivers running north. The eastern part of the Balkan Range is the widest and runs to the Black Sea, ending in towering cliffs near the cape of Sveti Atanas. The hills gradually decline in altitude to the south running into the Transition-Mountain-Depression region, in the west are many spectacular peaks. Faults throughout the region have created depressions and valleys, one is the famed Valley of Roses, where three-quarters of the attar-yielding roses in Bulgaria are grown.

The Upper Thracian lowlands is the largest plain in Bulgaria and throughout the Balkans. It consists of many very fertile alluvial plains, and to the south is the Sakar Mountain with its stepped, southern slopes and vineyards.

The final region is the Rila–Rhodope Massif. In the west the mountains rise to 2,251 metres (7,203 feet) with Ruen being the tallest peak. The Rila–Pirin area has the highest peaks in Bulgaria – Mussala 2,925 metres (9,360 feet) and Vihren 2,915 metres (9,328 feet). One could be forgiven when looking at Rila for thinking it was a Swiss mountain, it is so Alpine in shape and supports a flourishing ski industry. Peaks in the Rhodopes area rise to 2,168 metres (6,937 feet) and many of the mountain ridges are above 1,500 metres (4,800 feet) overshadowing deep river valleys. There are a number of unusual natural rock formations here including the Devil's Bridge on the Arda River and the Trigrad gorge.

The Black Sea coastline is rocky with many bays and capes, but there are fine sandy beaches and at Nessebur the sand dunes are 20 metres (64 feet) high.

The magnificent entrance to the 10th century monastery at Rila which lies sheltered beneath the mountains. Destroyed in the late 18th century, it was later restored in the early 19th century and represents one of the most important monuments in Bulgaria.

WILDLIFE Because of Bulgaria's position, it has an extremely varied fauna attracting species from Europe, Asia and the Mediterranean. Because the Ice Age did not affect many parts of the country, animals from northern Europe, driven south by the ice, survived here, and met animals from southwest Asia able to penetrate Europe across the Balkan land bridge.

Officially Bulgaria boasts 92 species of mammals, 337 species of birds, 35 species of reptile, 16 species of amphibian, 177 species of fish and 30,000 species of insect.

Many insects and butterflies are relict animals, survivors of the cold spells during the Quaternary Period, or dating back to the Tertiary Period. Holarctic species, from the northern temperate regions and Arctic, include red deer, wolf, mallard, common raven and common tern, while the Palaearctic species include fox, marten, yellow necked mouse, sparrowhawk, greater spotted woodpecker, skylark and common toad.

There are six types of fauna. Euro-Siberian accounts for more than half of Bulgaria's fauna and covers virtually all the country, except some areas in the far south. These are cold-climate species, and Bulgaria marks the most southerly distribution limit for almost all. Species include capercaillie, nutcracker, coal tit, bank vole, and in the high meadows, common lizard, adder and wall creeper. In open country the Orkney vole, water vole, partridge and grass snake can be found and in the woods the red squirrel. Although now regarded as Euro-Siberian fauna there are species like the pine marten, the edible or squirrel-tailed dormouse, crested tit, fire-bellied toad and crested newt, which originated in the western zone of the central European fauna.

Arctic-Alpine and Boreal Alpine: there are about 60 arctic-alpine species in Bulgaria, of which 90 per cent are insects, mostly butterflies and beetles living in the Alpine meadows, or woods over 2,400 metres (7,680 feet).

Steppe fauna: this classification of fauna is really restricted to the Dobrudja area, the country's only primary steppe. Found here is the great bustard, little bustard, polecat, hamster and a wide range of steppe insects. The bustards are threatened with extinction because of human activity.

Pontic fauna is found in the easternmost part of the country in the sea, lakes, river estuaries and swamps. Although mostly worms, snails, mussels and crustaceans, there are a number of fish species including the sturgeon, herring and gobies. Land species include the red necked pheasant, pygmy cormorant, Levant sparrow hawk and grass snake.

Mediterranean fauna covers a large list including black-eared wheatear, sub-Alpine warbler and many other birds, insects and spiders. Typical of the eastern Mediterranean species are the olive tree warbler, masked shrike, and rock nuthatch.

Sub-Mediterranean fauna are found in the south, along the Black Sea and up to altitudes of about 500 metres (1,600 feet). It consists of many species, including bats and birds.

Many of the birds in Bulgaria are migratory including ducks, geese, cranes and even rooks which summer on the Scandinavian tundra and winter in Bulgaria. Woodcock and great bustards are partial migrants and many other species overfly Bulgaria, especially waders and seabirds on their way to breeding grounds further north. Storks, golden orioles, bee eaters, rollers, nightingales and cuckoos all winter in Africa and summer in Bulgaria, and even pelicans, cranes and west African songbirds can be spotted.

The bear, wolf, jackal, wild goat, raven, bustard, most vultures and eagles have all been severely depleted by human activity, including hunting. Many species are now protected by law, and national parks and reserves have been created.

CLIMATE Bulgaria has a complex climate, influenced not only by the mountainous nature of the country but by weather systems on three continents. Generally, the climate is temperate with continental influences, therefore it has warm summers and cold winters, with substantial snowfalls in many areas. At different times of the year, climatic conditions coming from the Atlantic Ocean, Western and Central Europe, Asia Minor, the Mediterranean, Northern Africa and the Arctic Ocean can all play a part in determining the weather in Bulgaria.

The influence of the Black Sea is felt all year round and accounts for 45 per cent of all air currents flowing into the country, but the direct influence is only felt in eastern Bulgaria because the mountains block passage further west. The mountains also block much of the weather coming in from the Atlantic allowing continental masses to develop over the Balkans. The movement of air over the country is affected mostly by Icelandic low pressure systems which have an influence throughout the year and the Mediterranean low pressure systems, which are only a relevant factor during the winter months. These two systems, however, account for the constant movement of humid air currents towards Bulgaria and the changeability in weather.

Whenever the Mediterranean depressions move northeast and reach the Danube lowlands, a southwesterly air current is formed over the country. When the southerly winds reach the Balkan Mountains a foehn (hot dry wind) is created, sweeping down the mountain valleys. These foehns are particularly strong to the north of the Balkan Mountains and Danubian Plains, also occurring in the Sofia Valley, especially on the northern sides of the Vitosha and Lyulin Mountains. These winds can reach speeds well in excess of 100 kilometres an hour (62mph) and when they come into contact with cyclonic activity and cold fronts, violent storms occur. The Mediterranean cyclones which pass over Bulgaria bring heavy snowfalls in winter and rain at other times of the year. In the spring there can be torrential rains accompanied by thunder and hail. From the spring, cyclones penetrate northwards into the Black Sea and this also leads to very heavy rainfalls. On August 21 1951 more than 330 millimetres (13 inches) of rain fell in the 24 hour period because of this sort of cyclonic condition.

Rain falls throughout the year, with the north and central parts of the country driest in February and wettest in June, while the southern parts of the country and the southern sections of the Black Sea Coast are driest in August and wettest in November or December. The northern Black Sea Coast and western parts of the Upper Thracian Valley get the least rainfall and the northern foothills of the Balkan Range get most. The snow cover stays from about ten days on the Black Sea Coast to more than 200 days in the high mountains. In the lowlands, snowfalls can occur between October and mid-May, although regular snowfalls can be expected between December and March in the north. Hail can be expected any time between May and August but is most frequent and harmful to the vines and grapes in June and early July. Fog is a problem, especially during the winter months.

Much of Bulgaria is hilly or mountainous, and this has an enormous influence on local weather conditions. While the mountains influence the weather of the whole country, scores of different micro-climates can be found in their valleys. The Balkan Range which divides the country has a major influence, preventing cold air from the north penetrating into southern Bulgaria and stopping hot air from the south reaching the Danube plains.

The average temperature in the south is up to one degree centigrade higher than in the north of the country, while average rainfall in the north is higher than in the south. The average monthly temperature for the hottest month is between 20.1 and 24.4°C (69-76°F), although temperatures of over 35°C (95°F) have been recorded on a number of successive days during freak hot weather blowing in from the Sahara. During the year there is between 2,000 and 2,400 hours of sunshine in non-mountainous areas, with least in December and most in July. The average annual air temperature for the whole country is 10.5°C (50°F), but it averages 12°C (54°F) on the Danube and Thracian Plains, and 14°C (58°F) along the Black Sea coast and southernmost regions. There can be vast ranges between winter and summer temperatures. In Vidin the average January temperature is −1.6°C (30°F) and 23°C (74°F) in July. Inland temperatures in the spring are

higher than those along the coast, but colder during the autumn. The highest temperature ever recorded in Bulgaria was 45.2°C (113°F) in Sadovo in July 1916, the lowest was in 1947 in Trun when it fell to −38.3°C (−36.4°F).

The Black Sea and the mountain climates favour leisure and sporting activities, while most regions of the country have areas suitable for the cultivation of vines. In the southern parts of the country there is plant growth for about seven and a half months of the year, but for only six and a half months in the northern areas.

VEGETATION

Because of Bulgaria's diverse climatic conditions there are many different types of vegetation to be found and more than 3,500 plants have been catalogued. The most common trees are willow, white poplar, aspen, birch, white pine, fir and spruce.

In the south, Mediterranean species can be found and there are a number of species endemic to Bulgaria. Because this part of the eastern Balkans was not as badly affected by the Ice Age as central and northern Europe, there are still many plants which can be traced directly back to the Tertiary period.

The various vegetation belts are:

The Alpine Belt, 2,300 metres (7,360 feet) above sea level, consists mainly of herbaceous plants, low shrubs and bushes. There are also many rock plants. There are also many lichens and you can find edelweiss.

The Sub-Alpine Belt covers the area between 2,200 and 2,300 metres (7,040-7,360 feet) above sea level. Dwarf pines cover large areas, as do shrubs, blueberries and rhododendrons. In the past, many of the shrub dwarf pines were cut down for fuel or to make charcoal, or just to clear the alpine pastures, and these have been replaced by *Juniperus sibrica* and other Vaccinium species.

The Coniferous forest belt lies between 1,300 and 2,200 metres (4,160-7,040 feet). Pines predominate but where these have been cleared, birch, aspen and dwarf pine have emerged, together with shrubs and herbaceous plants. Large areas of this belt have been cleared for arable land and are used to grow potatoes, flax, oats and other crops.

The Beech forest belt lies at 1,000-1,700 metres (3,200-5,440 feet). These beech forests with their undergrowths of evergreens still predominate, although fir stands and mixed forests can be found, usually in rocky valleys. Again, much of this belt has been cleared for farming where potatoes form the main crop, followed by oats, flax and cereals.

The Hornbeam and Oak forest belt covers the land between 500-700 metres (1,600-2,240 feet) and 1,000-1,200 metres (3,200-3,840 feet). The original vegetation was deciduous forest. In

Strandja and the eastern Balkan Mountains there are still stands of oriental beech, the only place they are found naturally in Europe. It is further evidence that Bulgaria's vegetation survived the Ice Age. Much of the undergrowth consists of rhododendrons, laurel, ivy and vaccinium. In the Preslav there are still woods containing horse chestnuts, the only place in the Balkans where they are still found. They are unique in Europe because they have been growing there undisturbed since the Tertiary period. Much of this belt has been influenced by human activity: trees have been felled for housing, fuel and to clear the land for farming.

The Oak Belt, between 500 and 700 metres (1,600-2,240 feet) above sea level covers most of the hilly regions throughout the country but much of the original vegetation has been destroyed and replaced by crops such as vines, cereals, orchards and, in the south, tobacco.

Mediterranean vegetation can be found in the south of the country, along the Black Sea Coast, the Upper Thracian lowland and some of the river valleys. In most areas it has replaced the original forests which had been destroyed. Evergreen shrubs such as quercus, juniper and phyllirea can be found.

GEOLOGY AND SOILS

Bulgaria's plains, hills and mountains are a result of intense geological activity, mainly during the Mesozoic and Cenozoic eras. The whole of the Balkans area was affected as the earth's massive plates to the east, west and north moved against each other. The Balkan Range is part of the extensive line of mountains stretching from Europe into Asia, from the Alps to the Himalayas. The region, especially the Thracian Central Massif, contains many rifts which are still moving today, in particular, the rift zones of Kraishtides and the Vardar which trap the Dardan Massif between them.

The Thracian Central Massif includes the Rhodope Massif, incorporting Sredna Gora, the Strandja Mountains and the Pelagonic-Thessalian Cyclade. The Rhodope Massif is mainly formed from old metamorphic rock, and has suffered enormous erosion over many geological eras. The Stredna Gora region resulted from this erosion which led to huge ruptures in the earth's crust: magma flowed out, accumulated and formed the mountains.

The Moesian Platform extends in the east along the south of the Danube to the Black Sea. It is a stable lithospheric plate of Pre-Cambrian consolidation. The metamorphic rocks are covered by bands of shale and marine sediment up to 12 kilometres (seven miles) deep in places, and a number of carbonate layers laid down since the Middle Upper Devonian period.

The Stara Planina region is composed of mainly sedimentary

rocks containing deep faults, in places several kilometres wide. There are granite outcrops, and one such is the Botev Peak, the highest point in the Stara Planina.

The Southern Carpathians, in the northwest of Bulgaria, are formed of Cretaceous and Upper Cretaceous sediments, and the Kraishtides zone, which occupies much of the southwest, is a typical rift region, with a very complex series of rock blocks.

SOIL   There are many different types of soil in Bulgaria and this is one reason which helps to explain the diversity of its wine. The soils themselves are, of course, generally dependent on the rock structure below and on the climate which affects the erosion and weathering of the soil.

There are three soil zones: the first is the forest-steppe zone which covers Northern Bulgaria around the Danube Plain and the Fore-Balkans. The average altitude is between 60 and 100 metres (192-320 feet) and the area has a temperate continental climate with forest steppe and forest vegetation. Most of the Danube Plain is composed of loess, or loamy deposits, while the southern part of the Plain and the Fore-Balkans consists of grey forest soil from Cretaceous and Quaternary deposits.

The second soil zone is southern Bulgaria which is covered by the Xerothermal zone. This is an area of plains and low hills rising to 700 metres (2,240 feet). There is a mixture between continental and Mediterranean climates and the vegetation is primarily forest shrub and meadow, with elements of Mediterranean flora in the south. The most common types of soil are cinnamonic forest soil and the smolnitas.

There is a sub-zone in the south, taking in part of the Struma river valley, south of the village of Krupnik in the Blagoevgrad district, part of the Mesta river valley, the Eastern Rhodopes, the Sakar Mountain, the Dervent Upland and the Strandja Mountain. The rocks here are very varied but the soils are rich and mainly alluvial and diluvial. The Strandja Mountain is the only place in Bulgaria where you can find yellow soil.

The third is the mountain zone, covering areas over 700 metres (2,240 feet). The vegetation is forest and meadows and the soils are generally brown forest and mountain meadow. The forest belt stretches throughout Bulgaria and includes the beech, coniferous and mixed forests between 800 and 2,000 metres (2,560-6,400 feet) above sea level. Here, there are mineral soils and brown forest soils.

The woodless, sub-Alpine belt, is found above the tree line, higher than 1,800-2,000 metres (5,760-6,400 feet). Mountain meadow soils, rich in organic matter, predominate.

The main soil types used for cultivating vines are:

The *chernozems* which cover almost all of the western and central Danube Plain, the Dobrudja Plateau and most of the Ludogoric Region. The soils, which have developed mostly on loess, have a highly stable, granular and crumbly texture, high water holding capacity and good water permeability. In texture terms they are described as sandy loams, loams and silty loams. The soils are slightly alkaline in calcareous and typical chernozems, and neutral or slightly acid in leached or degraded chernozems. The soils usually contain between 2.5 and 5 per cent humus, sufficient nitrogen, but only negligible amounts of phosphorous and potassium. The natural fertility of chernozems is high, and about 86 per cent of this soil is under cultivation, much of it to vineyards.

The *Smolnitzas* occur together with the cinnamonic forest soils in the valleys and low fields of central and southern Bulgaria, the Thracian Valley, the lowlands of the Tundja Hilly region, the Burgas Valley and some areas of southwest Bulgaria. They have been formed on the flat slopes of low elevations where there is insufficient surface water run–off, and under hydrophylic meadow and meadow swamp vegetation. They are heavy, colloid–rich soils with quite good water resistance, high water holding capacity and low aeration. They are loamy and have a humus content of about 6 per cent in non–cultivated soils, about half that when farmed. The soils range from slightly acid to slightly alkaline and have sufficient quantities of nitrogen and potassium, but are poor in phosphorus. They are very fertile and are used for growing a wide range of crops, including vines.

The *Cinnamonic* forest soils occur over 700–800 metres (2,240–2,560 feet) to the south of the Balkan Mountains in the Tundja Hilly region, around the Stredna Gora Mountains, in the Eastern Rhodopes, in the valleys of the Struma and Mesta rivers and around Sofia. The soils have developed in arid, or semi–arid sub–tropical to transitional continental climates under deciduous forests, mainly of oak and hornbeam. The soils are crumbly, have low water permeability and poor aeration. They are heavy textured and hard to cultivate. They have a humus content which can reach 9 per cent, but averages about 6 per cent and ranges from slightly acid, through neutral to slightly alkaline. They contain very small amounts of nitrogen, moderate amounts of phosphorus and large amounts of potassium so fertility is not high. Before irrigation they are suitable for growing vines and when irrigated are used for orchards, cereals and cotton.

The *brown forest* soils occur between 800 and 2,000 metres (2,560–6,400 feet). They have developed in a temperate climate with plentiful rainfall under beech, mixed and coniferous forests.

The soils have low water holding capacity, high water permeability and good aeration. The soil is acid, has a humus content of up to 7 per cent, low nitrogen, potassium and phosphorus. The soils have low fertility and are used for growing potatoes, rye and soft fruit.

The *dark-coloured forest* soils occur in the mountains and sub-Alpine zones between 1,600 and 2,200 metres (5,120-7,040 feet). They are under high mountain forest vegetation such as spruce, white fir, dwarf pine and beech. The soils are peaty and chernozem-like, sandy loam, with a high humus content up to 20 per cent and are acid. The soil is rich in nitrogen and is used to grow potatoes, soft fruits and currants.

The *meadow* soils are alluvial deposits. They are found on the floodplains and floodplain terraces. They occur in the Danube lowlands, the valleys of the Lom, Ogosta, Iskur, Vit, Yantra, Rositsa, Maritsa, Tundja and Struma. The soils are loose, do not form a crust, have low water holding capacity and high water permeability. They contain about 1.5 per cent humus but large concentrations of nutrients. They have high fertility and are used to grow a wide range of crops, especially vegetables.

The *rendzinas* owe their formation to calcareous rocks – limestone and marble in particular – and occur in small areas in northern Bulgaria, and near cinnamonic forest soils in southern Bulgaria. They are very crumbly because of their high humus content and high water permeability. The soil is neutral to alkaline, has significant levels of nitrogen and phosphorus and high levels of potassium. It is used for growing vines and stone fruits.

Neat rows of vines cover the rolling plains of the Russe region. This vineyard is near the village of Trastenik where both Cabernet wines (in the distance) and Muscat Ottonel vines (in the foreground) are grown.

HISTORY

Bulgaria has one of the richest histories of any European country and can trace it back a good deal further than most. The earliest evidence of man comes from as far back as the Old Stone Age, and flint implements and blades have been found around the Rhodope Mountain and in the north.

There are many more traces of man's activities stemming from the Middle Old Stone Age, from between 100,000 and 40,000 BC. Much of the history has been unearthed by exploring caves, particularly in the Devetashkja Cave in the Lovech district, the Bacho Kiro cave near the monastery at Dryanovo and the Samuilitsa 11 cave near the village of Kunino in the Vratsa area. Many other prehistoric sites have been excavated in northern Bulgaria. Caves have also yielded much evidence of settlements abounding during the Upper Old Stone Age, from about 40,000 to 10,000 BC. Many camps have been discovered on the slopes of the Balkan Range, in the valleys of the Iskur, Vit, Ossum and Yantra. It was at this time that man advanced spiritually and developed fetishes and rituals, as relics and drawings illustrate.

Throughout this period, there was considerable progress, especially in the shape of tools and the techniques used to make them, and these resemble the civilizations of the Mediterranean lands rather than other settlements in central and western Europe. This development continued during the Middle Stone Age between 10,000 and 7,000 BC. Tools and weapons were now made of stone, wood or bone. The New Stone Age (6,000 to 5,000 BC) and Copper Stone Age (4,000 to 3,000 BC) saw the emergence of agriculture and the rearing of animals. Tells, or habitation mounds, can be spotted in many areas, made up of different layers, each representing a new culture developing on the site of the old.

It was during the Copper Stone Age that ordered communities emerged. Many of the settlements were fortified, and gold and copper were used to produce jewellery and religious items. From sites excavated, it is clear that the people living in the lands that now form modern Bulgaria were among the most civilized in Europe at the time, with cultures similar to those of their contemporaries in Egypt and Mesopotamia.

The ethnic origins of the Bulgarian people have not been firmly established, but because of the advanced civilization many peoples were attracted to the region. Between 3,000 and 2,000 BC bronze was used for tools and weapons, and trading links were established with tribes in Asia Minor, along the Danube, the coast of the Black Sea and into Greece. At this time the Kingdom of Thrace extended as far north as modern-day Bulgaria, and it was Thracian craftsmen who taught their bronze making skills to the people of the eastern Balkans.

There were many Thracian tribes living in what is now Bulgaria and the capital Sofia is built on the site of one such settlement. Spartacus, the slave who led the greatest rebellion against the Romans, came from one such tribe. These tribes established permanent settlements and adopted agriculture, and many of the modern towns and cities of Bulgaria still stand on sites first cleared by Thracians 3,000 years ago. For example, during the first century BC the major town of the Thracians was Blizye, the present day town of Vize.

While the Thracians were developing settlements inland, the Greeks and tribes from Asia Minor were establishing city colonies along the Black Sea Coast. The most important were Apollonia (now Sozopol), Messambria (Nessebur), Odessos (Varna), Dionysopolis (Balchik), Bizone (Kavarna), Tomis (now the Romanian town of Constanta) and many others. Many of the Greek settlements were founded on the sites of much older Thracian towns, first as trading posts and then as city states and major cultural centres.

Separate inland Thracian settlements got together to form a state towards the end of the sixth century BC. The powerful Odrysae tribe founded the Odrysae Kingdom in the fifth century, which eventually extended as far north as the Danube. Although the kingdom continued to extend its boundaries, rivalry between the tribes prevented a totally united state with a central government. The first known ruler of the Odrysae Kingdom was Teres who ruled from about 480 to 440 BC. He was an accomplished statesman and forged friendly links with neighbouring nations, and his son Sitalkes (440-424 BC) continued this policy by marrying a Scythian princess. He signed a military pact with Pericles of Athens against the Macedonians and led a military campaign against their joint enemy. The power of the Odrysae Kingdom began to ebb and at the end of the fourth century BC it split into two. Despite a brief reunion, it split again into three parts in the middle of the third century.

This period was dominated by wars with neighbouring states, but at home farming, stock breeding, viticulture and mining were being developed, especially mining for gold. Excavation of Philippopolis has uncovered well built fortified cities, with grand tombs and much jewellery in gold and silver. The tombs also revealed some magnificent murals, now on the UNESCO list of the world's natural and cultural heritage. The Thracian civilization bridged those of the east and the west. The

language came from the Indo-European family, and hundreds of words from this time survive in modern Bulgaria.

Constant battling with Macedonia weakened the Thracian economy during the third and second centuries BC, and the country became prey to its neighbours. The Celtic Gaelatae tribe established a kingdom in the second century, but this was wiped out, and the Roman Empire gradually absorbed most of the land. Tribes in northern Bulgaria withstood the Roman legions for two centuries, but by 45 BC all the Thracian tribes to the south of the Danube had been conquered by the armies of Rome. The tribes of northern Bulgaria were incorporated into the new province of Moesia in AD 15.

Many Roman cities were built throughout Bulgaria – Serdica (Sofia), Philippopolis (Plovdiv), Augusta Trajana (Stara Zagora), Pautalia (Kyustendil), Ratiaria (the village of Archar), Oescus (near the village of Gigen), Nove (near Svishtov), Sexaginta Prista (Russe), Durostorum (Silistra), Montana (Mihailovgrad), Abritus (near the town of Razgrad), Marciamopolis (near Devnya), Nicopolis ad Istrum (near the village of Nikyup), and Nicopolis ad Nestrum (near the town of Gotse Delchev).

The Romans introduced ordered towns and a road network, and promoted their culture and religion. They also improved winemaking techniques. But by the middle of the third century AD the fortunes of Rome were ebbing, and the region was being attacked by barbarians from the north and east. A new province of Thrace was formed and became subject to its capital, Constantinople, later to become Byzantium, the heart of the Eastern Roman Empire.

In AD 378 the Roman legions were defeated by the Gothic tribes, and in AD 395 the Roman Empire was split into two and Thrace officially became part of the Eastern or Byzantine Empire. It was during this period that the seeds of modern Bulgaria were sown. The region was attracting wandering people from many lands, and for some time Slavic tribes had been establishing settlements around the fringes of Bulgaria to the north of the Danube. During the fifth and sixth centuries, they started making inroads into the country. The Byzantines reacted by building massive fortifications, but the raids grew more frequent and by the end of the sixth century, the Slavs had reached the Adriatic and the outskirts of Constantinople.

While the Byzantines were at war with the Persians in the seventh century, the Slavs used the chance to pour their people into the Balkans. There was mass colonization, the Slavs became the majority group and their political and cultural ways started to take over. A new type of Medieval European civilization was being created.

THE BIRTH OF THE FIRST BULGARIAN KINGDOM

The other important event during this period was the arrival of the Proto-Bulgarians, a people of Turkish origin. Although some had settled in Bulgaria in the third century, they were driven out during the Hun invasion. They allied themselves with the Byzantines against the Ostrogoths and made frequent forays into the Balkans, but in the wars of AD 567 the tribal union of the Proto-Bulgarians was defeated by the Western Turks. After a resistance campaign lasting more than 60 years, they finally won their freedom and established, under Khan Kubrat, the powerful military and tribal alliance known as Great Bulgaria. After his death in the mid seventh century, the tribes disbanded and some moved to the confluence of the Kam and Volga and formed the independent state of Bulgaria.

In AD 680 Khan Asparuh led his Proto-Bulgarians against the Byzantine armies and defeated them. He chased them back across the Danube and within a few months had taken all the north-eastern parts of the Balkan peninsula. He negotiated with the Slav tribes and founded Bulgaria.

The following year a joint force again beat the Byzantine armies, this time in Thrace and the empire became bound by treaty to pay annual tribute to Bulgaria. In AD 685 the Slav tribe in the Timok Valley was freed from the rule of the Avar Khagnate and it too joined the state of Bulgaria. While the state was a powerful political and military body, Bulgaria was the outpost of

Slavdom and in the front line of its continuing struggle with the Byzantines, Avars and Franks. Wars were waged with the Byzantines for centuries, but gradually Bulgaria extended its borders, incorporating more Slav tribes to the south and west.

Despite these bloody times, the state prospered, universal written laws were introduced and the steady Slavonization of the culture continued. However, Christianity was persecuted.

In AD 827 war broke out between Bulgaria and the Frankish Empire, the Bulgarians were victorious and Khan Omurtag celebrated by rebuilding the capital of Pliska which had been destroyed by the Byzantines. He built a massive palace and fortress on the river Ticha, near the present day village of Khan Krum in the Shumen district. In AD 837 Slav tribes in the south rose up against the Byzantines. Supported by Bulgaria, they were victorious, and so the tribes in the southwestern part of the peninsula also joined the Bulgarian Kingdom. In AD 863, after being defeated by the Byzantine army, Bulgaria adopted Christianity, heathen religions were abolished and temples destroyed. It took almost a year to baptise the nation, and the process sparked off a rebellion by boyars (noblemen) opposed to the conversion, which was cruelly suppressed.

This was a time of great learning in Bulgaria, coupled with military might. Bulgaria in the early ninth century stretched from the Adriatic to the Black Sea and the Aegean and covered most of the Balkan peninsula. Literature flourished, as did architecture and the arts, and this period is now known as the "Golden Age".

Throughout the ninth century hostilities continued with the Byzantines, and for a time with Hungary. In AD 971 the Bulgarian army was defeated and much of the country was overrun by the Byzantines. To the west of the Iskur, the Bulgarians successfully resisted the invasion, but after 40 years of war the Bulgarian armies were finally defeated and Bulgaria once again became part of the Byzantine Empire. This was a time of great oppression. Harsh taxes were imposed, the aristocracy was exiled, and much of the land was given to the church. Despite popular uprisings, the Byzantine rule lasted for 169 years. Byzantium however, was unable to stop attacks from Hungary, Normans from Italy and the First (1096) and Second (1147) Crusades.

THE BIRTH OF THE SECOND BULGARIAN KINGDOM

The Byzantine decline started in 1185 when a popular uprising was sparked off by the imposition of harsh taxes. It started in Turnovo and because the Byzantine armies had already suffered major defeats at the hands of the Hungarians, they quickly retreated. Ivan Asen was declared Tsar of Bulgaria and within two years Constantinople was forced to sue for a peace treaty, and the Second Bulgarian Kingdom was born.

Although often nearly brought to its knees by wars and internal struggles, Bulgaria always managed to survive, and by the middle of the twelfth century had emerged as one of the major political forces in eastern Europe, dominating the Balkans. The capital Turnovo was re-developed, many churches, fortresses and palaces built and during the reign of Tsar Ivan Asen II (1218-1241), the first Bulgarian coins were minted. Craft and trade flourished, as did literature and the arts. A year after his death, the country was overrun and devastated by the Tartars and obliged to pay taxes to their ruler Khan Batu. While civil war broke out at home, neighbouring states took advantage of the unrest to annexe parts of the country. There were repeated invasions by the Hungarians, Tartars and Byzantines and the peasants and nobility, who had joined forces to overthrow the Tsar, fell out and fought each other. The country divided into a number of feudal states and, unable to defend itself, it succumbed to the Tartars.

THE MEDIEVAL PERIOD

In 1300 a power struggle broke out in the Tartar court. Khan Nogay was killed and his son Chaka accompanied by Todor Svetoslav, the Bulgarian Tsar's son who had been a hostage in the Tartar court, fled to Bulgaria. Todor Svetoslav killed Chaka and siezed power. He managed to restore peace within the country, and then waged war with the Byzantines, winning back much of the country's lost territories. His son continued his work, but when he died unexpectedly in 1322, Bulgaria was plunged yet again into crisis. For a year the nobles fought among themselves and then they elected as Tsar the Despot of the Vidin Principality, Mihail Shishman, and thus the Shishman dynasty was created.

Although the culture and especially the art of the country continued to develop over this period, Bulgaria was under constant attack in the west from the Hungarians and Serbs, while the Ottoman Empire to the southeast (the Turkish successor to the Byzantines) was steadily growing more powerful. The latter part of the fourteenth century was dominated by constant attacks from the Turks. Sofia fell in 1382, and in 1393, after a heroic resistance, Turnovo was captured, the aristocracy slaughtered and the clergy and population driven into exile or sold as slaves.

Despite a Crusade led by King Sigismund of Hungary and backed by the Pope, the Turks defeated the Bulgarians and their allies from western Europe in 1396 at the Battle of Nikopol. The independent state of Bulgaria ceased to exist and it was absorbed into the Ottoman Empire.

The Bulgarian culture was crushed or forced underground, a

Turkish system of government and justice was imposed, and the people were deprived of all civil rights. Many of the young boys were taken away to be trained as fanatical Muslim soldiers. Heavy taxes crippled any hope of prosperity and prompted a number of uprisings all of which were savagely crushed. By the eighteenth century, however, feudal lords had taken much of the power away from the central Ottoman authorities, and the start of the nineteenth century saw a period of anarchy throughout the Balkan Ottoman lands. The Bulgarian people, although oppressed, managed to retain their national identity, keeping their language, traditions and religion, even if in secret.

THE BULGARIAN NATIONAL REVIVAL

The Bulgarian national revival can be traced back to the beginnings of the eighteenth century. It was a time when the country was slowly moving from the medieval to the modern, when capitalism was emerging, and with it a new middle class. It was they who fired the nationalist spirit and fostered the idea of a new independent state, free of Turkish rule. The struggle lasted until 1878 when the yoke of Ottoman domination was finally thrown off. Bulgarians today are very proud of this epic story.

It was the bourgeoisie who started manufacturing, utilizing raw materials such as minerals and wool. Clothes, leather goods,

The typically distinctive golden domes of a church near the village of Shipka.

handicrafts and wine were exported. The works of Bulgarian artists and craftsmen were in great demand in Istanbul and Europe. Companies were formed to make exporting more efficient and trading links were established as far afield as Britain and Russia. In 1834, the first woollen mill was opened. The merchants, artisans and farmers felt the Turkish oppression most because of taxes and forfeiture, and it was this emerging class which led the revolution. Bulgarian exiles enlisted in foreign armies to fight the Turks. The first political circles were formed, and printing centres were set up to publish books about the country's proud past and urging people to join the revolution.

Schools were set up to revive secular teaching, introduce literacy and to promote Bulgarian national consciousness. The first such school was opened in Gabrovo in 1835 with the first textbooks of the Bulgarian language and grammar. The first school for girls was opened in 1840 in Pleven and by 1856 there were 35 such schools. Students who had been taught abroad returned home to open more schools funded entirely by the Bulgarian people, and this process escalated after the Crimean War (1853-56). By 1878 there were more than 2,000 schools throughout the country and education was free. It led to an explosion of literary works written by people such as Petko Rachev Slaveikov, Lyuben Karavelov, Hristo Botev, Vassil Drumev, Dobri Voinikov and Ivan Vazov, all of whom are now remembered by Bulgarians for their contribution to the country's literary development.

This period was also a remarkable time for artists and craftsmen of all types, including builders and architects. Many fine buildings, bridges and houses survive to bear testament to this.

In 1860, after a 30-year struggle, the Bulgarians succeeded in re-establishing their own independent church, which until then had been under the domination of the Greek Bishops, but it took a further 10 years for the Turkish government to accept this.

Bulgaria had established friendly relations with Russia and other neighbouring states but none offered help during the many uprisings of the mid-nineteenth century. While there was popular support for Bulgaria in Russia, Tsar Nikolai I refused to back the uprisings, in case the success of a revolution might start his own people thinking.

After the Crimean War the country's industrial growth continued, capitalism spread and the middle class were able to consolidate their power. The declining Ottoman Empire tried to squeeze even more taxes from the Bulgarian nation, and this hardened its resolve to achieve independence. The idea of a national uprising was the inspiration of Georgi Stoikov Rakovski. Armed groups were trained outside the country. The First Bulgarian Legion was established in Serbia in 1862 and, in the same year, Rakovski declared a Provisional Bulgarian Administration with him as its head. Between 1867-68, the Second Bulgarian Legion, which had been founded in Belgrade, crossed into Bulgaria to organize the uprising and establish a provisional government. After many battles, the Legion was wiped out but its actions had succeeded in focusing European attention on Bulgaria.

In 1869 a joint revolutionary organization was set up, one section outside the country and one operating secretly inside through a network of committees. The revolutionary committee in exile operated from Bucharest, while inside Bulgaria hundreds of revolutionary committees were established in towns and villages. In 1870, under Vassil Levski, the Bulgarian Central Committee was convened in Bucharest but uprisings in 1875 and 1876 were uncoordinated and quickly and brutally suppressed by the Turks (an event known to history as "The Bulgarian Atrocities"). A new revolutionary committee was set up in Bucharest, the Bulgarian Central Charity Society, this time with the open support of Russia, and the tacit support of many other European nations.

When Russia declared war on the Ottoman Empire on April 12 1877, thousands of Bulgarians enlisted and were in the army which crossed the Danube on June 15. The southern offensive was launched on January 1 1878 and within weeks the road to Constantinople was clear and the Turks sued for peace. The Treaty of San Stafano, signed on February 19 1878, created a new enlarged Bulgaria, and immediately the other major European powers objected, fearing that Russian influence in the Balkans had grown to a point where the balance of power was threatened. On June 1 1878 these powers convened the Berlin Congress and dismembered Bulgaria. Only that part of the country north of the Balkan Range was allowed to call itself Bulgaria, the eastern part of the country and lands to the south reverted back to being an autonomous province of the Ottoman Empire, while Romania and Serbia also shared in the spoils.

The new independent Bulgaria immediately set about ousting all traces of the Turks. New political and legal measures were introduced, elected local government was established as well as city councils, and there was a major land reform. The land was returned to the peasants, and the huge farms, vineyards and estates split up. The Bulgarian Army was formed and an officer's college established in Sofia in 1879. The first Bulgarian parliament, the Constituent National Assembly, met in Turnovo on February 10 1879 and adopted the country's first constitution on April 16 1879. A few days earlier, the Great National Assembly had elected as Bulgaria's new leader, the Kynaz, the Prussian Prince Alexander Battenberg, a nephew of the Russian Tsarina. He assumed power on June 25 1879 and on the same day all Russian troops garrisoned on Bulgarian territory were recalled. For a time the Prince tried to ignore the Constitution, but the Liberal Party, which had enormous public support, forced him to abide by it.

Under the Berlin agreement, Eastern Rumelia had been returned to the Ottoman Empire although it was run by Bulgarians and was virtually autonomous. In 1885 the secret Bulgarian Central Revolutionary Committee was set up in Plovdiv to plan an uprising leading to its re-unification. The people rose in September, met no resistance, and Bulgarian troops entered Eastern Rumelia. Neighbouring states, including Russia, argued that the balance of power had been disturbed, and once again, Serbia declared war on Bulgaria. Serbia, backed by the Austro-Hungarian Empire, was crushingly defeated, and at the Bucharest peace treaty in February 1886, the unification of Eastern Rumelia with Bulgaria was internationally accepted. The union wrested back from the Turks most of the land they had held in southern Bulgaria.

In 1886 a coup by senior army officers forced Prince Alexander to abdicate and flee the country. The coup lacked popular support, and although the Prince returned, he had lost the backing of Russia and a new leader was sought. On June 25 1887 the Prussian Prince Ferdinand of Saxe-Coburg-Gotha was elected as Ferdinand, Prince of Bulgaria, and stability was restored. During his 30-year rule more than 80 new factories were opened, foreign trade was expanded and new companies formed. New roads, railways and ports were built. There was large scale construction in Sofia and other leading towns and cities, and the first university was opened in Sofia in 1888.

The country was run by a rich ruling class, taxes were high and any unrest was quickly stamped out by the police. Conditions got so bad that in 1901 Ferdinand abolished the government and took direct control. It was during this period that the first trade unions were formed. Between 1894 and 1900 more than 70 were established and in the countryside the agrarian movement also became an important force, eventually becoming a political party, the Bulgarian Agrarian Union. While agriculture prospered, industry was fragmented and backward. From this period Dimiter Blagoev is remembered as the founder of socialism. The revolutionary Marxist Bulgarian Workers Social Democratic Party (BWSDP), led by Blagoev, started to recruit among the workers.

The People's Liberal Party, which supported the Prince, was asked to form the government in 1903 and it immediately restricted the right to strike, introduced child labour and raised taxes. It was so unpopular that in 1907 the Prime Minister, Dimiter Petkov, was shot in the street. In the general elections in

1913, the revolutionary BWSDP won 18 seats in the National Assembly having made big gains in the municipal elections.

During this time, Bulgarians in Macedonia and the Adrianople region were still under Ottoman rule. In 1903, on July 23, the people of Macedonia revolted, and on August 6 there was an uprising in the Adrianople region. Their campaign for independence raged for years, becoming embroiled in the Balkan Wars and then the First World War. The Bulgarian government decided the only way it could regain the territories held by the Turks was to wage war on the Ottoman Empire. On September 22 1908 it defied the Berlin Agreement and declared itself an independent state, sparking off the Balkan crisis. The following day, Austria-Hungary annexed Bosnia and Herzegovina and war with Turkey was only averted because Russia and the other Great Powers publicly backed Bulgaria. In 1912 peace treaties were signed with Serbia, Greece and Montenegro in readiness for a united war against Turkey. War was declared by the allies against Turkey on October 5 1912 and raged until May 1913 when peace was agreed. Turkey was defeated and the Turks were expelled from all but a small corner of their European domains. Although Bulgaria should have received all her territories held by the Turks, her former allies occupied them.

On July 16 1913 Bulgaria attacked the combined armies of Greece and Serbia and the Second Balkan War broke out. Serbia and Greece were backed by Montenegro, Romania and the Turks, and surrounded on all sides, Bulgaria was forced to surrender. Instead of unifying the country, the war left Bulgaria in a worse position. She lost more land, her economy was ruined and parts of the kingdom were now ruled by the Serbs and Greeks. In August, Bulgaria signed a secret treaty with Germany. In return for attacking Serbia she would regain all her lost territories. The First World War began in August 1914, with Turkey on the German side and Russia and Serbia joining Britain and France. Bulgaria declared war on Serbia on October 15 1915, but after initial successes the army became bogged down and trench warfare continued until 1918. There was considerable domestic opposition to the war.

In September 1918 the retreating Bulgarian army rebelled and declared the country a republic, but loyal government troops, backed by the Germans, put down the Soldiers' Mutiny. On September 29, the Armistice was signed and the Bulgarian army disbanded. Ferdinand I was forced to abdicate, to be succeeded by his son Boris III, who was to reign until 1943. At the peace treaty in 1919 Bulgaria again suffered enormous territorial losses to Greece, Romania and Serbia, and the country was once again plunged into an economic and political crisis.

A woodcarving (symbolizing the harvest) depicts peasant girls carrying a huge bunch of grapes back home.

In the resulting conditions of the shortages and high taxation, the Marxist BWSDP flourished. Mass strikes were organized against rising prices and unemployment, and the party started to gain election successes. The ruling Agrarian Party set out to improve foreign relations and Bulgaria was admitted to the League of Nations. The Agrarian government was toppled in 1923 by a coup led by the army and the Constitutional Bloc, an alliance of all the Bourgeoisie parties. Despite uprisings against the coup, the army supported the new right wing government which had the backing of the king.

An anti-fascist uprising took place in September 1926 and by September 23 had spread throughout the country. As each town was taken, a revolutionary committee was formed, but the rising was not co-ordinated, and was eventually crushed and state oppression intensified. It was not until 1931, after many years of consolidation, that the workers' parties came to power in Bulgaria.

In May 1934 the right wing staged another coup and overthrew the government, establishing a Fascist administration which was to stay in force until the 1944 revolution. An alliance with Germany was established by which the Bulgarian regime hoped to regain the lost territories. Bulgaria joined the war on the German side in 1941 – but only against the Western powers, not the USSR. But in 1944 the advancing Russian forces invaded. Bulgarian towns suffered heavily from Anglo-American bombing raids during 1943 and 1944. On September 8 1944, faced with invasion from the Russian army, the Bulgarian government broke off diplomatic relations with Germany. The threat of the Russian advance sparked off the workers' rebellion and by September 9 Sofia had been overrun and the Russian troops were welcomed as liberators. On September 10 the government was overthrown and the Socialist State of Bulgaria came into being. The Constitution of the People's Republic of Bulgaria was adopted in 1947 and treaties of friendship were signed with neighbouring states.

The Great National Assembly nationalised private industrial and mining enterprises and banks in December 1947, and in December 1948 launched the first Five Year Economic Plan. Cooperative farms were formed and socialist reforms continued. In 1955 Bulgaria was one of the signatories of the Warsaw Pact, and in December of that year joined the United Nations. In 1959 a new administrative regime was introduced, and in 1971 a new constitution was approved consolidating the new social system. Today, Bulgaria is a member of the world socialist community and the Bulgarian Communist Party is in control of the country's development – with the declared aim of the building of an advanced socialist society.

WINE IN BULGARIA

Although many countries lay claim to the title, Bulgaria could well be the oldest wine producing country in Europe. Extensive archaeological surveys carried out in the last 10-15 years show that the climate during the Neolithic Period (6,000 to 3,000 BC), was suitable for the cultivation of the *Vitis vinifera* Silvestris Gonol and there is a wealth of evidence to show that wine was being produced in the eastern part of the Balkan Peninsula during this time. There are relics to show that festivals were held to the god of wine, Dionysus.

For thousands of years before the Romans invaded the territories that now form Bulgaria, the land was settled by Thracian tribes, who introduced winemaking techniques. The tribes held lands on both the northern and southern slopes of the Balkan Range, known then as Hemus. Today, vineyards are still gracing these slopes. The wines of Ancient Thrace were made famous by Homer who mentioned them in both the Iliad and the Odyssey – the 11th Song of the Iliad says that the tents of Atride are full of wine brought by the Acheians from Thrace across the sea. In Song Nine of his Odyssey, the hero tells that his ships contain amphoras and skins filled with sparkling red wine taken from the Thracian tribe of Kikoni which populated Izmar.

The favourite God of the Thracians was Dionysus, perhaps because the celebrations allowed the people to eat, drink and be merry in his honour. His cult spread throughout Ancient Thrace and many archaeological treasures survive attesting to the cult's widespread appeal. Monuments were erected depicting vines, bunches of grapes, vintage scenes and various aspects of the winemaking process. These monuments have been discovered in virtually all parts of the country but the most interesting is a marble relief of Dionysus from the district of Plovdiv, preserved today in the National Archaeological Museum in Sofia.

Again, in many parts of the country archaeologists have unearthed specially hollowed out stones used for crushing the grapes. Some of these stones were clearly designed to be moved, perhaps the first mobile grape presses.

The murals from the famous Kazanluk tomb and gold artefacts from the Panagyurishte treasure show that grapes and wine played a very important role in the life of the Ancient Thracians. They developed many special tools both for the

A fresco from the Kazanluk Thracian tomb representing Dionysus, the god of vines and wines, most revered by the Thracians. A prominent Thracian chieftain is thought to have been buried here in the 4th-3rd century BC.

cultivation of the vines and the making of the wine and many examples of these, including pruning knives, barrels, wine skins, and amphoras have been discovered during excavations.

While the Thracians were responsible for starting wine production, it was the Romans who expanded it and introduced new techniques of viticulture and viniculture. They are credited with planting vineyards throughout the Balkan Peninsula and they surveyed the land, picking out the best sites. Special vine growing areas were established and the wines were exported to Greece, Asia Minor and Egypt. The Romans introduced order into all aspects of the wine industry. Lists in Latin have been found showing that they carefully categorized the grape varieties, noted the success of each vineyard and recorded the production of each winery. Skilled winemakers were introduced into the area who brought new equipment, and the importance of wine to the local economy grew.

Bulgaria can also boast some of the oldest wine laws in the world because in the second century AD during the reign of Antonius Pius, Emperor of Rome, an edict was proclaimed to protect the vineyards in Lower Mizia, now northern Bulgaria. The law, upheld by the Emperor's two successors, also laid down severe punishments for anyone caught damaging the vines.

From the Roman period there is also evidence of a large winery in Madara in northeast Bulgaria, built between the second and fourth centuries AD; from the extent of the buildings, winemaking must have been conducted on a large scale even then.

Wine production continued over the centuries and the techniques were passed down to the new tribes settling the country – the Slavs and the Proto-Bulgarians – who established themselves in the northeastern part of the Balkan Peninsula. The first Bulgarian state was established in AD 681 and 200 years later came the Golden Age of Bulgaria. By this time wine production was so widespread and wine so plentiful that the country found it had a drinking problem and vineyards were ordered to be destroyed.

There is a record in the Vatican library from a Byzantine merchant which reports that when the conquering Emperor Nikiphorus entered the Bulgarian capital of Pliska, he found many wine barrels in the palace cellars which he ordered be given to his troops to celebrate their victory.

Wine production continued to grow and flourish in medieval times. Wine may even have figured in the downfall of the Bulgarian state and the subsequent domination by the Turks. According to the archives, during the eleventh century Cosmas the Priest lectured the Bogomils and reproached the clergy for their excessive drinking. It was a problem affecting many groups

It was during the reign of Khan Kroum that a law was passed ordering the destruction of the vineyards to try to curb the drinking excesses. There is a legend that one night, one of the Khan's lions escaped from his cage in the palace grounds. There was panic in the street but the lion was tracked down and slain. The Khan decreed that he would reward the person who has shown such courage. A mother told the Khan that her son Mavrud had killed the beast. Khan Kroum asked what was the secret of Mavrud's great strength and fearlessness, but the mother was too afraid to answer. It was only after the Khan promised that no harm would come to her that she admitted she had disobeyed his law about destroying all vines and had kept one in her garden. She had secretly made wine, which had given her son the courage and strength to slay the lion. Khan Kroum was so impressed that he rescinded his law and vineyards were once again established throughout the country. To this day, the valour of the son is still remembered by the Mavrud vine, which produces one of the best quality red wines in Bulgaria.

in the population and one of the reasons for the general decline of the Bulgarian state. It was during the Middle Ages that the influence of the church and monasteries grew. Many of the vineyards were absorbed into the monasteries' ever-growing land holdings and their winemakers and cellar masters established a reputation both at home and abroad.

The nobles, or boyars, and the senior clergy kept the best quality wines for themselves although the poets and writers must have had the chance to taste them, because the wines were frequently praised in their writings. Theophylact enthused in his writings about the light and pleasant wine he had drunk in south Bulgaria. The knights in the crusading army led by the Emperor Frederick Barbarossa also praised the quality of the Thracian wine in their accounts of their journey to the Holy Land.

Excavations at dozens of settlements around Bulgaria have revealed just how widespread vineyards and wineries were during the Middle Ages. Between the ninth and fourteenth centuries iron pruning shears were developed and many are preserved in museums. During this time the winemakers also realized the importance of storing the wine in cold cellars. This discovery may have been made after tasting the monastery wines kept in cellars below the thick-walled abbeys and priories. Wine cellars were built in the capital of Pliska, in Preslav and Turnovo and parts of these still remain.

Even under Turkish domination winegrowing continued to flourish although the Koran outlawed wine. The reputation of Bulgarian wines was such that exports brought in valuable revenue, and allowing the population access to wine may have helped them forget the atrocious conditions to which they were subjected. The Turkish pashas appointed to rule the various districts introduced dessert grapes from Asia Minor to satisfy their sweet tastes.

Bachkovo Monastery stands on the steep banks of the river Chepelarska, near to Assenovgrad. Founded in 1083, as a centre of education, the monastery was extended in 1604 under Ottoman rule and the church of the Virgin Mary was built. The monastery was again enlarged in the 18th century. Now only the original Georgian church of the Archangel Michael remains.

There are many records of travellers visiting the country between the eleventh and nineteenth centuries who praised the quality of the wines. In 1664 the Englishman John Burbury travelled through Bulgaria on his way to Constantinople. He wrote of the wines of Philippopolis (now Plovdiv) and how "superb and plentiful" they were. The French physician and traveller Paul Lucas who visited Bulgaria in 1712 wrote of Stanimuka (now Assenovgrad): "this is a significant small town, populated only by Christians. Its surroundings are covered with fine vines which yield excellent wines. The vats in which the wine is made are as large as a square room and are plastered with concrete mixed with olive oil which looks like red marble."

Another writer, an Austrian called Jenke, passed through Bulgaria in 1785. He wrote about the wines in Pazardjik in southern Bulgaria. "The wine here is very good and very cheap. A bottle costs two Kreuzer (a small denomination German coin). In Vienna one can find the same type of wine delivered from Enidje which is considered the best wine in European Turkey". The Greek consul in Varna, Vretos (1849-1851), writing about viticulture in Bulgaria, said: "vines grow well in the southern part of Bulgaria and yield an abundance of excellent wines which could successfully rival the wines of western Europe."

After Bulgaria's liberation from Ottoman rule in the late nineteenth century, the vine growing areas quickly expanded. But then disaster struck when phylloxera broke out. The disease had been steadily moving east after devastating the vineyards of France, Germany and Italy and it reached Bulgaria at the end of the nineteenth and beginning of the twentieth centuries. The outbreak did enormous damage but it did force the growers to re-plant. They used phylloxera resistant rootstocks with the native vines grafted to them.

Once again the vineyards expanded, but most were owned by small landowners not prepared or able to introduce modern methods. The wineries themselves were primitive and unsuitable for making fine wines. Much of the best wine at this time was being produced by the newly formed cooperatives. It was these wineries, using the latest techniques and equipment, which started to create specific types of wine using varieties such as Gamza, Dimiat, Misket, Broad Melnik and Pamid. It was these cooperatives which laid the foundation for Bulgaria's modern wine industry.

AGRICULTURE IN MODERN BULGARIA

Although Bulgaria has always engaged in agriculture, including vineyards and wineries, the farms were too small to be profitable and too scattered to be efficient. Because of this in the years leading up to the 1944 revolution Bulgaria was at the bottom of the list of Europe's rural economies. There were over a million farms cultivating more than 12 million plots of land, each averaging less than half a hectare (one acre). Mechanization was virtually unknown. The wooden ploughs were pulled either by draught animals or the people themselves. In 1944 there were 518,000 wooden ploughs, 310,000 carts and only 3,000 tractors.

Most farms barely provided a living for the families working them. The large estates were often run by owners living miles away in the cities and any profits that were made were taken by the state which imposed heavy taxes. As the peasant farmers went more heavily into debt they were forced to sell out and they swelled the growing ranks of the unemployed rural workers. In 1940 more than 1.2 million peasants were unemployed and 35 per cent of the income of working farmers went to pay state taxes. Between 1935 and 1939 more than 14,000 farms were auctioned to pay the farmers' taxes.

The government at this time could see the damage that was being caused to agriculture and various measures were proposed. It was suggested giving each peasant farmer their own cow which would provide milk and serve as a draught animal. Attempts were also made to merge the farms into more productive units, in many cases by forceably moving the farmers. Not surprisingly, these measures did not succeed but the farmers did start to defend themselves and rural cooperatives were formed, usually with the help of the Bulgarian Communist Party. Although only 29 cooperatives survived to the revolution, they did set the pattern for agriculture for the next four decades.

In 1946 the country's agriculture was reformed. A law was passed restricting a farming family's holding to 30 hectares (74 acres) and any land above this was distributed among the 128,000 landless and poor peasants. In 1948 all big farming machinery was compulsorily bought from the large landowners and given to state machine and tractor stations which were set up.

Over a period of 15 years the state cooperative farms were established in three separate stages. Firstly the scattered farms were organized into larger enterprises. By 1958 there were 3,290 cooperative farms involving more than 1,250,000 families and 4 million hectares (9,884,000 acres) of land. It meant that 93 per cent of all the arable land subject to collectivisation was already pooled in the collective farms, which averaged 1,260 hectares (3,114 acres).

At the same time state farms were also set up as model agricultural enterprises to show the cooperatives the way. They also supplied the cooperatives with the best seeds, breeding stock, vines and latest agricultural techniques. Between 1959 and 1970 the state farms and the cooperatives were further merged. There were now about 800 cooperatives, each approximately 4,100 hectares (10,131 acres) and involving about 1,120 farmers. The number of state farms was reduced to 150, each about 4,400 hectares (10,872 acres) in size and employing about 1,000 workers. New orchards and vineyards were planted and large animal farms set up. Productivity increased by about four per cent a year, faster than any other European country.

Since 1971 the third stage of development has been introduced, the evolution of what are called agro-industrial complexes. These are designed to make use of the latest scientific and technical developments in order to boost productivity, efficiency and competitiveness. The state farms and cooperatives were phased out and replaced by 170 agro-industrial complexes, each with about 25,000 hectares (61,775 acres) of land and employing some 6,200 people. The complexes allowed the introduction of large-scale production techniques. Cereals which up to 1970 had been grown on 45,000 plots averaging 40 hectares (98 acres) each were now grown in plots between 200 and 500 hectares (494 and 1,235 acres) each. New modern vineyards and orchards of 1,000-2,500 hectares (2,471-6,177 acres) each were planted. A similar pattern was adopted for all other crops and vegetable production.

This industrialization of agriculture has led to massively increased productivity in all areas especially in wine production. Today, there are 274 agro-industrial complexes, each linked to a local municipality, together with ten industrial-agrarian and eight research and production complexes. Each has an average of 15,000 hectares (37,065 acres), 25 million levs of fixed capital, and 3,500 full time workers. Bulgaria now boasts one of the most concentrated agricultures in the world with some of the most advanced agricultural machinery plants and scientific research stations which will allow it to go on developing. Cereal production has more than trebled since the revolution, the number of agricultural workers has been reduced by two thirds, but productivity per worker is seven times higher than it was in 1944. Food Production has increased almost sixfold in the last 20 years.

WINEMAKING TODAY

Because of the scattered nature of the farms in pre-revolutionary times, many of the farmers used the grapes to make wine only for their own consumption. But these farms continued a wine tradition sketching back, as we have seen, to ancient times.

Indigenous grape varieties such as Pamid, Mavrud, Shevka and the Broad Melnik vine have certainly been used since the time of the First Bulgarian Kingdom (681-1018) and probably for many centuries before that. After the fall of the Kingdom to the Turks, the Ottoman commanders introduced several dessert varieties from Asia Minor such as Afus-ali (Bolgar), Chaush, Kadun

Parmak and Al Zeinel. As was the case throughout Europe vines were grown on their own roots before the phylloxera outbreak but a rapid transformation took place in the years afterwards. The phylloxera outbreak forced the vineyards to switch to disease resistant rootstock and the acreage under vines increased enormously. This initial expansion programme continued until well after the end of the First World War.

In 1919 there were 43,413 hectares (107,273 acres) under vine and this had grown to more than 143,103 hectares (353,607 acres) by 1944. Today there are about 166,000 hectares (410,186 acres) of vine under cultivation. In 1927 the commercial production of dessert grapes began and by the late 1930s Bulgaria was one of Europe's leading exporters of table grapes with more than 50,000 tonnes (49,200 tons) being sent abroad annually.

Since 1944, vine growing in Bulgaria has changed enormously. Perhaps the most important development was the planting of large-scale vineyards on the most suitable sites. Traditionally vineyards had often been planted on small plots not needed for other forms of agriculture. The new vineyards were established on the state farms and cooperatives. There were 4,000 major vineyard sites, each of between 25 and 35 hectares (61 and 86 acres).

In 1962 the first scientific classification of vine-growing by zones was carried out. This enabled the authorities to pinpoint particular areas especially suitable for specific varieties. New high quality grape varieties were introduced. Cardinal and The Queen of Vines were two of the major introductions for dessert grapes,

while many of the classic wine vine varieties from France and Germany were introduced. These included Cabernet Sauvignon, Merlot, Chardonnay, Riesling and Ugni Blanc. Varieties such as Rkatsiteli were also introduced from Russia. By the mid-1960s the Bulgarians were producing about 200 million rootstocks per annum and about 100 million engrafted rooted vines.

There has been a steady expansion of viticulture since 1944 and the process is still continuing. All of Bulgaria (except the countryside around the capital Sofia) has been declared by the government as a wine growing area. In the early 1970s the vineyards switched from a low growing system of cultivation to trellis-training, with the stems reaching a height of between 1 and 1.2 metres. There are now 435 major vineyard groupings in the public sector. There is heavy reliance on mechanization so that one worker can manage between eight and nine hectares (19 and 22 acres) of vines. The switch to trellises also meant a reappraisal of the varieties grown because the vines were now more susceptible to cold. This led to a much more widespread distribution of Cabernet Sauvignon, Merlot, Rkatsiteli, Riesling and Musket Ottonel varieties. The local varieties are still grown, however, on specially selected sites. The area under cultivation of Pamid, Mavrud, Gamza, Dimiat and Red Misket has all increased in the last ten years.

In 1982 vineyards covered three per cent of the cultivated area in the country and 50 per cent of the area given over to perennial crops. Today Bulgaria is the second largest exporter of bottled wines in the world and the fifth largest wine exporter, after Italy, France, Spain and Germany. More than 80 per cent of the country's wine is exported, Bulgaria leads Europe in the production and export of wine seedlings and its research stations have produced many new varieties. New wine grape varieties include Buket, Bulgarian Riesling, Thracia Bisser, Mavrud, Branch 1, Pomorie Bisser, Plovdiv Malaga and Varna Misket.

Before 1944 there was little application of fertilizers and insecticides and crop losses due to pests and diseases was up to a quarter of total production. Because of the size of the new vineyards, large-scale mechanical spraying by helicopters and aircraft is now possible, but scientists have also developed biological techniques for controlling pests.

Predicting and giving advance warning are another important feature of vine protection. Scientists issue bulletins warning specific areas of threats from plants or diseases and advising on the optimum time to spray. In recent years the application of pesticides has come under increasing scrutiny and an integrated approach to pest management has been introduced. This involves a new range of chemicals, applied in lower volumes, that are more effective but harmless in the environment. Other controls include better hygiene, seed disinfection and disinfection of empty storehouses and so on. Biological pest control is now widespread using parasites to prey on pests dangerous to the vines or grapes.

The emphasis on pest control is to develop methods which do not harm the environment. Approaches being developed include a method of ray sterilization and homosterilization, and genetically creating plants with their own built-in immunity to disease.

The great strides that have been made in the vineyards with new systems of cultivation, varieties and better grape handling, have been mirrored in the wineries. There has been an enormous investment in winemaking and bottling. There are university courses in wine production at Plovdiv and students travel the world studying the most up-to-date techniques. The research institutes at Pleven and Sofia are recognized internationally.

While the latest equipment is used to make the wines, there is still a reliance on traditional skills and crafts. It is this blend of new and old that helps produce wines of character and breeding. Pickers are still used to harvest all of the grapes, because despite mechanization trials, the wine makers insist there is no substitute for the delicacy of the human hand. The use of oak casks to mature the wines is still practiced. The blenders often come from families with generations of experience in winemaking.

At every stage of winemaking there are stringent quality controls. A classification system, similar to the Appellation Côntrolée (AC) of France has been introduced and the first wines to carry this distinction were released in 1982. There are also the country's wine laws, some possibly the oldest in the world, whose purpose is to guarantee the quality and pureness of all wines and spirits and products derived from grapes and vine.

There is roughly equal production of reds and whites. In the 1950s most of the red wines were made from the Gamza grape, but today the majority are made from the Cabernet Sauvignon which is now the dominant variety in Bulgaria. Today there are about 200 state-owned producers. All the wine is made in the wineries of collectives and about 85 per cent of production is controlled by Vinprom, the state-owned economic organization, set up in 1952 to replace the State Monopoly of Alcoholic Drinks which had been established five years earlier. All Bulgarian wine exports are handled by Vinimpex, set up specially to handle sales abroad.

WINE TRADITIONS The vineyards and wineries have an important place in Bulgarian life and wine is featured in all major events – wine is drunk to celebrate a birth or a wedding and the dead are toasted in their absence. For thousands of years wine has played such an important role in the lives of the people that it has become enshrined in the folklore.

One of the most important, and enjoyable, wine festivals is Trifon Zarezan – Vine Growers' Day – which is celebrated on February 14. On that day everyone involved in winemaking, no matter how young or old, dresses in their best clothes and, accompanied by bands of musicians, go to the vineyards. They decorate themselves with flowers, especially crane's bill (a variety of wild geranium) and boxwood (an evergreen shrub). The people then select the best vine grower as leader of the festivities and he opens the proceedings by symbolically pruning vines in different parts of the vineyard and pouring wine over them to encourage a rich vintage. The pruned cuttings are woven into girdles which are worn by the men over their shoulders. The festivities, which have not changed in hundreds of years, continue long into the night. When the families have returned to their village, the master of each house brings out wine, first for the leader of the festivities and then for all the other guests. A few drops of wine are always spilled on to the ground as part of the ritual to encourage fertility both in the vineyard and the village.

There are also festivals for the land and for the vines, and to celebrate the start of the vintage, young girls carry the first of the picked grapes to the wineries accompanied by music and dancing.

THE REGIONS   Virtually the whole country has been officially designated by the government as a grape-producing area and even though Sofia and its environs are excluded, vines can still be found there.

There are five main wine growing regions – Eastern, Northern, Southern, Southwestern and Sub-Balkan – and all are dealt with in detail in following chapters.

The Eastern Region comprises about 29 per cent of the country's vineyards and includes many famous sub-regions, the most notable of which are Varna, Aytos, Burgas, Khan Krum, Novi Pazar, Shumen, Tolbuhin, Preslav, Targovishte, Pomorie and Razgrad. The famous Euxinograd wines are also produced here. The area concentrates on the production of high quality white and sparkling wines and spirits. The main grape varieties are Riesling, Rcatzitelli, Aligoté, Chardonnay, Misket, Muscat Ottonel, Ugni Blanc, Dimiat and Fetiaska.

The Northern Region consists of the central belt, northwestern zone and the Danube belt. In the central belt are the towns of Suhindol, Pleven and Veliko Tarnovo. The Danube belt includes the territories of Nikopol, Svishtov and Russe, and the northwestern zone includes the districts of Vratsa, Mikhailovgrad and Vidin. The celebrated Gamza wine is produced in the region of Novo Selo, and the Veslets semi-dry wines and Vratsa Misket dessert wines are produced around Vratsa. The area is known for its red quality wines and the main varieties are Gamza, Cabernet Sauvignon and Merlot. White varieties are by Rcatzitelli, Aligoté and Muscat Ottonel.

The Sub-Balkan region is found south of the Balkan range and contains two sub-regions. The eastern belt includes the famous Sungurlare valley where the Red Miskat variety is grown. The western belt contains the Valley of Roses whose slopes have been planted with a number of grape varieties. This sub-region also produces the white Slavjanci dessert wine and has the important Karlovo wine producing centre. Predominant varieties are Cherven Misket, Rcatzitelli, Muscat Ottonel and Riesling, although there have been extensive plantings of Cabernet Sauvignon in recent years. The entire area specializes in the production of white quality wines and vermouth, although the red wine percentage is increasing rapidly as the Cabernet matures.

The Southern Region comprises about 33 per cent of the country's vineyards and is divided into three sub-regions. The eastern part includes the territories of the towns of Jambol, Korten, Sliven, Sakar and Nova Zagora; the central part is noted for such territories as Stara Zagora, Oryahovitsa, Chirpan, Haskovo, Stambolovo, Assenovgrad, Brestnik, Ljubimetz and Perushtitza producing excellent reds, semi-dry whites and dessert wines. The western part includes the towns of Pazardjik and Septemvri producing high quality blended red wines. The whole region is known for its red wines, made from Cabernet Sauvignon, Merlot, Mavrud and Pamid, and for whites using Rcatzitelli, Cherven Misket and Muscat Ottonel.

The Southwestern region includes the territories of Blagoevgrad and Kjustendil, and the controlled denomination of Harsovo. Although small in size it produces some excellent wines because of its special climate. In the valley of the Struma River early ripening grapes are cultivated for dessert wines, mostly Shiroka Melvishka Loza from which the Melnishko and Melnik 13 wines are produced. The red and white wines tend to have southern characteristics because climatic conditions are similar to those of the Mediterranean. The main varieties are Cabernet Sauvignon, Pamid, Rcatzitelli and Aligoté.

The sheer scale of the vineyards takes the breath away. While the average vineyard in Bordeaux is only half a hectare (1-2 acres), in Bulgaria "vine massifs" can cover more than 484 hectares (1,200 acres). These industrial vine growing techniques have been very successfully introduced in the districts of Stara Zagora, Pazardjik, Burgas, Plovdiv, Sliven, Varna, Shumen, Blagoevgrad and Haskovo. While the traditional grape varieties are still grown, especially Pamid, Dimiat, Gamza, Red Misket, Mavrud and Broad Melnik, imported classic varieties now account for 40 per cent of plantings. These varieties include Cabernet Sauvignon, Merlot, Rkatziteli, Muscat Ottonel, Riesling, Aligoté, Chardonnay and Ugni Blanc.

The enormous size of the winery complexes are also staggering, especially those such as the ones at Novi Pazar and Sliven. There are few places anywhere else where industrial technology has been applied to winemaking on such a scale while still retaining the essential human input. Since the foundation in 1947 of the State Monopoly of Alcoholic Drinks, which was reorganized in 1952 into Vinprom State Economic Association, the wine industry has mushroomed from a backward, fragmented enterprise into a modern, highly efficient and important sector of the food industry. The expansion of production created ideal conditions for starting again, making use of the latest technology, equipment and expertise. The existing wine cellars were expanded and new wineries built for processing the grapes and making the wine. Capacity for wine production and storage has increased several-fold. Stainless steel tanks with a capacity of 400 cubic metres (392 cubic yards) are not unusual.

The Bulgarian wine-producing industry is now equipped with mechanized flow lines, necessary for processing the high tonnages of grapes normally harvested. Yields of between 20 and 40 tonnes a hectare (19 and 39 tons an acre) are common. This increased storage capacity, the introduction of flow lines, controlled fermentation, application of the latest technology and automation have all contributed in raising Bulgaria to its present impressive position in the wine world. For the last three or four

Left *Chardonay and Riesling vines forming part of the vast winery complex at Novi Pazar.*

Right *The stablization plant at the Russe winery.*

years techniques have been developed for the controlled fermentation of white wines, and 60 per cent of reds are now produced with vinificators which improve colour extraction and the fermentation process. New bottling lines have been built, and new bottling techniques developed to guarantee prolonged stability of the bottled wine. This was an important development because it enabled Bulgaria to switch from the export of bulk to the export of bottled wine.

The government research stations are constantly striving to improve and develop the existing technologies to enhance the wide range of wines, vermouths and spirits produced.

THE RANGE OF WINES PRODUCED

Apart from the white, red and rosé wines for which Bulgaria is best-known abroad, and which are listed in the margin, a range of other drinks is made.

Conditions in Bulgaria are ideal for the production of dessert wines. There are 15 labels and they include the quality white dessert wines Varna, Bisser, Slavianka, Vratsa Misket, Tamianka and Vladislavovo. The red dessert wines are also of good quality and are characterized by a mild balanced taste and specific bouquet. They include Turnovo, Pomorie, Roubin, Chirpan, Haskovo, Lozen, Sliven and Korten.

There are many naturally sparkling wines produced including the white, red, and rosé Iskra and Magoura, only differing because of sugar content. The naturally sparkling Lazour and Simfonia muscat wines are particularly pleasant, as is Malina with its characteristic raspberry flavour. The list also includes Iskra-Maritsa, Biliana and Iskra-Zvezditsa.

The Bulgarian wine industry produces a rich variety of vermouths, differing in colour, flavour and taste. Apart from the white and red Vinprom vermouths, the other labels available are Orpheus, Cio Cio San, Cossara and Amaro. Original Bulgarian vermouths made with local herbs are the white Aglikaand and the red Rouen. Other Bulgarian apéritifs include Ropotamo, Bitter Sofia, Bitter Rozari and Apéritif 22 which contains an extract of 22 local herbs.

WHITE WINES
The list of dry white wines is constantly growing and at the time of writing included 18 labels, such as Misket from Soungourlare or Karlovo, Riesling from the Valley of Roses, Chardonnay, Aligoté, Slanchev Bryag, Dimiat, Loudogorsko and Emona. The list of semi-dry and semi-sweet white wines include 14 labels, including Hemus, Zlatni Kapki, Riesling Superior, Targovishko Margareshko Mlyako, Loznitsa, Kamchiiski Misket, Manastirska Izba, Madarski Konnik, Shoumen, Veslets and Tamianka.

RED WINES
The list of red wines includes 24 labels. Of particular high quality are the Gamza from Souhindol and Pavli-keni, Mavrud from Assenovgrad, Cabernet Sauvignon from Svish-tov, Mehandjiisko, Cabernet Sauvignon from Pleven, Gamza from Novo Selo, Merlot from Sakar, Zagore, Nestinarsko, Voevodsko and Pamid. The list of red semi-dry wines covers seven labels – Kadarka, Manastirsko Shoushoukane, Melnik 13, Assenitsa 1230, Balkanski Ogan, Mecha Kruc and Rouino.

ROSÉ WINES
Among the dry and semi-dry rosé wines are Agalina, Ralitsa, Rosé Trakia and Sredets.

BULGARIAN WINE IN ROUND FIGURES

Area under grape cultivation	166,000 hectares (410,186 acres)
Wine production	4 million hectolitres a year
Wine exports	3.5 million hectolitres a year
Wine imports	0-60,000 hectolitres a year
Consumption per head of population	22 litres (4.84 gallons) a year

The local spirit drink, Rakiya, is produced in great variety throughout Bulgaria. It is a brandy with an alcohol content of 40° and produced mainly from grape marcs; however, it can also be made by the distillation of fermented fruit juice, chiefly plums, apricots and pears, although a wide range of fruits may be used.

The most famous of the fruit and grape brandies are Troyanska Slivova, Silistrenska Kaisieva, Viliamovo brandy, Omourtashka Slivova and Slivenska Perla. Spices are sometimes added to brandies to give them special flavours and examples of these include Troyanska Bilkova, which contains Troyan herbs, and Lovdjiiska. There are also a number of old brandies now being produced as the industry develops and builds stocks. The most famous of these are Pomeria and Preslav, produced from five-to eight-year-old distillate, and the brands Pliska 1300 and Pliska Aheloi, produced from 12-year-old distillate.

BULGARIAN WINE LAW AND CLASSIFICATION

In July 1978 new wine laws were introduced by the Bulgarian National Assembly. The aim was to increase the guarantees of the quality and naturalness of the wines, drinks and products made of grapes or wine, in keeping with the specific natural conditions and production traditions. The classification is based on the area of cultivation, the grape variety cultivated, the winery technology applied and quality ratings. After assessment, all the wines are graded into one of three Definitions of Quality – standard, high quality and special, which includes sparkling, dessert, fortified, fruit and the new range of country wines.

Standard wines are the lowest category and are defined according to typical qualities found in the grape variety and the characteristics found in a specified wine-producing region.

High Quality wines constitute the next level of quality and are again judged by the varietal characteristics of the grape and the particular characteristics of specified wine-producing areas. This category is further sub-divided into three groups:
(1) wines without declared origin but of declared variety or registered brand name.
(2) wines of declared geographical origin.
(3) wines of "Controliran Region", corresponding to appellations such as Apellation Contrôlée (AC) in France, Denominazione di Origine Controllata (DOC) in Italy, and Qualitätswein in Germany. There are currently 20 such designated regions but the number is increasing as quality and consistency improves.

The Controliran Region wines have distinct characters and features, based on the specific natural conditions and production traditions of a particular region. The conditions which govern production of these Controliran Region wines have to comply

with the Regulations issued by the Government. The main points are that the grapes for the wine have to originate from a defined geographical micro-region with specific and uniform soil and climatic conditions; the wine must be produced from grape varieties approved for the region; the cultivation of the vines must follow a defined technique and the wines must be produced under strictly defined vinification technology; and the wines must be within tight limits on quantifiable aspects such as alcohol, acidity, sugar, extract, colour, flavour and taste. These are checked by physical-chemical tests and by tasting.

A wine is approved as a Controliran Region wine by the National Tasting Committee, appointed by the Minister of Agriculture. Each wine has a dossier containing the full information of the region, soil and climatic conditions, the winemaking technology, the varieties and a tasting evaluation of the wine from three consecutive vintages proving consistency of quality. The National Tasting Committee also controls the production of these wines, representatives of the committees being present at the harvest to verify that the grapes comply with the regulations. The Committee issues a certificate of approval after tasting and also before bottling. The first Controliran wines were approved in 1978.

In 1985 additional regulations were passed defining a new classification for Bulgarian wine production under the title Reserve – itself an addition to the Bulgarian Wine Law of 1978. The regulation specifies that two categories of High Quality wines – those with declared geographical origin and wines of Controliran Region – can also be classified as "Reserve" provided that:
(1) for the Controlian Region wines the vintage is superior to the average vintage and has been aged in barrel for a minimum period of three years for whites and four years for reds. Additionally, wines of this category which have noticeably improved in bottle after being released for sale can be up-graded to this classification.
(2) for wines with declared geographical origin similar conditions apply with the exception that the minimum ageing period is two years for white wines and three years for red wines.

Therefore, the Reserve category defines wines which have shown the best potential for ageing and have been matured in oak barrels to further improve their outstanding qualities.

Depending on the variety, the wines are aged in Bulgarian or imported new and old oak. The first wines imported into the UK in this category were of declared geographical origin and were single varietals. They were aged in 220 litre (48 gallon) barrels made from American and Bulgarian oak for up to 18 months and then transferred to larger casks for the stipulated period. The final ageing process is in bottles. The labels are numbered and carry the signature of the particular cellar master and also have details of the vintage and the wine producing region.

Special Wines always originate from regions in which specified varieties are grown. The vineyards have been planted only after the most thorough analysis to ensure suitability of the variety and the highest quality wine. The wines are distinguished by original properties and characteristic features determined by the specific natural conditions and the production traditions of the designated area. The labels on the bottles of these wines bear the details of the vintage and the words "Wine with a denomination of origin" plus there is a guarantee mark which assures compliance with the provisions of the Bulgarian Wine Laws relating to production. There are 38 denominated regions in Bulgaria.

The Wine Laws are enforced at local, regional and national level. This control includes the drafting of technological maps for viticulture, surveying and developing special technologies for processing the grapes and producing the wines with controlled labels of origin. The first Bulgarian wines with controlled labels of origin include Suhindol, Pavlikeni, Novo Selo, Svishtov, Ljaskovets, Lositza, Targovishte, Khan Krum, Novi Pazar, Prissad, Brestnik, Sakar, Oryahovitsa, Stambolovo, Varna, Sungurlare, Harsovo, Assenovgrad and Karlovo.

UNDERSTANDING THE LABEL

There are more than 80 different wines produced in Bulgaria and most are described either by grape variety or place or region of production. Blended wines are often sold under brand names.

The following list will help you understand the wine labels:

Byalo vino	white wine
Butiliram	to bottle
Cherveno vino	red wine
Estestveno penlivo vino	sparkling wine
Lozia	vineyard
Naturalno	natural
Sladko vino	sweet wine
Sort grozde	grape variety
S ostatachna zahar	with residual sugar for example semi-sweet or sweet
Vinimpex	State trading company for wine and spirit imports and exports
Vinoproizvoditel	winery, wine producer

EASTERN REGION

BURGAS The Vinprom Burgas enterprise occupies the southern coastal strip of the Cherno Morie (Black Sea), extending inland between 50 and 60 kilometres (31 and 37 miles). The sub-regions include Kraimorski (sea coast), the most south-easterly part of the country and the micro-regions producing the Controliran Region wine Rosé ot Juzhnija Brjag, the AO wine Mlado Cabernet and other high quality reds, and the district producing Sozopol, a dessert wine akin to Marsala. Prossenishko is an historic wine district where the vines are grown in deep sand on their own roots. This district produces the AO wine Prossenishko. Many of the vines pre-date the phylloxera outbreak (1895-1910). Aitos, which occupies the most eastern slopes of the Stara Planina hills, has vineyards with a southern exposure. This region is only planted with grapes for high quality white table wines, the most prestigious of which is perhaps the AO Aitoski Muscat.

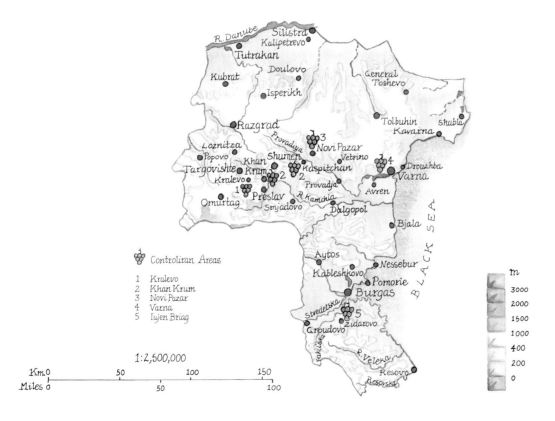

Controliran Areas

1 Kralevo
2 Khan Krum
3 Novi Pazar
4 Varna
5 Iujen Briag

1:2,500,000

The vineyards vary in altitude between sea level and 250 metres (820 feet). The soils are mainly woodland with the exception of the Prossenishko micro-region where the soils are deep sands. The land is generally inclined to the southeast and enjoys more sunshine than any other part of the country. It is also one of the hottest regions and the soil retains this heat. The region enjoys a special climate because of the influence of the Black Sea and to a lesser extent the Mediterranean, which is not far away to the south. The winters are mild, rainfall is evenly distributed throughout the year, and although it is hot in the summer, the sea has a cooling influence.

Wine has always been an important commodity here both for drinking and trading, and grapes have been grown in the region for thousands of years. The traditional varieties of Pamid, Dimiat, Misket and Mavrud dominated for centuries. Until 1945 the vineyards were small, privately owned and unco-ordinated. After nationalization in 1947 two new modern cellars were built, one for the processing of grapes for high quality white wine, and the other for the production of white, rosé and red table wines. The enterprise has since added a thermo-processing plant for stabilizing the wines, and two bottling lines, one for the cold sterile bottling of quality wines, and the other for mass production. Other agriculture in the area includes fruit, especially citrus, vegetables, cereals, fodder crops and livestock in the surrounding hills and mountains.

The vintage takes place during September and October when the region has generally warm, dry weather. The picking is done by hand and the grapes collected in pails. The grapes for Controliran Region and AO wines are taken to the wineries in containers, while the grapes for the rest of the wine is transported in large skips that are unloaded automatically on arrival.

The winemaking follows a pattern which has been traditional in the region for centuries. The skins of the grapes are removed before crushing and the filtration-pressing equipment is designed to produce a clear must with as little suspended material as possible. The wine makers believe this produces more elegant wines. Selected yeast is added and controlled cold fermentation takes place. The young wines are filtered, stabilized and then transferred to tanks or wooden barrels for holding or ageing. Because of the stable climate, the vintages between 1977 and 1986 have been fairly uniform both in terms of quantity and high quality.

There is an experimental wine station in Pomorie and a scientific research institute looking into both vine production and winemaking. An international wine exhibition is held in Slantchev Brjag every four years.

The district of Burgas occupies 6.6 per cent of the total territory of Bulgaria. The area planted with vines is about 16,000 hectares (39,536 acres) with 65 per cent white wine varieties and 35 per cent red. The main white wine varieties are Dimiat, Red Misket, Riesling, Ugni Blanc, Muscat Ottonel and Rkatziteli. The red varieties are predominantly Cabernet Sauvignon, Merlot and Pamid.

The average annual production of the enterprise is about 15 million litres (3.3 million gallons) of white wine and 10 million litres (2.2 million gallons) of red.

FOLKLORE AND CUISINE

The main celebration takes place on February 14 to commemorate the start of the vintage. It is also the holiday of fruitfulness and most of the rituals still performed are connected with wishes for a good vintage, health and a long life. The area is rich in folk songs and dances, and there are many legends and stories featuring the vines and wine.

The cuisine of the region is very varied and alongside traditional meat dishes there are many fish specialities, originating, it is believed, from ancient Greek cooking. Flat sausages (Strandzhansko djado) are another speciality.

TOLBUHIN

Tolbuhin is a city in the far northeast, close to Romania and the Black Sea Coast. The Vinprom Tolbuhin enterprise includes the two small wine-producing sub-regions at Kavarna and Shabla. Kavarna is a rather exposed plateau about 300 metres (984 feet) above sea level with black soils and a continental climate. It is an area of 36,000 hectares (88,956 acres) of which 500 hectares (1,235 acres) are planted with vines. Shabla is also a plain with black earth and a continental climate, but the average height above sea level is only five metres (16 feet). Although Shabla's total cultivated area is 23,000 hectares (56,833 acres) only 60 hectares (148 acres) are planted with vines. Other agriculture products in the area include cereals, vegetables and beans. The region has cold springs, cool summers and warm autumns with variable winters that have occasional, but not lasting, snowfalls.

White wine varieties predominate, mainly Rkatziteli, Muskat Ottonel, Riesling and Fetjaska; with some Cabernet Sauvignon for reds. The dessert vineyards adopt a development of the Moser system of training with a stem height of 50-70 centimetres (19-27 inches) before branching, while the table wines are trained on the Umbrella system to a height of 1.2 to 1.3 metres.

The region is noted especially for its Dobrudzhansko wines, and Dobrotitza and Shablensko from declared geographical regions. About 60 per cent of production is in varietals: Rkatziteli 700,000 litres (154,000 gallons); Muskat Ottonel 650,000 litres (143,000 gallons); Riesling 300,000 litres (66,000 gallons); Fetjaska 40,000 litres (8,800 gallons); Cabernet 100,000 litres (22,000 gallons).

Harvesting is by hand and the grapes are still collected in pails. Here, the pickers empty grapes into large containers ready for transport away from the vineyards.

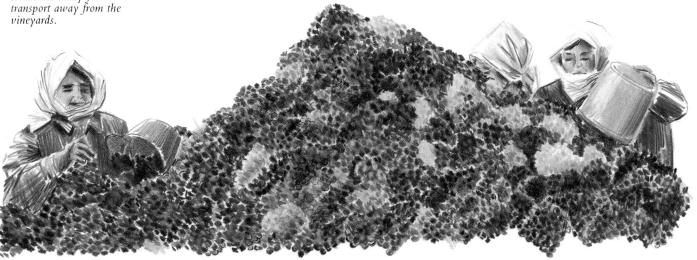

Quality and quantity of the vintages over the last few years has varied enormously because of some very cold winters and droughts during the summers. Climate is an ally in the fight against disease and about 90 per cent of the grapes received at the winery are top quality.

Experimental work in the vineyards is directed at pruning techniques and different methods of training to boost yields, or at least make them more uniform. There have been particular problems with the Rkatziteli vines which have had very irregular yields.

Although vines have been cultivated in the area for many centuries, the vineyards were always in private hands and production was small. The wine industry only really started to develop after 1960 and a major step forward occurred in 1970 when the two new wineries in Tolbuhin and Kavarna were completed. The aim since then has been to produce high quality white wines, wines from designated geographical regions and drinks with names characteristic of the district. Many of the winemaking processes have been automated including fermentation, more moderate sulphation, racking, filtration and removal of the marc. New plants for stabilizing and storing the wine have been built as well as new bottling lines.

TARGOVISHTE

The Targovishte wine area includes all the lands to the southeast of the city as far as the foothills of the Targovishte heights, to the southwest and west as far as the district of Veliko Tarnovo and to the north as far as the border with Razgrad. The land is a rolling plain, with an average altitude a little over 200 metres (656 feet) above sea level and the plain is cut by rivers which have carved out ravines, gorges and caves. The general exposure of the land is to the north, northeast and northwest.

The area has a moderate continental climate with mild winters and warm summers, although temperatures between 1984-87 were well above average for several weeks during the summer months. The average annual temperature is 11.1°C (51°F), the coldest month is January with an average temperature of just above freezing, although the lowest temperature recorded is -28.8°C (-19°F). Frosts can occur between October 27 and April 11.

The soils of the region are characteristically black earth and grey woodland, although there are areas of alluvial meadow and diluvial soils. Although the area generally has favourable conditions for viticulture, the terrain prevents the development of large vineyards as the middle to heavy soils are difficult to cultivate and production of wine here is very expensive in comparison with the rest of the country.

Rainfall levels in June are high enough to bring risk of mildew and oidium, and the total rainfall for September and October, while the grapes are ripening, averages about 90 millimetres (3.9 inches). In some years it is higher and creates favourable conditions for the noble rot.

Because of the difficult terrain, an enormous amount of work has taken place in selecting specific varieties for particular sites, and this research continues unabated. Where possible the vineyards are planted in wide rows to allow maximum mechanization. Most of the experimental work is now concentrated on boosting yields and quality through the introduction of improved varietal strains, new growing techniques, the scientific application of fertilizers, pesticides and other sprays, and more mechanization. The aim is to further increase the economic efficiency of production and reduce the labour force required.

Although conditions are not ideal for the cultivation of dessert grapes, about 45 hectares (111 acres) were planted in 1986.

Mildew and oidium are the greatest problems in the vineyards and are treated by applications of copper sulphate and sulphur dust respectively. The vineyards have developed a system of fine droplet spraying which ensures the plants are treated but the minimum quantity of chemicals is needed. Applications are about 300 litres a hectare (66 gallons an acre) and an even finer spraying technique has recently been introduced which allows effective applications as low as 15 litres a hectare.

The vintage usually starts about September 15 with the earliest-ripening varieties and it continues until the end of

Vines planted and percentage of total production		
	hectares/acres	per cent
Bolgar	73/180	3
Dimiat	185/457	7
Italian Riesling	544/1,344	22
Tamjanka	16/39	
Rkatziteli	996/2,461	40
Pamid	23/56	1
Riesling	10/24	
Cabernet Sauvignon	93/229	4
Misket Ottonel	343/847	14
Chardonnay	119/294	5
Aligoté	102/252	4
Hamburger Misket	6/14	
Perla	3/7	
Thracia Misket	3/7	
Total	2,516/6,211	100

Wine production by variety or type	
Muskat Ottonel	1,200,000 litres/264,000 gallons
Dimiat	1,000,000 litres/220,00 gallons
Rkatziteli	6,000,000 litres/1,300,000 gallons
Riesling	2,600,000 litres/572,000 gallons
Aligoté	300,000 litres/66,000 gallons
Chardonnay	700,000 litres/154,000 gallons
Rozova Tamjanka	50,000 litres/11,000 gallons
Fetjaska	500,000 litres/110,000 gallons
Sparkling wines	6,000,000 litres/1,300,000 gallons
Blended white and reds	6,000,000 litres/1,300,000 gallons

October. The grapes are picked by hand, collected in pails and transferred to two-ton trailers pulled by tractors. They are then emptied into four-ton containers aboard lorries and transported to the wineries. On arrival about a third of the grapes are selected for high quality wines. They are transferred to a Dieme line consisting of a four-cylinder crusher and a 600 millimetres (23 inch) press, with a capacity of 20 tonnes (19 tons) an hour. After filtering, the wine is cooled and racked. The young wine is then transferred to 30,000 litre (6,600 gallon) ferro-concrete and 50,000 litre (1,000 gallon) metal tanks with cooling jackets for the fermentation. Selected yeasts, usually Eperne and Moskovska, are added. After controlled cold fermentation the wine is passed through a Kieselguhr filter.

After three months the wines are treated with tannin, gelatine, salt and bentonite and filtered again. The semi-dry wines are dosed with *süssreserve* to the required sugar level, chilled and then filtrated sterile through two filters.

For Controliran Region wines, those of declared geographical origin and all wines for export, fermentation is controlled between 14 and 16°C (57-60°F). The required sugar content is achieved by cooling to stop fermentation. The wine is filtered through Kieselguhr, treated with tannin, gelatine, salt and bentonite and filtered again. It is then cooled down by passing through a chilling unit and held in 18,000 litre (3,960 gallon) insulated tanks for between one and two weeks. It is then filtered again and cold sterile bottled. The wine is blended in minimum 400,000 litre (88,000 gallon) batches in the production cellars in Targovishte and Popovo. About 14 million litres (3 million gallons) of varietals are produced.

There is an experimental vineyard of five hectares (12 acres) in the Strazha area under the control of Dr Zdravko Zankov, of the Plovdiv Agricultural Institute. Bulgarian wine and dessert varieties are tested for genetic resistance to disease and levels of fertilizer required. There are also on-going trials to develop treatment systems to combat pests and diseases. Wines made from the grapes produced at the experimental farm are carefully analysed and tasted to see whether mass plantings are viable.

Wine has been produced in the region since Thracian times but always on smallholdings. Before the Second World War a number of cooperative cellars were established, the most notable of which were those in Makariopolosko, Palamartzi, Voditza and Podgoritza. In 1944 there were 57 privately owned inns in Targovishte, the biggest being Bjalata Metchka (the White Bear), run by a famous wine maker, Hristi Tzanev. It is still considered a great compliment to a local wine maker if you say his wines are as good as those of Bjalata Metchka.

Between 1977 and 1986 the average yield of grapes at Targovishte was approximately 19,500 tonnes (19,188 tons), the lowest being 14,845 tonnes (14,607 tons) and the highest 26,000 tonnes (25,584 tons). The vintages of 1977, 1979 and 1984 were classified as good, and 1980, 1985 and 1986 as very good.

After nationalization three state wine enterprises were established at Targovishte, Popovo and Omurtag. In 1956 the three were united under Vinprom and consolidated in Targovishte. A viti-vinicultural complex was founded in 1976 with specialized vine growing areas around the villages of Kralevo, Ovtcharovo, Strazha, Pevetz and Dalgatch. The winery in Targovishte specializes in stabilized wines for export and the home market. It also produces table wines, sparkling wines, brandy and vodka. In 1976 a second plant was opened to produce the naturally sparkling herb wine Biljana and it now produces another sparkling wine called Albena. The winery in Popovi specializes in processing the grapes from the micro-regions, and produces wines, and brandy and wine distillates. Omurtag specializes in fruit brandies.

The Controliran Region area is around the village of Kralevo, about 17 kilometres (28 miles) from Targovishte. It includes the countryside to the southwest known as Kajadzha which stretches up into the foothills of the most northern branch of the East Stara Planina. This micro-region covers 200 hectares (494 acres). Riesling is grown for the production of the white semi-dry Sakrovishteto na Kralevo (Kralevo's Treasure) which comes from a 26 hectare (64 acre) vineyard.

It is hoped that other Controliran Regions will be designated shortly, especially around the village of Strazha, where new plantings of Chardonnay now cover more than 100 hectares (247 acres), and around the village of Ovtcharovo in the Bataklaka district, where 80 hectares (197 acres) have been planted.

FOLKLORE AND CUISINE

The region celebrates all the national folk holidays, but also has some special ones of its own. The festival Triffon Zarezan marks the start of the pruning and has been celebrated in the district since Thracian times. The people gather to parade around the villages and vineyards, wearing garlands made from the newly cut vines, before sitting down to a feast, music and dancing.

Enchovden is celebrated on June 24 when all the young girls go out and pick herbs to prepare potions to give good health. On a Sunday in June, Water Nymph's Sunday (Russalska nedelja) is commemorated. The herb rossen is gathered by the young girls and it used to be said that if a girl could collect enough it would guarantee a long and healthy life.

During long periods of drought, the villagers hold a "german" (an ancient pagan festival). A doll is made of mud and carried by young girls who sing laments as if at a funeral. The doll is then thrown into the river as a sacrifice to bring rain. Other festivals are Lazaritza and Brada. The first takes place in the summer when the young girls play, dance and sing to wish everybody health, happiness and fruitfulness. Brada takes place at the end of the harvest when a wreath is made of the last wisp of straw which is presented to the farmer as a charm to bring a good harvest the following year.

The main dishes of the region fall into two categories – stews and roasts. Specialities include hotch potch, casseroled chicken with vegetables, and meatballs. There are also sharp, peppery soups. Favourite desserts are baklava and strudels.

SILISTRIA   Silistra is a town on the lower Danube, which forms the frontier with Romania. The wine district covers the sub-regions of Aideemir, Kalipetrovo, Sreburna, Smiletz, Kainardzha, Sitovo, Dobotitza and Tutrakan. Most of the soil is leached black earth. The area is a plateau with an average altitude of 110 metres (360 feet) above sea level, while a second area along the river valley of the Danube is between 15 and 20 metres (49-65 feet) above sea level. Apart from vinegrowing other agriculture includes cereals, vegetables, stock breeding and apricots. The region has a continental climate with hot dry summers and cold winters. Summer temperatures can reach 38-40°C (100-104°F) and there are often droughts. Winter temperatures can fall to -15 to -20°C (5 to -4°F).

Vines have always been grown in the region but during the Turkish occupation many growers abandoned their vineyards because of the high taxes imposed or they cultivated small areas to produce wine for their own consumption. Apart from commercial vineyards in Silistra and Tutrakan, most of the holdings were small until the 1930s. Even the largest vineyard was rarely more than 1.5 hectares (3.7 acres) and the village elders would meet each autumn to decide when the vintage should start. The grapes were transported from the vineyards in wooden tubs on horse drawn

The region extends over 160,000 hectares (39,536 acres) of which 1,637 hectares (4,045 acres) are covered by vines. About 1,150 hectares (2,841 acres) are planted with wine varieties and the remainder with dessert grapes.

carts. The tubs were too heavy to remove from the carts so the men would climb into them and crush the grapes with their feet. The must escaped from the tub through a hole drilled in the bottom into a wooden vessel placed beneath the cart. This vessel was carried down into the cellars and the must poured into casks for fermentation.

If the wine was mainly for home consumption it was rarely decanted from the casks, but if it was for sale it would be decanted in March into clean casks. The marc from the barrel would be added to the marc left over from the pressing and distillation. The wine was usually sold to local innkeepers who would collect it themselves, driving to the winery on carts containing large casks. During the Second World War, the vineyard owners sold the grapes while they were still on the vines and the innkeepers had to harvest and make the wine themselves.

Wine has always been drunk in the region and for a long time was considered more healthy than water. The children used to eat bread soaked in wine, a dish known as wine sops.

After nationalization, wine production developed around Silistra, Tutrakan, Alfatar, Ishirkovo and Kainardzha. The equipment was primitive, with manual grape crushers, small wooden vessels for filtration and fermentation and manual pumps for transferring the must and the wine. In 1958 two overground cellars with concrete tanks were built at Silistra and Tutrakan. Since then capacity has been increased, more sophisticated machinery introduced and new vineyards planted. In 1966 a further overground cellar was built in Silistra, and this was extended with more tanks, a new pressing section and five processing lines between 1972-76. At present a new line of cold

At present, out of the 1,637 hectares (4,045 acres) there are about 283 hectares (700 acres) of bearing vines, and the rest should be yielding grapes by 1990. Varieties grown are as follows:

Variety	area hectares/acres	wine produced per cent	total vineyards per cent
Rkatziteli	214/528	18.6	13.07
Muscat Ottonel	288/711	25.05	17.60
Dimiat	102/252	8.86	6.23
Chardonnay	100/247	8.70	6.10
Riesling	80/197	6.95	4.88
Fetijaska	36/88	3.14	2.20
Red Misket	40/98	3.48	2.44
Pamid	113/279	9.83	6.90
Cabernet Sauvignon	112/276	9.74	6.84
Merlot	65/160	5.65	3.96

fermentation tanks is being installed in Silistra for the production of still higher quality wines.

The grape-growing villages are Aidemir, Kalipetrovo, Sreburna, Smiletz, Kainardzha, Sitovo and Dobrotitza and the town of Tutrakan. There are two wine cellars in Silistra and Tutrakan.

The vintage normally starts on September 20. Picking is by hand. At the winery, the degree of pressing depends on the quality of wine to be made and once the must has been produced strict controls are enforced to ensure it is transferred to the correct processing area. The must is allowed to stay in contact with the grapes for up to six hours to enhance its bouquet. After settling and fining, the must for high quality wines is cold-fermented in metal tanks. The temperature during fermentation is not allowed to rise above 22°C (71°F), by the use of water cooling. Other wines are fermented in concrete tanks.

Grapes for red wines are crushed and transferred to ferro-concrete tanks where fermentation takes place. The young wine is separated from the marc during fermentation and transferred to other tanks for it to be completed. It is then filtered, filtered again after 15 days when sulphation and fining takes place. Some fermentation also occurs in controlled fermentation tanks where agitators keep the must separated from the marc.

The enterprise produces about four million litres (880,000 gallons) of wine annually, and this is expected to rise to about seven million litres (1.5 million gallons) by 1990 when the new vineyards start to bear fruit.

Production for the last three years was hit by very hot summers and droughts although sugar quality was high and quality excellent.

There is a considerable amount of experimental work being carried out in the area in conjunction with the research stations at Han Krum in the Shumen district, Varna and Pleven. There is no Controliran Region in the area at present but it is planned to introduce them shortly for the villages of Kalipetrovo, Aidemir, Smilets and Sitovo.

WEDDING TRADITIONS IN SILISTRIA

Among the region's many traditions, the two most elaborate and important are those to do with weddings and Christmas, the rituals dating back centuries.

The wedding ritual, from engagement to marriage, follows the seasons and is inexorably linked with the farming year. The wedding usually takes place after the harvest and the season lasts until Christmas. When a man has decided who he wants to marry the ritual begins. The whole of his household has to give their blessing so they visit the family of the bride. If they approve the man formally proposes, and if she accepts the wedding formalities start. The bride-to-be gives each of her relatives present a towel which they wrap around their fur caps. The future father-in-law gives her a bunch of flowers, a wooden wine vessel and a gold vessel. This signals the start of the "little engagement".

The engagement proper is formalized on the eve of the holiday to celebrate the gathering of the vintage. All the relatives of both families gather and the fiancé is given three symbolic gifts, a piece of string, a bunch of flowers and a piece of bread. Once the girl has accepted these she hands out small presents and the couple exchange rings. She also offers those present a drink of wine from the wooden cup given to her by her father-in-law. They are now considered truly engaged. All the details of the wedding are now worked out and the date fixed. The girl is no longer able to go to dances alone, although she can go accompanied by her fiancé's female relatives.

In the week before the wedding many rituals have to be observed and special food prepared. The brothers and sisters of the couple help to sift flour which is baked into ritual breads. There is also a ritual wedding tree, wedding flag, wedding cock and wedding garlands. The flour is sifted using three sieves and three basins. The dough, once kneaded, is then scraped from the basins using gold or silver ornaments or coins to bring future wealth. Once the loaves have been baked they are covered with honey and eaten after a horo has been danced. Two pieces of dough are left, one for the groom-to-be (who is not allowed to be present) and the other for the bride who will knead it into her special wedding loaf. The fiancé's family makes the wedding cock from a string of red peppers, a sack of grain and towels.

Before sunrise the next day, the wedding flag is made, a bright red banner with an apple impaled on the top of the pole. To

Varieties produced at present, and production expected by 1990		
	1988 litres/gallons	1990 litres/gallons
Rkatziteli	500,000/110,000	1,300,000/286,000
Muscat Ottonel	300,000/66,000	1,500,000/330,000
Dimiat	200,000/44,000	600,000/132,000
Chardonnay	60,000/13,200	600,000/132,000
Riesling	200,000/44,000	500,000/110,000
Fetijaska	200,000/44,000	500,000/110,000
Misket	150,000/33,000	600,000/132,000
Pamid	200,000/44,000	600,000/132,000
Cabernet Sauvignon	500,000/110,000	500,000/110,000
Merlot	60,000/13,200	300,000/66,000

dancing, it is paraded around the houses and then fixed to the roof of the house of the groom-to-be. It is never allowed to stay outside after sunset, so each dusk it is taken indoors, again to singing and dancing, and the ritual is repeated next day just before sunrise. Throughout there is feasting and dancing. At the house of the groom-to-be a special feast is hosted by his godfather where his relatives are lavishly plied with food and drink.

The wedding usually takes place on a Saturday and Sunday and on that day, before sunrise, the groom is shaved by his sisters-in-law. Relatives assemble from far and wide for the marriage and festivities. The wedding flag is removed from the roof and heads a procession which goes from house to house calling on the wedding guests to follow it. When they reach the house of the groom they find it barred by the bride's brothers.

Traditionally the godfather has to pay for the door to be opened, and then the groom's flag at the top of a four or five metre high pole has to be removed before the wedding can take place. There is never a shortage of volunteers willing to climb the flagstaff.

The groom, accompanied by his godmother and brothers, then have to pay the bride's sisters before she appears. The bride hands over gifts. including the wedding tree to the godfather and other relatives, and then drawing her veil over her face she gets on a horse drawn cart to be taken to the house where the wedding will take place. A few of the groom's relatives stay behind to move the bride's trousseau to her new home.

After the wedding ceremony, the couple are taken by cart to the groom's house. The procession is escorted by singers and dancers. On arrival the couple stay in the cart while his mother dances a ritual dance around them, holding bread, flour and wine. Then the presentation of gifts begin. The groom's father is first, then the mother (who gives household gifts and poultry) and then all the other relatives. The groom escorts his bride into his house

Ritual breads are specially prepared before a wedding. Bread dough is scraped from the basins using gold and silver ornaments and even coins as implements. It is believed this will bring future prosperity to the couple.

over white cloths that have been laid on the ground. As he enters the house the groom is symbolically beaten by the bride's brothers for having stolen her away. It is then time for more feasting and dancing. The wedding feast always consists of richly decorated ritual bread and boiled chicken.

CHRISTMAS SILISTRIAN STYLE The celebration of Christmas has also become an established ritual, starting on December 20. On that day all the children go from house to house with a stick in their hand and a bag over their shoulder. At each house they are given small loaves of bread, dried fruits, nuts or boiled maize. If the household has a daughter, she bakes a special loaf. A special round loaf is baked for Christmas Eve and only meatless dishes are eaten during dinner – boiled beans, boiled wheat, cabbage, pickles and compote of fruits. The oldest man of the household breaks the bread to signal the start of the meal. At midnight the young bachelors of the village, aged between 16 and 20, and occasionally a bridegroom married for less than a year, get together and appoint a "king". He divides them into small groups called "Koledari", which between them will visit all the houses of the village. There is usually a lot of rivalry as the young men vie to get in the group delegated to visit the homes of their girlfriends. One member of each group is elected the "donkey" to carry the gifts they receive during their visits. Each group is led by the youngest member who goes ahead to warn of their coming. The groups sing songs and hand out wine, and in return receive gifts of food or special bread. When all the houses have been visited, the groups re-assemble and the "king" conducts an auction. The young men each bid for the bread baked by their sweethearts.

After Christmas, the festival of Survaki is celebrated on January 1. The men weave a basket of twigs for their children and during the morning the Survakari, or well-wishers, arrive to greet

the family and the New Year. Each well-wisher is given a small gift of bread, walnuts, dried fruit, sweets, coins or home made presents.

The main wine festival celebrated in the region is Triffon Day on February 14, the holiday of the vine-growers and wine makers. Everyone dresses in national costume and gathers in the vineyards where the first vines are pruned. Garlands are made from the cuttings and at first worn around the hats of the vine growers. Later, they are removed and "watered" with wine from a wooden jug to try to ensure a good harvest. The rest of the day is spent feasting, dancing and singing.

There are a number of speciality dishes, many of them involving fish because of the proximity of the River Danube. There are also a number of light meatless dishes which seem to have developed because of the hot climate.

POMORIE

The Vinprom Pomorie enterprise consists of four main growing districts – Pomorie, Kablenkovo, Galabetz and Bata. The region extends in the east to the Black Sea, in the west to the mountains between the villages of Brajastovetz and Muglen, in the north to the Stara Planina and in the south to the Atanassovsko Lake.

Wines have certainly been grown in the region since Thracian times, especially in the warm valleys and the hill slopes exposed to the sun. In the Hermitage museum in Leningrad there is a tablet from Pomorie which was used in rituals to worship the wine god Dionysus. It was discovered in Anhialo, transferred to the Odessa museum in 1829, and to the Hermitage in 1869. It depicts a female figure standing over a sacrificial altar. In one hand she is holding a wine vessel and in the other a bunch of grapes. The inscription in Ancient Greek reads: "Good luck Avludsena. The daughter of Avludsen presents to the god Appolonius a gift of thankfulness for her own survival and for the survival of her vineyards on the slopes." There are records that report that there was a Thracian named Avludsena living in Anhialo at the turn of the millenium, and quite clearly the prosperity of the town came from its wine.

The Greeks introduced new grape varieties from the south and new winemaking techniques. A flourishing trade developed and amphoras bearing the seals of Anhialo and Messambria were found in Heraklia, an ancient town in the Asian part of Turkey. Coins minted in Anhialo at the time showed the God Hermes holding in his arms the child Dionysus, or the fertility goddess Demetra holding a bunch of grapes.

When the Romans came to the Balkan Peninsula in the first century AD they abolished the decrees that only wheat could be planted on the land along the Black Sea coast. Many white varieties were planted to cope with the demand for lighter, more easy drinking wines. Special ships were built capable of carrying hundreds of amphora containing wine, and the remains of one such vessel have been discovered on the seabed just off Pomorie. Many giant clay jars have been unearthed during excavations at Nessebar, Sozopol and elsewhere. The amphoras were buried up to their necks in the earth to maintain constant temperatures.

The vineyards continued to prosper under the Slavs and most of the land was planted with vines, according to the Greek chronicler Anna Comnena who wrote about Anhialo in the eleventh century. There were huge wine warehouses in Anhialo and Messambria and the wine was exported throughout Europe and the Middle East.

Under Ottoman rule, there was a general decline in agriculture but the vineyards survived. The Turkish regional governers encouraged the planting of dessert varieties.

At the turn of the century the main wine varieties were Pamid, Dimiat and Mavrud. Phylloxera hit the area in 1906 but its impact was limited because the growers had already started to introduce resistant American rooting stock. In 1927 the first cooperative was established in Anhialo called Dimiat. A wine cellar was built with a total capacity of almost two million litres (440,000 gallons). Pumps were imported from Italy, continuous presses installed as well as 30,000 litre (6,600 gallon) fermentation tanks. Wine maker Martchevski, who was an expert in French winemaking techniques, ran the cellar. The wines sold throughout Bulgaria and were even exported to Germany. Almost all the other producers at this time had small vineyards and sold their wines locally.

Vinprom Pomorie brought together all the private producers, distillers and Dimiat. Between 1948-50 two overground cellars were constructed to increase processing and storage capacity.

Between 1955 and 1960 a new cellar was built in Pomorie with a nine million litre (1.9 million gallon) capacity, and the cellars in Nessebur and Bata were rebuilt with two million (440,000) and one and a half million litre (330,000 gallon) capacity.

In 1958 the region produced 30,000 tonnes (29,520 tons) of grapes, but the wineries could not cope with this rapid expansion. Water tanks in Aheloj and Kableshkovo had to be used as emergency holding tanks. Consequently, between 1960-62, the capacity of all the cellars was increased. Since the 1960s there has been a steady updating of the latest winemaking equipment with Italian filtration machines, French presses, German separaters and Bulgarian technology. Today the latest equipment is used to produce the high quality dessert wines and red and white table wines that the enterprise specializes in.

The area comprises of three distinct zones, the plain, hills and mountains. The region around Pomorie is flat, while the terrain around Kableshkovo, Bata and Galabetz although undulating is not too steep for mechanized equipment in the vineyards. The land around Kositchino is mountainous and difficult to work and has prevented the planting of large vineyards.

The Pomorie Plain has an average altitude of only nine metres (30 feet) above sea level and is slightly sloping. The River Aheloj crosses the region and both it and its tributaries are used for irrigation. The region is relatively dry and the annual total rainfall is between 400 and 500 litres a square metre (88–110 gallons a square yard), evenly distributed throughout the year. The plain has mild and humid winters, long and cold humid springs, hot, dry summers and long, warm autumns. The soils are predominantly leached black earth, black meadow and alluvial meadow. Most of the plain has a humus covering of between 50 and 80 centimetres (19–31 inches), and in some cases is more than a metre (3.2 feet) deep. The vineyards are planted in the areas where the humus content is lowest, between 1.5 and 2.5 per cent. Other crops are autumn cereals, fodder crops, sunflowers and vegetables.

The hilly zone is between 50 and 150 metres (164–492 feet)

above sea level with flat river valleys and gentle slopes. The main soils are leached woodland covering 40-50 per cent of the land, with an average humus depth of between 20 and 30 centimetres (7-11 inches), and maroon woodland slightly acid soils are found around the villages of Poroi, Galabetz, Bata, Stratzin and Gorishta. There are also areas of leached black earth and alluvial meadow soils, which are very fertile with deep humus layers. Dams on the rivers Poroi, Tankovo and Aheloj provide water for irrigation of both the vineyards and vegetable crops. The region is dry, but the annual rainfall total is higher than that of Pomorie, between 500 and 550 litres a square metre (110-121 gallons a square yard). Most of the vineyards are planted on terraced, eastern facing slopes.

The mountainous zone is between 350 and 600 metres (1,148-1,968 feet) above sea level, with an annual precipitation of between 500 and 600 litres a square metre (110-132 gallons a square yard). The soils are leached and mainly woodland earth.

The enterprise concentrates on wine production although increased mechanisation and efficiency has meant more labour available to boost fruit and vegetable production both for the

complex and the surrounding regions. More than 90 per cent of the total vineyards are for wine production – 3,653 hectares (9,026 acres) are fruit bearing, 475 hectares (1,173 acres) are recently planted vines.

The four main wine growing districts – Pomorie, Kableshkovo, Galabetz and Bata – are complemented by the agro-industrial complex of Nessebar, which also has three grape producing areas around Nessebar, Orizare and Obzor, and these include 22 specialized technology sites. The vineyards are between 200 and 400 hectares (494-988 acres) each and the average yield is between 10 and 12 tonnes a hectare (9.84-11.8 tons an acre). In some years the total yield has topped 40,000 tonnes (39,360 tons) of grapes. The table grapes are grown mainly on slopes and areas of lighter soils, while the wine varieties and grapes for brandy and sparkling wines are found mainly on the plain and areas of richer soils.

There are four main wine cellars, two in Pomorie, one in the town of Kableshkovo and one in the village of Bata. Pruning starts in the late autumn and continues until the end of March. Since 1985 there has been some mechanical pruning using both Italian Campanela and Bulgarian equipment. The Bulgarian machines were developed at the Hydravlica works in Kasanluk. Weeds are controlled between the vines by ploughing but not deep enough to disturb the sub soil. Herbicides and sprays are used to control perennial weeds and mildew, and there can be up to six treatments with sulphur dust to control oidium. Insecticides are also applied throughout the growing season, especially against the grape moth.

The vintage normally starts between September 10 and 15 depending on the ripeness of the grapes. Most picking is by hand: the pickers are divided into groups of 60 people, each group operating between 200-250 pails and having its own tractor and trailer, and lorry to keep supplied. Depending on the variety, a picker can gather about 1,000 kilogrammes (2,205lb) of grapes a day, and the entire complex at its heights is picking between 800 and 1,000 tonnes (787-984 tons) a day. Two Soviet and one French harvesters are being experimentally used to collect grapes from 70 hectares (172 acres) of suitably prepared vineyard, but the results to date have not been impressive. The quality of the picked grapes is not satisfactory and a lot of leaves and twigs are also gathered by the harvesters.

The grapes for the white wine are crushed and passed through presses. Sulphation of the must takes place in separation tanks after 24 hours. The must is then racked and pumped into fermentation tanks for the initial vigorous fermentation, and then transferred to ferro-concrete and steel tanks for the remainder of the fermentation.

The Pomorie region covers 25,300 hectares (62,516 acres) of land, of which 17,120 hectares (42,303 acres) are cultivated – cereals 7,000 hectares (17,297 acres), arable land 1,700 hectares (4,200 acres), vegetables 320 hectares (790 acres), fodder crops 3,600 hectares (8,895 acres), fruit 1,700 hectares (4,200 acres) and vineyards 2,800 hectares (6,918 acres). Sheep and cattle are also reared.

Left Above *Stabilization tanks inside the winery buildings; (below) wine is bottled at the laboratory and bottling plant in Burgas.*

Above right *A modern building in Pomorie used for the ageing of brandy. Below wine is rigorously tested in the Burgas laboratories.*

Grapes for red wines are crushed and controlled fermentation is carried out between 25 and 28°C (77-82°F). The wine is separated at a relative weight of between 1035 and 1045. The marc is removed and pressed again for distillation, and the wine is transferred to tanks for ageing.

Each year the enterprise produces about 13 million litres (three million gallons) of table wines and about nine million litres (two million gallons) of wine for distillation into brandy at Pomorie. Between 1976 and 1986 the enterprise was hit by bad weather and suffered considerable losses because of hailstorms and drought. There were also problems with diseases and pests which the current measures have been designed to eradicate. Because of drought the enterprise lost 2,500 tonnes (2,460 tons) of grapes in 1983, 1,700 tonnes (1,672 tons) in 1984, 7,000 tonnes (6,888 tons) in 1985 and 700 tonnes (688 tons) in 1986.

POMORIE: GRAPE VARIETIES GROWN

	vineyard size hectare/acre	productive vines hectare/acre	young vines hectare/acre
Dessert varieties			
Super Ran Bolgar	3.8/9.3	1.4/3.4	2.4/5.9
Cardinal	68.1/168.2	46.5/114.9	21.6/53.3
Tzaritza	11.3/27.9	11.3/27.9	
Tchaush	13.2/32.6	13.2/32.6	
Italia	34.3/84.7	18.8/46.4	15.5/38.3
Bolgar	4.1/10.1	4.1/10.1	
Hambourg Misket	72.4/178.9	29.0/71.6	43.4/107.2
Servan	7.4/18.2	7.4/18.2	
Alfonce Lavelle	1.1/2.7	1.1/2.7	
Pleven	19.1/47.1	2.2/5.4	16.8/41.5
Brestovitza	18.1/44.7		18.1/44.7
Maritza	1.7/4.2		1.7/4.2
Zagore	6.6/16.3		6.6/16.3
Dunav	1.0/3.2		1.0/3.2
Ran Misket	3.1/7.6		3.1/7.6
Veren	3.0/7.4		3.0/7.4
Vjara	1.3/3.2		1.3/3.2
Tcherna Perla	0.6/1.4		0.6/1.4
Buljana	0.4/0.9		0.4/0.9
Alfonce x Thracia	0.3/0.7		0.3/0.7
Experimentals	2.2/5.4		2.2/5.4
Wine varieties			
Pamid	781.2/1,930	722.4/1,785	58.8/145.0
Aligoté	51.8/127.9	51.8/127.9	
Shevka	70.7/174.6	7.0/17.2	63.7/157.4
Cabernet	74.3/181.1	74.3/181.1	
Merlot	129.3/319.5	129.3/319.5	
Dimiat	418.8/1,034	400.8/990.0	18.0/44.0
Red Misket	14.0/34.5	14.0/34.5	
Rkatziteli	251.2/620.7	251.2/620.7	
Musket Ottonel	256.6/634.0	256.6/634.0	
Riesling	11.3/27.9	11.3/27.9	
Ugni Blanc	381.4/942.4	357.4/883.1	24.0/59.3
Kamtchia	26.5/65.4	2.0/4.9	24.5/60.5
Chardonnay	13.7/33.8		13.7/33.8
Varna Misket	9.2/22.7	6.3/15.5	2.9/7.1
Tamjanka	7.4/18.2	7.4/18.2	
Herbus	0.9/2.2		0.9/2.2
Trakijski Bisser	0.3/0.7		0.3/0.7
Dunavski Lazur	9.3/22.9	9.3/22.0	
Srebrostruj	1.1/2.7	1.1/2.7	
Pomorijski Bisser	9.4/23.2	9.4/23.2	
Kailashki Misket	1.8/4.4	1.8/4.4	
Pleven Kolorit	0.4/0.9	0.4/0.9	
Sortiment	8.2/20.2	5.1/12.6	3.1/7.6

The area does not have any wines of Controliran Region as yet but is hoping some might be approved by Vinprom and the Central Tasting Commission in Sofia shortly.

FOLKLORE AND CUISINE

Before the start of the vintage each year, the priest led a procession of villagers past the home of each vine grower and wine maker. The priest would say a prayer and sprinkle holy water over the casks, the cellars and winemaking equipment.

People used to travel to the region from far away to help with the vintage and it was a time of great festivity. Before the vintage got under way there would be singing, dancing and feasting.

The holiday of the vine grower is celebrated on February 14 with processions, a ritual pruning of the vines and prayers. The women bake special loaves and bury them in a hole dug in the vineyards to bring a good harvest.

Winemaking, salt production and fishing have been the occupations in the region for thousands of years and have determined the pattern of local cuisine. There are very special ways of preparing fish which constitute the main dishes of the region. These include belted bonito where the dried fish is baked, soaked in oil and vinegar and grilled. Each autumn grey mullet (plakija) is popular. The fish is baked in an oven with sour cabbage and served with vine leaves. There are many salt fish dishes and caviars, but salted mackerel liver is a speciality. Another special delicacy is made from the caviar of the turbot, which is pressed between two pieces of wood and then allowed to dry in the sun. Also famous are the region's soups, again usually made with fish. Other traditional dishes include turkey with blue plums, veal with blue plums and veal with okra.

Table grapes are used in the preparation of many desserts and

Production according to variety		
Dimiat	1,900,000 litres	(418,000 gallons)
Ugni Blanc	1,700,000 litres	(374,000 gallons)
Misket	200,000 litres	(44,000 gallons)
Riesling	200,000 litres	(44,000 gallons)
Rkatziteli	1,500,000 litres	(330,000 gallons)
Muscat Ottonel	2,400,000 litres	(528,000 gallons)
Bjalo ot Pamid	3,100,000 litres	(682,000 gallons)
Pamid	300,000 litres	(37,000 gallons)
Cabernet	700,000 litres	(154,000 gallons)
Merlot	1,000,000 litres	(220,000 gallons)
Other reds	400,000 litres	(88,000 gallons)

drinks. Specialities include treacle quinces, grape treacle, white khalva, walnut kernels dipped in grape must and then flour, Kulikja loaves boiled in must, and narden (a drink made from the boiled must). During the vintage, the towns and villages are filled with the fragrant smell as each house prepare its narden and other delicacies.

SHUMEN

The Shumen district is one of the most famous wine producing areas of Bulgaria and has been producing quality wines for centuries. A series of excavations around Preslav has unearthed many artefacts dating from between the ninth and the fourteenth centuries AD connected with the cultivation of the vines and the making of wine. Many large clay fermentation pots called Vinarka, dating from the ninth century, have been found near Patleina, as well as gold and silver wine goblets. Many of the terraces still used were built hundreds of years ago to create more vineyards as wine became the most important local product.

Situated in the central part of northeast Bulgaria, the countryside varies enormously and there are many different soil types. There are plateaux, river valleys and semi-mountainous slopes and a multitide of micro-climates suitable for growing vines and giving the wine special qualities. The phylloxera outbreak hit the Shumen district at the end of the last century, devastating the vineyards, but the growers quickly replanted with resistant root stock. The first wine cooperatives were formed in the 1920s and there were some private firms selling both wines and dessert grapes to European customers.

After the war a programme was started to modernize the wineries and extend the vineyards, although it was not until the 1960s that many of the new varieties were introduced. In 1965 the first automated bottling line was installed in Preslav with a capacity of 2,500 bottles an hour. The first distillery was built in 1967. In 1979 the first cold sterile bottling line was opened in Khan Krum, also the first in Bulgaria, with a capacity of three million bottles a year. It now exports to the UK, the United States, Canada, Japan, East and West Germany, the USSR, Poland, Cuba, Sweden and Denmark.

There are three micro-regions – north, central and south. The north region covers the southern slopes of the chain of hills which divides the Ludogorsko and Madarsko plateaux from the central zone. It includes the settlements of Stan, Novi Pazar, Pamuktchi, St Michailovski, Voivoda, Isbul and Praventzi on the Ludogorsko Plateau, and Zlatna niva, Pliska, Kaspitchan, Madara and Kjulevtcha on the Madarsko Plateau. The soil is carbonate black earth and high in limestone, and the region enjoys a very mild climate

because of the penetrating influence of warm winds. The total temperature during the growing season is between 3,300 and 3,400°C (5,972-6,152°F) and the total annual rainfall is the lowest in the region at 500 litres a square metre (110 gallons a square yard). This micro-region specializes in quality white wines. The main variety is Rkatziteli but the acreage under Chardonnay and Riesling is growing fast.

The central micro-region takes in the middle hills and includes the settlements of Belokopitovo, Srednja, Lozevo, Shumen, Divdjadovo, Salmanovo, Marash, Dibitch and Ivanski. The enterprise at Novi Pazar plans to have 800 hectares (1,976 acres) of Chardonnay in the next few years which will account for more than 40 per cent of all production. The vineyards are planted on the hill slopes and the soils are eroded black earth, rich in organic matter. The average total temperature during the growing season is between 3,400 and 3,600°C (6,152-6,512°F), depending on the exposure and the slope. The average annual rainfall is between 570 and 600 litres a square metre (125-132 gallons a square yard). The climatic and soil conditions here are also ideal for white wine grapes. The main varieties are Rkatziteli and Musket Ottonel, although Traminer rosé and Sauvignon are now being extensively planted.

The south micro-region is bordered by the southern slopes of the Shumen plateau and the river Vrana. It includes the settlements of Khan Krum, Troitza, Osmar, Kotchovo, Imrentchevo, Preslav, Dragoevo, Zlater, Smjadovo, Jankovo and Kulnovo. The vineyards are mostly planted on grey soils. The total temperature during the growing season is between 3,400 and 3,600°C (6,152-6,512°F), and the average annual rainfall between 650 and 700 litres a square metre (143-154 gallons a square yard). This micro-region has both the highest temperatures and the highest rainfall and is ideal for the cultivation of Rkatziteli, Dimiat, Muscat Ottonel, Chardonnay and Traminer rosé. The highest quality table wines are produced as well as grapes for wine distillate.

The viti-vinicultural region of Novi Pazar-Shumen – Preslav

White wine accounts for almost 95 per cent of production.

The main street in the village of Osmar.

Major white grape varieties and their production	
Rkatziteli	28.4 per cent
Dimiat	15.9 per cent
Muscat	14.6 per cent
Riesling	13.2 per cent
Chardonnay	10.4 per cent
Aligoté	6.2 per cent
Traminer rosé/Sauvignon	3.8 per cent

can be divided into two main geographical zones. Firstly, the Samuil Heights and plateaux, situated in the north and central part of the region. This is a region of high plateaux, about 250 metres (820 feet) above sea level, which divides the regions of the Danube and the Black Sea; and second, the Preslavsko-Dragoevski Heights, a region of hills and deeply cut river valleys, with an altitude varying between 250 and 300 metres (820-984 feet).

Between 35,000 and 40,000 tonnes (34,440-39,360 tons) of grapes are processed annually in the wineries at Preslav, Novi Pazar, Shumen, Khan Krum, Gragoevo, Osmar and the brandy distillery in Khan Krum. The wineries in Preslav, Khan Krum and Shumen also bottle wine – 14 million bottles annually in Preslav and 3 million bottles each at the other two plants. Preslav also handles 14 million bottles of brandy a year.

The region has a growing period of between 190 and 200 days with favourable conditions, it is frost-free between April 10-18 and October 25 to November 5 and there are between 1450 and 1650 hours of sunshine. Under these conditions the grapes start to ripen in the second half of August and are ready for picking, depending on variety, between September 15 and October 20.

Pruning starts early in the new year and continues until March when the sap starts to rise in the vines. Most of the pruning is by hand although mechanical pruners have been introduced in some areas. The vines are trained according to the Ombrassa or Improved Moser system with the stem height varying between 60 centimetres (23 inches) and 1.2 metres (3.9 feet) and the rows 2-3.4 metres (6.5-11 feet) apart. Very occasionally the Guyot system is used for dessert grapes.

The vintage usually starts with the gathering of the earliest ripening varieties – Chardonnay, Traminer and Sauvignon. It is followed by Riesling, Aligoté, Muscat Ottonel and Muscat, and finally by the late ripening Dimiat and Rkatziteli. The vintage starts in the second half of September and continues for about 45 days. From about the middle of August the scientists study the ripening grapes, analysing them for sugar content, acid and fruit acid. All the grapes are picked by hand, not only because quality control is critical, but because much of the terrain would not lend itself to mechanical harvesters. The grapes for the highest quality wines are gathered in buckets, the remainder in larger containers and tubs. The grapes are all in the cellars within two to three hours of picking. They are checked for quality and sugar content and the technologists decide how they are to be used.

The grapes are pressed and then passed through rotto-filters under controlled temperature to separate the must. The wines are cold fermented under strictly controlled conditions. The tanks are cooled in a variety of ways, either by refridgeration units, running

The Shumen region has 153,000 hectares (378,063 acres) of land under cultivation of which 5,680 hectares (14,035 acres) are vineyards – 5,270 hectares (13,022 acres) producing wine grapes and 410 hectares (1,013 acres) producing dessert wines. Other agricultural products include cereals 70,900 hectares (175,193 acres), fruit (apples, plums, cherries and apricots) 3,500 hectares (8,648 acres), and vegetables (tomatoes and peppers) 2,650 hectares (6,548 acres). Fodder crops account for 30,700 hectares (75,859 acres).

In the years between 1977 and 1987 the amount of grapes gathered each vintage has varied from 31,500 tonnes (30,996 tons) in 1977 to 53,000 tonnes (52,152 tons) in 1982. Hailstorms, droughts and very high summer temperatures hit yields in 1985 and 1986 – 34,000 and 27,600 tonnes (33,456 and 27,158 tons) respectively.

cold water down the outside of the fermentation vessels, or using cold air jets. After fermentation the wine is filtered and transferred to holding tanks. The wineries usually produce about 60 litres (13 gallons) of wine from each 100 kilogrammes (220lb) of grapes.

Experimental work is undertaken by the research station in Khan Krum and concentrates on the bioclimate of specific vineyards (the relationship between soil and climate) to obtain stable yields and high quality. They have established a number of small experimental vineyards to test the performance of different varieties, and this data is then translated into instructions for the commercial vineyards. There is also work on pruning methods, and the correct levels of nutrition feeding.

The area is suited to the production of high quality wines and the following varieties have been chosen after many years of trials as the most suitable – Chardonnay, Aligoté, Riesling, Sauvignon Blanc, Traminer rosé and Muscat Ottonel. There are two Controliran Region areas, producing Chardonnay from Novi Pazar and Traminer from Khan Krum. The eighth vintage from both these areas was produced in 1987.

A new Controliran Region area producing Sauvignon Blanc is expected to be announced shortly. There are very promising results from experiments in Khan Krum where Chardonnay is being fermented in small oak barrels. The cellar is already leading the way with the cold fermentation of Chardonnays. Fermentation in steel tanks takes place at between 12 and 14°C (53-57°F) and produces very high quality wines with masses of aroma and elegance. Other wineries are now following this example.

FOLKLORE   The villagers celebrate the Holiday of the Vine Grower on February 14. In this region all the villagers go to one vineyard to a carefully chosen vine which is then ritually pruned by the oldest wine grower. The vine is then "watered" by wine poured from a wooden vessel as part of a traditional ceremony to ask for a good harvest. Then all the people cut a twig and carry this with them for the rest of the day which is spent feasting and dancing.

Plans are going ahead to build a museum to the vine and wine at Mogilata, on the southwest outskirts of Preslav. It is planned to build the museum in the centre of a vineyard with its own winery and tasting centre. Both new and old varieties will be planted.

RAZGRAD   The Razgrad enterprise is in the northeast part of the country, neighbouring the districts of Silistra, Shumen, Targovishte and Russe. The terrain is hilly at an altitude of between 200 and 495 metres (656-1,623 feet) above sea level. The hillsides vary from gentle slopes to plunging cliffs. The soil is mostly leached grey woodland, but on the upper slopes of the hills there has been a lot of soil erosion bringing many mineral salts to the surface.

Vines were introduced to the region in the Middle Ages, and the Pole Samuil Tvardovski, who accompanied Prince Cristophor Zbarski through the region in 1621, wrote "we arrived in Razgrad, famous for its vineyards." The Turkish travel writer Evlija Tchelebi visited Razgrad between 1651-56 and said the vineyards were famous for their succulent grapes. The real story of winemaking, however, starts in 1907 when the vineyards were replanted after the phylloxera outbreak. In 1911 a syndicate of local growers was formed to import Amercian resistant root stock and get the industry back on its feet. Every family owned a vineyard, no matter how small and the main varieties grown were Pamid, Misket, Shikla, Gamza and Dimiat.

The vineyard expansion continued steadily until the Second World War with wine varieties ousting many of the table grapes. In 1939 there were 8,000 hectares (19,768 acres) of vineyards and in 1943 the growers established their own cooperative, building a cellar with a 600,000 litre (132,000 gallon) capacity.

After nationalization, new vineyards were planted and many of the old ones dug up. The first wine factories were built in 1966 in Razgrad (five million litre/1.1 million gallon capacity) and in Kubrat (two million litre/440,000 gallon capacity). The two plants were expanded in 1972 doubling their capacities.

The region covers 262,370 hectares (648,316 acres), of which 162,800 hectares (402,278 acres) are cultivated, 80,000 hectares (197,680 acres) are covered by forests and 225 hectares (555 acres) by lakes. The Beli Lom dam has been built as part of a major irrigation scheme. Other agriculture includes cereals, sunflowers, sugar beet and tobacco and livestock (pigs, poultry, sheep and cattle). Bee keeping also plays an important role in the agriculture of the region.

Main grape varieties			
Reds	hectare/acre	**Whites**	hectare/acre
Gamza	3.0/7.4	Aligoté	253.8/627.1
Pamid	3.0/7.4	Rkatziteli	804.6/1,988
Cabernet Sauvignon	60.0/148.0	Dimiat	73.3/181.0
Pinot Noir	12.0/29.6	Pink Traminer	30.0/74.0
Hamburger Misket	5.0/12.3	Italian Riesling	27.0/66/7
Merlot	30.0/74.0	Muscat Ottonel	52.8/130.4
Senzo	5.6/13.8	Chardonnay	8.0/19.7
Saperavi	8.0/19.7	Red Misket	3.0/7.4

There are nine vine producing districts, each organized into a brigade and the grapes are processed at Vinprom Razgrad in Kubrat. There are nine agro-industrial complexes, an experimental sheep breeding centre, and a state seed station. The wine industry is well developed with 126.6 hectares (312.8 acres) of vineyards producing grapes for red wine, 1,252.5 hectares (3,094 acres) producing grapes for white wine and 112 hectares (276 acres) for dessert wines.

The total temperature during the growing period is between 3,100 and 3,700°C (5,612-6,692°F). The average monthly temperature in the hottest summer months of July and August is 22 and 23°C (71-73°F), and there are about 195 frost-free days. Pruning takes place between January and March, and there is a regular programme of spraying to combat disease and pests.

The vintage usually starts between September 15 and 20, and the first grapes to be picked are those for the sparkling wines, and the last, after November 1, are those for dessert wines. The grapes are picked by hand. On arrival at the winery, the grapes are tested for sugar content, quality and weight. The grapes are then crushed and the must allowed to run off into cooling tanks before it is filtered and transferred to fermentation tanks. All the white wine is produced using controlled cold fermentation, and ten such tanks were installed in 1980. There has already been an appreciable improvement in quality. The annual total production is about seven million litres (1.5 million gallons).

The quality of wine over the last few years has been good but quantity has been hit by bad weather, especially hailstorms and

Production		
Sparkling wines:		
Aligoté	600,000 litres	(132,000 gallons)
Riesling	200,000 litres	(44,000 gallons)
Rkatziteli	150,000 litres	(33,000 gallons)
Chardonnay	30,000 litres	(6,600 gallons)
Table wine:		
Aligoté	400,000 litres	(88,000 gallons)
Riesling	100,000 litres	(22,000 gallons)
Rkatziteli	2,000,000 litres	(440,000 gallons)
Muscat Ottonel	400,000 litres	(88,000 gallons)
Cabernet Rosé	200,000 litres	(44,000 gallons)
Gamza	100,000 litres	(22,000 gallons)
Blended reds	100,000 litres	(22,000 gallons)
Blended whites	800,000 litres	(176,000 gallons)
Wine vinegar	300,000 litres	(66,000 gallons)

frosts. There has been a tendency to reduce the vineyard amount and consequently the grape tonnage to improve quality. The region is noted for its Aligoté and Rkatziteli wines which are characterized by freshness, fruit and elegance. Cabernet rosé with its excellent colour, good varietal characteristics and taste is becoming popular.

The region produces one Controliran Region wine, Momina Tcheshma. It is a pure varietal made from Aligoté, produced around Razgrad and has a yellow-greeny colour and strong varietal characteristics. It is aged for two years in special cellars to produce a distinctive bouquet, rich scent and taste.

In 1987 the wine Loznishko Bjalo was also approved as a declared geographic origin. It is a white wine blended from 85 per cent Dimiat and 15 per cent Muscat Ottonel, and produced in the town of Loznitza. It is noted for its fruitiness and balance.

VARNA

This wine enterprise is in the Black Sea division and is noted for producing high quality table and sparkling wines, mostly from Dimiat, Italian Riesling, Aligoté and Chardonnay. The area has always been involved in producing grapes, and the ancient motto of Varna was "sun, sea and grapes".

There are archaeological relics to show that the Thracians were producing wine in the area of Odesos. In medieval Bulgaria, between the sixth and fourteenth centuries, the wines of the region had an international following. Even under the Turks, the wines of Varna were exported. In 1860 Nikola Provadaliev from Varna founded the first distillery and in 1875 the first wine society was formed in Varna. The first cooperative, called Dimiat, was formed in 1920, the following year it became a member of the Bulgarian Central Cooperative Bank and in 1925 it started to sell its produce, of grapes, wines and fruit. It won its first export order in 1927 for a wine produced from the Dimiat grapes. In 1933, in the summer resort of Saint Constantin, the country's first plant health institute specially for vines was opened.

Disease problems between 1936 and 1941 led to a decline in vine growing and there was a substantial decrease in the vineyard area. After nationalization wine continued to be produced in the former warehouses of private firms on a small scale. The first vintage of Vinprom Varna was sold in 1951 and by 1954 the enterprise was processing 1.2 million tonnes (1.1 million tons) of grapes. The vineyards were extended and an extra processing capacity had to be introduced, so new processing cellars, laboratories and storage capacity were built. In 1963 hot bottling was introduced and for the first time in Bulgaria new low alcohol whites were produced, mostly from Dimiat, Ugni Blanc, and

Above *A vineyard in Varna where Varna Misket grapes are used to make white wine.*

Below *Experimental research cellars.*

Rkatziteli. They had an alcoholic strength of between 6-7½ per cent, and a sugar content of between 4½-7½ per cent. Since then there has been a steady programme of modernization and expansion. A new cellar with a 7.2 million litre (1.5 million gallon) capacity was built, new equipment introduced and new bottling lines, capable of producing four million bottles a year. New ranges of wines were created such as Lazur, Iskra-Zvezditza and Dionisievo. Cold fermentation and cold sterile bottling were also introduced in readiness for the granting of AIC designations.

The district is divided into five sub-regions (Avren, Bjala, Provadja, Dalgopol and Vetrino) each managed by an agro-industrial complex and they all come under the control of the viti-viniculture complex of Varna. The area has milder and windier winters in comparison to the rest of the region, and a colder and longer spring which means a slower start for the vines. Most of the vines are planted on stony black earth which only has a depth of between 40-50 centimetres (15-19 inches). The soil is acidic with good water retention but poor organic content.

The area can be split into three zones: coastal belt at sea level taking in the territory between Beloslav, Sindel, Bozvelijsko and Gradinarovo; the hills and plains along the rivers Kamchia and Provadiya as far as Burgas; and the plateau and hills including the Frangen Uplands between Aksakovo, Suvorovo and Belogradetz.

The area managed by Vinprom Varna covers 2,534 hectares (6,261 acres) of cultivated land apart from the vineyards, of which 1,208 hectares (2,984 acres) are for cereals and 1,881 hectares (4,647 acres) for perennial crops. The area is suitable for cereals, fruit, vegetables and stock breeding, cattle, pigs, poultry and sheep, but wine production is still a major enterprise. The main grain production is for bread wheat which is concentrated in four areas – Aksakovo, Valtchi dol, Suvorovo and Vetrino. Fruit, especially apples and peaches are grown around Dalgopol, Georgi Traikov, Provadia and Vetrino. Main vegetables grown are tomatoes, peppers, onions, carrots and potatoes in Aksakovo, Vetrino, Provadia and Valtchidol.

The area of vineyards in the region now exceeds 5,234 hectares (12,933 acres), of which 92 per cent are the dominant varieties of Dimiat, Rkatziteli, Riesling, Muscat, Chardonnay and Aligoté. Dessert vineyards cover 497 hectares (1,228 acres), mostly with Bolgar, Hamburger Misket, Cardinal and Trakijski Misket. The ratio between wine grapes and table grapes is changing and it is planned to arrive at a proportion of 88 per cent to 12 per cent respectively.

In the Varna wine complex micro-region there are 1,523 hectares (3,763 acres) of vineyards, 1,411 hectares (3,486 acres) for wine and 112 hectares (276 acres) for dessert grapes.

About 15,000 people are employed directly in the vineyards, wineries, laboratories and allied industries. Apart from the Vinprom enterprise there are about 3,000 hectares (7,413 acres) of privately owned vineyards in the region mainly growing Dimiat, Pamid, Bolgar, Hamburger Misket and Cardinal. There are three Vinprom cellars for making wine at Varna, Provadia and Bjala, and experimental cellars in Vladislavovo, Vetrino and Evksinovgrad.

Work in the vineyards starts immediately after the harvest with autumn ploughing. This continues up to December 10. Spring ploughing takes place until April 25 and then there is regular rotavation between lines through the summer. Manure, phosphates and calcium fertilizers are added as necessary, and pruning begins as soon as the leaves start to fall and continues until the end of March. Some of the leaves are also removed before the grapes start to ripen and unwanted bunches are also removed. Perennial weeds are sprayed in the early spring and there are regular sprayings throughout the summer to control other weeds, diseases and insects.

The vintage is divided into two, the picking of the grapes for wine, and those for the table. The vintage for wine grapes usually starts in the first or second week of September after the technologists have visited the vineyards to test for ripeness. Before picking starts the leaders of the AICs meet to determine how the grapes should be picked, in what order, and how deliveries are to be made to the different wineries.

Grapes for sparkling, AO and Controliran Region wines are picked by hand and placed in wooden boxes. Grapes for other

---

Main wine varieties

Dimiat	571 hectares	(1,410 acres)
Muscat Ottonel	146 hectares	(360 acres)
Pamid	139 hectares	(343 acres)
Ugni Blanc	126 hectares	(311 acres)
Chardonnay	122 hectares	(301 acres)
Rkatziteli	78 hectares	(192 acres)
Varnenski Misket	88 hectares	(217 acres)

Dessert varieties

Bolgar	34 hectares	(84 acres)
Hamburger Misket	18 hectares	(44 acres)
Trakijski Misktet	44 hectares	(108 acres)
Super ran Bolgar	2 hectares	(4.9 acres)
Maritza	1 hectare	(2.4 acres)
Veren	1 hectare	(2.4 acres)

Production of varietals

Ugni Blanc	576,000 litres	(126,720 gallons)
Rkatziteli	2 million litres	(440,000 gallons)
Fetiaska	178,000 litres	(39,160 gallons)
Misket	305,000 litres	(67,100 gallons)
Dimiat	3.1 million litres	(622,000 gallons)
Varna Misket	310,000 litres	(68,200 gallons)
Riesling	976,000 litres	(214,720 gallons)
Muscat Ottonel	1 million litres	(220,000 gallons)
Pamid	1 million litres	(220,000 gallons)
Cabernet	457,000 litres	(100,540 gallons)
Merlot	60,000 litres	(13,200 gallons)
Chardonnay	194,000 litres	(42.680 gallons)
Sparkling wines	3.7 million litres	(814,000 gallons)
Others	121,000 litres	(26,620 gallons)

wines are also picked by hand but put into larger containers which are then emptied into specially equipped trucks and trailers for transport to the wineries. All vehicles arriving at the winery are weighed and the grapes checked for quality and sugar content. There are special requirements for grapes picked by hand and destined for quality wines.

The crushers can handle up to 15 tonnes (14.7 tons) of grapes an hour. The must, together with the skins, stems and so on, is then transferred to tanks where it is sulphated. The sulphur is applied manually and gradually as the must enters the tanks. The must is then separated from the marc, fined by using sulphur dioxide and bentonite, and then allowed to settle for up to 24 hours before filtering.

Fermentation takes place in metal tanks and temperature is controlled by water. About 24 hours after the vigorous fermentation, the young wine is decanted off and transferred to other tanks for the final stages of fermentation which takes between ten and 14 days. During this time the tanks are constantly topped up. The young wines are then drawn off, filtered and stabilized using sulphur dioxide.

The enterprise produces 20 million litres (four million gallons) of wine a year, of which about 3.5 million litres (770,000

At Varna, sparkling wine is first fermented in rows of temperature controlled metal tanks before transferral to other tanks for the final stages of fermentation.

gallons) is sparkling wine. There is an experimental station in Varna and a great deal of research work is conducted into both vine growing and wine-making. The station was the first in the country to plant and try imported varieties such as Italian Riesling, Ugni Blanc, Pinot Chardonnay and Aligoté. There has been a lot of work into ways of controlling oidium and grape moths, and of particular interest, how to maximise plantings and yields from terraced vineyards.

In 1968 the region was also the first to introduce the high stem system of training, and in 1972 a high-stem, widely spaced line system was introduced to facilitate automation. The distance between vine rows was between 2.4 and 3.5 metres (7.8-11.4 feet). All this work was pioneered in Varna and has now been widely implemented, not only throughout Bulgaria but in other countries.

In 1962 a separate facility to research winemaking techniques was introduced under Nikolai Spirov. It has developed ways of producing sparkling, semi-dry low alcohol wines; introduced new strains of yeast, especially "Varna 1"; found the best methods of winemaking for varietals grown in the district; and conducted extensive research so that it can now advise on the best techniques for stabilizing wine with sulphur. The success of the research station can best be judged by the 32 gold and 36 silver medals won by its wines in international competitions.

In September 1986 the enterprise was awarded its first Controliran Region wine, Varna Chardonnay, and AO Varna Misket and Silistra Fetjaska. The Chardonnay comes from around the village of Sluntchemo, in the micro-region of Pripek.

The vines are grown on the high-stem broad line Umbrella system. The lines are 3 metres (9.8 feet) apart and the height of the stem is 1.3 metres (4.9 feet) with one leading wire. The vines are fertilized as necessary and there is small volume spraying to combat diseases and pests. The grapes are picked by hand and placed in wooden crates and taken immediately to the winery. The grapes are crushed and the must filtered using a rotto-strainer. The infusion takes between four and six hours, and is then sulphured, cooled down and filtered again. Fermentation takes place in water cooled metal tanks at a temperature between 16 and 22°C (60-71°F). After fermentation the tanks are constantly topped up and the young wine sulphured according to the wine maker's instructions.

Before the wine is bottled, samples are sent for official analysis and tasting. After official approval, the wine is bottled on a cold, sterile line and then stored for two months, necks down in a cool cellar. Bottles have been held back from each vintage and stored in the Dimiat cellars for three years. They are then labelled and offered for sale. In 1986 the first Controliran Region

In the last few years production has been hit by adverse weather conditions, particularly hailstorms and summer droughts. Production for 1984 was 33,707 tonnes (33,167 tons), 1985 26,315 tonnes (25,893 tons) and 1986 25,423 tonnes (25,016 tons).

Chardonnay of Varna was released on the market, having come from the 1983 vintage.

FOLKLORE AND CUISINE

The main festival is the holiday of vine-growing, celebrated on February 14 which can be traced back to worship of the Thracian God Sabasij or Dionysus. The celebrations always start the night before when special flat cakes are baked, a chicken boiled and a wooden wine vessel washed and set aside. The next morning it is usually the men who go into the vineyards, either on foot or horseback. As music is played, the vines are ritually pruned. According to local tradition the vines in the four corners of the vineyard are pruned, and the one judged to be most productive is put in the centre. After pruning, wine is poured over the vines and their roots to promote fertility and a good harvest. After the pruning the gaiety and feasting starts. On one of the tables a bunch of sweet basil is held together with a red thread and tied to three vine rods. The villagers then elect the King of the Vineyards, usually the owner considered to have produced the best wine the year before. He is decorated with a garland made from the vine cuttings and is led back to his home astride a horse. On the way he stops at each house and the owner comes with a copper wine jug. He gives everyone present a drink and if any wine is left, he throws it over the king. There is always a drop or two left.

In some villages of the region, it is traditional to slaughter a ram for the celebrations and make a special soup. All the food and wine is taken into the vineyards for the party which can last for 24 hours. All the wine has to be drunk before the people can return home, to leave a drop is considered bad luck.

Traditional dishes of the region include fish with fresh cabbage, grilled fish with mushrooms, mussels in wine sauce, crab soup, beef with plums, grilled suckling pig, stuffed vine leaves and Varna baked beans. There are also many vegetable specialities, but the area is especially noted for its fish, shellfish and crab dishes because of its location near the Black Sea.

NORTHERN REGION

SUHINDOL

The Suhindol wine-making enterprise is in central northern Bulgaria and in the southwest part of the district of Veliko Tarnovo. It produces the finest reds and is regarded as the country's leading winery.

Wine has certainly been produced in the region since Roman times and excavations of ancient burial sites and settlements have revealed artefacts from a previous primitive winemaking culture. Registers still exist to show that wine making continued during the period of the Turkish domination. In 1909 the first wine cooperative on the Balkan peninsula, called Gamza, was formed. It had 50 members and was founded by Marko Vatchkov from

The courtyard, shaded by vines, at the Suhindol winery.

Suhindol. After nationalization in 1947 there was extensive modernization and replanting which is still continuing. The complex includes the town of Suhindol and the villages and land around Krasno Gradiste, Bjala Reka, Gorsko Kalugerovo, Gorsko Koosovo and Koevtzi. The complex is divided into five brigades each responsible for their own vineyards, and there are two wineries – one in Suhindol and the other the Vinenka complex.

Most of the land is between 180 and 350 metres (590–1,148 feet) above sea level and the soils are primarily leached black earth, grey woodland and alluvial, on rock and limestone. The complex covers 6,000 hectares (14,826 acres) of which 1,500 hectares (3,706 acres) are planted with vines. Red wine varieties dominate with 60 per cent of the vineyards planted with Cabernet Sauvignon, 20 per cent Merlot, 10 per cent Gamza and 5 per cent each Pamid and Dimiat. Other farming includes cereals, fodder crops and stock rearing. The area enjoys a moderate continental climate with mild winters, wet springs, hot summers and dry autumns.

Pruning takes place in February and March, and in May the vines and runners are tied up, the soil between the lines ploughed to clear weeds, and the first sprayings to combat disease and pests take place. The vintage starts about September 20 and continues until November 1. All the grapes are picked by hand. The grapes are tested for quality and sugar content on arrival at the winery, crushed and transferred to fermentation tanks. After this stage of fermentation is complete, the young wine is drawn off into secondary tanks where the fermentation is completed. The wine is

The complex produces about 10 million litres (2.2 million gallons) of wine a year in the following volumes:

Cabernet Sauvignon
6 million litres
(1.3 million gallons)

Merlot
2 million litres
(440,000 gallons)

Gamza
1 million litres
(220,000 gallons)

Dimiat and Pamid used in blending
1 million litres
(220,000 gallons)

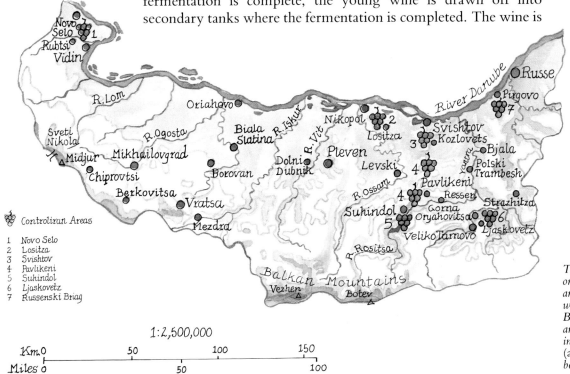

Controlirun Areas

1 Novo Selo
2 Lositza
3 Svishtov
4 Pavlikeni
5 Suhindol
6 Ljaskovetz
7 Russenski Briag

1:2,500,000

Km. 0   50   100   150

Miles 0   50   100

The Suhindol winery is one of the most beautiful and long established wineries in Bulgaria. Brightly coloured flowers and trellised vines intertwined with roses (above) complement the beautifully kept gardens.

then racked, stabilized with sulphur and transferred to oak barrels for ageing. After ageing, it is stablized and then allowed to rest before bottling, and further ageing in bottles.

The region specializes in quality wines and yields are restricted. This starts at the pruning stage and the aim is to produce a harvest of between 6,500 and 8,000 kilogrammes a hectare (14,332-17,640lb an acre). Yields within these levels have been achieved over the last ten years.

The enterprise has the Controliran Region Suhindol and produces stunning Cabernet Sauvignons, Merlots and above all the Gamza wines which would find favour with any connoisseur. The Gamza, the local variety, has the greatest promise because it is so little known internationally – as yet. It is a full bodied wine with a big scented nose and tremendous ageing potential.

FOLKLORE AND CUISINE

The main festival is the Holiday of the Vine Grower, celebrated here as in many other parts of the country, on February 14.

The area is noted for fish soups, banitza pastries and pork steaks. Fruit is stored in the well-ventilated spaces under the roofs, and in this way apples and grapes can be served well into late spring.

LJASKOVETZ

The Ljaskovetz complex includes Pavlikeni and Svishtov and is in the hilly and mountainous Veliko Tarnovo district.

The Thracians introduced the vine to the region and winemaking has been continued through the centuries. It is known that the men of Ljaskovetz fought in Asia Minor in ancient times and they could have brought the first vines back. A beautifully decorated wine vessel excavated locally is on display in Sofia. It shows clusters of grapes and ivy – the symbol of eternal youth. The Turks encouraged winemaking under their domination because they could impose taxes on production, and there are records of wine exports to Egypt in 1847. In 1851 a distillery was opened, with the equipment and technical expertise being imported from Belgrade and Hungary. In 1872 there were 942 hectares (2,327 acres) of vineyards in the region and 1,130 families.

In the 1890s the vineyards were devastated by phylloxera, but American rootstocks were introduced via France and by the First World War the vineyard area had increased to 1,800 hectares (4,447 acres). Production was on a small scale with each family growing and processing their own grapes. In 1912 the region became the first in Bulgaria to produce dessert wines, which were exported to Vienna. By the mid-1950s production of dessert wines topped 60 million litres (13.2 million gallons), most of it exported to the USSR, but this trade has now virtually died out because of the new anti-alcohol campaign in the USSR.

The 1958 dessert wines made from the Dimiat grape, a massive mouth-filling succulent wine, were still drinking very well when tasted in 1988. Production of dessert wines is increasing again and there is a very interesting dessert wine now produced from the Cabernet Sauvignon grapes.

The first growers' cooperative, Ptchela, was formed in 1921 and the first cooperative to produce wine was formed in 1935. It opened in Ljaskovetz with a 370,000 tonne (364,000 ton) capacity in 8,000 and 10,000 litre (7,872–9,840 gallon) ferro-concrete tanks. Pump and presses were imported in 1940 which led to an immediate improvement in the quality of the wines.

After nationalization the enterprise concentrated on white and red table wines and fruit brandies. In 1949 the first dessert wines were introduced and a distillery was opened with a continuous still with a throughput of 20,000 litres (4,400 gallons) of wine a day. Modern laboratories were also installed. A new wine cellar was built in Ressen in 1953, and those in Strazhitza, P. Trambesh and Svishtov in 1959. The modern cellar in Ljaskovetz was also opened in 1959 with a 5.5 million litre (1.2 million gallon)

capacity, and with continual improvements is now the most modern in Bulgaria. It has four French Vaslan presses as well as the latest equipment from West Germany and Italy.

After research by scientists from Sofia, Ljaskovetz was chosen as the most favourable site for vineyards to produce grapes for high quality sparkling wines and in 1955 production of *méthode champenoise* sparkling wines was introduced. At an international wine festival in Ljubljana in July 1963 49 samples of *méthode champenoise* wines from many countries were exhibited. Only the two samples from Ljaskovetz won gold medals. At the Budapest exhibition in 1966, only the Ljaskovetz entry won a gold medal. In 1960 special facilities were also opened specifically to handle wines for export. These wines have now won 61 gold and 75 silver medals in international competitions around the world. In 1965 a new plant to produce sparkling wines was opened, and in 1986 production topped six million bottles, all produced in tanks.

There are 11 wine cellars – the central one in Ljaskovetz and the others in Ressen, P. Trambesh, Strazhitza, Pavlikeni, Varbovka, Dimtcha, Lesitcheri, Vishovgrad, Svishtav and Kozlovets. The four wineries for pressing and primary production are in Ljaskovetz, Ressen, P. Trambesh and Strazhita. The microregions are Ljaskovetz, Resen, P. Trambesh, Strazhita, Pavlikeni and Svistov.

The area takes in a section of the hilly part of the Danube plain and the foothills of the Balkan Mountains. The average altitude is between 100 and 200 metres (328-656 feet) above sea level. Because of the terrain, there are many different soils and rock formations, and most are favourable for vine growth. The region has a temperate continental climate: winters are mild,

Grape varieties planted in private vineyards and their percentage of production		
	hectares/acres	per cent
Cabernet	45.0/111.0	7.04
Aligoté	109.8/271.3	17.17
Dimiat	210.0/518.9	32.93
Rkatziteli	58.9/145.5	9.21
Merlot	26.7/65.9	4.18
Gamza	48.0/118.6	7.51
Pamid	39.5/97.6	6.18
Muscat Ottonel	20.0/49.4	3.13
Vratsa Misket	6.0/14.8	0.94
Riesling	15.0/37.0	2.35
Chardonnay	55.0/135.9	8.6
Traminer	5.0/12.3	0.78

Ljaskovetz Agro-Industrial Complex varieties and their share of production		
	hectare/acre	per cent
Cabernet	521.3/1,288	39.45
Rkatziteli	321.6/794.6	24.33
Aligoté	48.3/119.3	3.66
Riesling	15.0/37.0	1.14
Dunavski Lazur	50.0/123.5	3.78
Dimiat	20.0/49.4	1.15
Pamid	10.6/26.0	0.80
Gamza	169.2/418.0	5.24
Merlot	79.6/196.6	6.02
Bolgar	175.0/432.4	13.24
Cardinal	11.0/27.0	0.83

springs are warm and wet, summers are hot and dry, and autumns are cold. The area has a mainly southeast or southwest exposure. There is good natural drainage, and early spring and autumn frosts are rare. It is seldom foggy and very cold winter winds are extremely uncommon. It is not a hailstorm region. The average temperature of the coldest month is −1.2-1.8°C (30-35°F). A characteristic of the climate of the region is the relatively fast warming up in spring and the cooling down in the autumn.

In the hottest months the temperature averages between 20.3 and 23.8°C (68.5-74.8°F) with the hottest temperatures recorded in July. In the winter the precipitation is mostly as snow with the first snow falling about December 3-10 and the last about the middle of March. The number of days with snow cover is between 47 and 50 on average, and its average depth in January is about 15.5 centimetres (6 inches).

There are about 1,961 hectares (4,845 acres) of vineyards in the region, of which 639.5 hectares (1,580 acres) are privately owned vineyards while the Ljaskovetz complex has 1,327.6 hectares (3,279 acres). Other farming includes cereals, fodder crops, fruit, vegetables and stock rearing. Around Kilifarevo the production of vine rootstocks is the main enterprise.

There are four agro-industrial complexes in the region: AIC Oryahovitsa, which includes the settlements of Orjachovitza, G. D. Trambesh, G. G. Trambesh, Draganovo and Streletz; AIC Ressen which includes Ressen, Vodolei and Ditchin; AIC Trambesh which includes Lipnitza, Obedinenie, P. Trambesh, Orlovetz, Kutzina and Strachilovo; and AIC Strazhitza which includes the settlements of Lozer, Vladislav Blagoevo, Assenovo, Mirovo and Gradiste.

The vini-viticulture complex in Ljaskovetz has 700 hectares (1,729 acres) of vineyards, and a further 400 hectares (988 acres) around Pavlikeni and Svistov. There are 636.5 hectares (1,572 acres) of vineyards in the Pavlikeni area of which 69.8 hectares (172 acres) are privately owned and mostly growing Gamza. There are 179.8 hectares of privately owned vineyards around Svishtov, growing Cabernet Sauvignon 55.62 per cent and Merlot 44.38 per cent.

Pruning starts after the vintage and continues over the winter to the end of March. Most of the vineyards have been planted with wide spaces between the lines so that machinery can be used to plough, spray and fertilize. The Chardonnay grapes for sparkling wine are the first to be gathered at the start of September. The grapes are picked selectively by hand and transported quickly to the winery cellar in Ljaskovetz, which specializes in the production of sparkling and table wines of high quality. The grapes for other wines are picked about the end of September and the vintage continues until the end of October. These grapes are picked by hand and then transferred via trailers to lorries with 4.5 tonnes (4.4 ton) containers.

The grapes for sparkling wines are pressed under strictly controlled conditions to obtain a must of very high quality which is then passed through a "rotto-drainer" and sulphated with between 5 and 10 grammes a 1000 litres of sulphur dioxide. The must is then cooled down and allowed to stand for about 24 hours before it is drawn off and transferred to controlled cold fermentation tanks where the yeast is added. Temperature during fermentation is controlled between 15 and 20°C (59-68°F). After the initial vigorous fermentation, the wine is drawn off and transferred to ferro-concrete tanks where the fermentation is completed. When this is over, the wine is decanted, stabilized and allowed to settle for a few weeks. It is racked again in the beginning of December and for a third time in February, then filtered ready for its dispatch to the sparkling wine plant for blending and the secondary stage of production.

Grapes for red wine are taken to the cellars in Ressen, P. Trambesh and Strazhitza where the grapes are separated from their bunches and crushed. The must is sulphated and then sent to metal or ferro-concrete fermentation tanks where the yeast is added. In both systems the fermentation temperatures are strictly controlled. After the vigorous fermentation, when the wine has

Varieties grown around Pavlikeni and Svistov, and their percentage of production

Pavlikeni
Cabernet 22.48 per cent
Rkatziteli 36.53 per cent
Gamza 10.5 per cent
Dimiat 11.52 per cent
Merlot 7.82 per cent
Pamid 3.88 per cent
Storgosia 4.68 per cent
Others 2.59 per cent

Svishtov
Cabernet 60.42 per cent
Merlot 15.31 per cent
Rkatsiteli 22.69 per cent
Dimiat 1.59 per cent

reached a relative weight of 1025-1040, it is drawn off into other ferro-concrete tanks for fermentation to finish. The wines are then desulphated, racked and left until the end of February or March when they are analysed and clarified. The wines are assessed and either go to 5,000 or 10,000 litre (1,100-2,200 gallon) oak casks for ageing, or to the bottling plant.

The Ljaskovetz complex processes about 13.5 million tonnes (13.2 million tons) of grapes from which 9.5 million litres (2 million gallons) of sparkling red and white wine is produced.

In 1982 the complex had 2,785.5 hectares (6,882 acres) of vineyards, of which 2,083.7 hectares (5,148 acres) were bearing fruit. There were about 355 hectares (877 acres) of dessert varieties. Production was 13,025 tonnes (12,816 tons). In 1983 the vines were hit by severe frosts and there were violent storms in May and during the summer which did considerable damage. Despite the adverse conditions, and thanks to an increased vineyard acreage and maturer vines, 21,246 tonnes (20,906 tons) of grapes were produced, of which 9,071 tonnes (8,925 tons) were bought by Vinprom for processing. About 4,022 tonnes (3,957 tons) was processed for sparkling wines.

The 1984 vintage produced 13,540 tonnes (13,323 tons) of grapes. This was followed by another harsh winter with very low temperatures when up to 60 per cent of the vines froze. Special pruning techniques were introduced the following spring to

Sparkling Wine Production

Aligoté	600,000 litres (132,000 gallons)	Merlot AO	100,000 litres (22,000 gallons)
Riesling	200,000 litres (44,000 gallons)	White blended	300,000 litres (66,000 gallons)
Dimiat	700,000 litres (154,000 gallons)	Red blended	300,000 litres (66,000 gallons)
Rkatziteli	480,000 litres (105,000 gallons)		
Chardonnay	200,000 litres (44,000 gallons)		
Gamza	200,000 litres (44,000 gallons)		

Pavlikeni

Gamza AOC	90,000 litres (19,800 gallons)
Gamza	200,000 litres (44,000 gallons)
Cabernet	400,000 litres (88,000 gallons)
Rkatziteli	800,000 litres (176,000 gallons)
Dimiat	400,000 litres (88,000 gallons)
Merlot	150,000 litres (33,000 gallons)
Pamid	100,000 litres (22,000 gallons)

Ljaskovetz Production Figures
Table Wines

Dimiat	500,000 litres (110,000 gallons)
Rkatziteli	2,000,000 litres (440,000 gallons)
Pamid	200,000 litres (44,000 gallons)
Merlot	300,000 litres (66,000 gallons)
Cabernet	3,000,000 litres (660,000 gallons)
Gamza	200,000 litres (44,000 gallons)
Aligoté (dry)	100,000 litres (22,000 gallons)
Dimiat AO	90,000 litres (19,800 gallons)
Aligoté AOC	90,000 litres (19,800 gallons)
Cabernet AO	100,000 litres (22,000 gallons)

Svishtov

Cabernet AOC	200,000 litres (44,000 gallons)
Cabernet	1,500,000 litres (330,000 gallons)
Merlot	600,000 litres (132,000 gallons)
Rkatziteli	600,000 litres (132,000 gallons)

encourage growth but then several areas were hit by violent hailstorms. Only 6,524 tonnes (6,419 tons) of grapes were bought for processing. Conditions in 1986 were favourable although early wet weather encouraged mildew which had to be treated. A total of 12,497 tonnes (12,297 tons) of grapes were processed, of which 4,071 tonnes (4,005 tons) were for sparkling wines. Quality was very high.

The area has several Controliran Region wines. In 1980 the appellation Aligoté from Ljaskovetz was introduced, plus Gamza from Pavlikeni, and Cabernet Sauvignon from Svishtov. The grapes for these wines come from special vineyards – 43 hectares (106 acres) for Aligoté, 52 hectares (128 acres) for Gamza, and 75 hectares (185 acres) for Cabernet Sauvignon. In 1983 the first quantities from these Controliran Region wines were released on the market. Production from these vineyards is limited to six tonnes a hectare (5.9 tons an acre), and the AOC regulations are strictly enforced by officials both locally and from Sofia.

Pavlikeni is probably the only winery in the world to have lace curtains in the bottling hall. Although the hall is run by women, the curtains are not purely for decorative purposes, they also have a very useful role in keeping out insects, especially during the intense summer heat.

FOLKLORE AND CUISINE

The region's main festival is the holiday of the vine grower, celebrated on February 14. It signals the start of work in the vineyards after the winter and is an occasion for music, dancing, singing and feasting.

The region's food is characterized by spicy and peppery food. Many dishes use pork and veal and there are special traditional flat sausages. Other specialities include Elenski leg of pork, knuckle of veal pot roasted, stuffed turkey, stuffed peppers, calf head cooked in tripe, and nearer the Danube, many fish recipes. The region is also noted for its breads and cakes.

PLEVEN

This enterprise contains some of the largest vineyard complexes in Bulgaria. The micro-regions include Pleven (800 hectares/1,976 acres of vineyards), Nikopol (1,500 hectares/3,706 acres), Belene (500 hectares/1,235 acres), D. Dubnik (500 hectares/1,235 acres) and Levski (700 hectares/1,729 acres). Wine has been produced in the region since ancient times and in 1890 a vini-viticulture school was opened. In 1893 the first experimental cellar affiliated to the school started operating and it had a capacity of 200,000 litres (44,000 gallons).

The area varies between 110 and 200 metres (360 and 656 feet) above sea level. The soil is mostly leached black earth, carbonated black earth and grey woodland. Pleven averages 160 metres (524 feet) above sea level, Nikopol 200 metres (656 feet), Belene 120 metres (393 feet), D. Dubnik 110 metres (360 feet) and Levski 140 metres (459 feet). The region has a sharply pronounced continental climate with long hot summers and cold winters. Summer temperatures can rise to 35°C (95°F) and winter temperatures often fall to −25°C (−13°F).

The vineyards are situated on high, flat, undulating plateaux and the area covered with vineyards totals 6,200 hectares (1,532 acres), of which 3,900 hectares (9,636 acres) are fruiting and 2,309 hectares (5,705 acres) are young, as yet unproductive vines. The enterprise has 5,500 hectares (1,359 acres) of vineyards of which 1,500 hectares (3,706 acres) are young and unproductive. Other agricultural enterprises include cereals and stock rearing.

Red wine varieties account for 70 per cent of production, covering 2,550 hectares (6,301 acres) of productive vineyards, mostly Cabernet Sauvignon, (808 hectares/1,996 acres), followed by Merlot (687 hectares/1,697 acres) and Pamid (460 hectares/1,136 acres).

The white varieties cover 1,110 hectares (2,742 acres) consisting of Rkatziteli (580 hectares/1,433 acres), Muscat Ottonel (186 hectares/459 acres) and Dunavski Lazur (241 hectares/595 acres). New areas of Chardonnay, Sauvignon Blanc, Aligoté and Italian Riesling are being planted. About 100 hectares (247 acres) of replacement vines are being planted annually.

The region is divided into 12 agro-industrial and vini-viticulture complexes, based on 35 viticultural brigades centred on the villages. There are nine wine cellars, seven attached to the wine factory, one attached to the VVC, and one belonging to the National Agrarian Union.

Pruning takes place early in the new year and continues until March. The earth around the vines is piled up and the rows between them ploughed to control weeds. There are frequent sprayings to combat insects and diseases. The vintage usually starts about September 20 and continues until the end of October.

On arrival at the winery, the grapes are tested for quality, ripeness and sugar content. The grapes are crushed and the must transferred to fermentation tanks. It is sulphated and, if necessary, the must is reinforced using sugar and grape concentrates. The fermentation is strictly controlled using either jets of cold air or cold water which is automatically released down the outside of the tanks if the temperature rises above set limits. After the initial vigorous fermentation, the wine is racked and transferred to separate tanks for the fermentation stage to be completed. The young wine is then racked and transferred to holding tanks for ageing, blending or bottling.

The average volume of wine produced in the last few years has been: 1982 24,570,000 litres (5,405,400 gallons), 1983 13,130,000 litres (2,888,600 gallons), 1984 22,355,000 litres (4,918,100 gallons), 1985 16,250,000 litres (3,575,000 gallons) and

1986 21,000,000 litres (4,620,000 gallons).

About two million litres (440,000 gallons) of wine was distilled for brandy, and about 1.3 million litres (286,000 gallons) used for the production of vinegar. Rubin, Bouquet, Storgozia and Danube Gamza are all new varieties.

In 1902 an experimental viticultural school was founded in Pleven which became the Vini-Viticulture Institute in 1944. This institute is now the leading research station for wine in the country, and the co-ordinating body for all scientific and development work affecting the industry. It carries out research into the selection of sites for vineyards, their planting and development, the economics and practice of vine growing, especially involving mechanization, control of the vine growth, production of new varieties and rootstocks, and winemaking techniques.

The region has the AOC Cabernet Sauvignon from Lositza. About 200 tonnes (196 tons) of grapes are produced from around the village of Lositza for this high quality wine producing about 900,000 litres (19,800 gallons) of wine. The vineyards have their own microclimate on a plateau at around 220 metres (721 feet).

VRATSA The region where this Vinprom enterprise is situated has been a

Pleven: production of wine in 1986		
White wines		
Rkatziteli	3,000,000 litres	(660,000 gallons)
Dunavski Lazur	1,000,000 litres	(220,000 gallons)
Muscat	600,000 litres	(132,000 gallons)
Dimiat	400,000 litres	(88,000 gallons)
White Pamid	1,000,000 litres	(220,000 gallons)
Misket	800,000 litres	(176,000 gallons)
Riesling and others		
Merlot blush	110,000 litres	(24,200 gallons)
Red wines		
Pamid	600,000 litres	(132,000 gallons)
Rubin	200,000 litres	(44,000 gallons)
Storgozia	1,600,000 litres	(352,000 gallons)
Bouquet	1,500,000 litres	(330,000 gallons)
Cabernet	3,500,000 litres	(770,000 gallons)
Gamza	1,000,000 litres	(220,000 gallons)
Merlot	1,413,000 litres	(310,860 gallons)
Mavrud	300,000 litres	(66,000 gallons)
Danube Gamza	300,000 litres	(66,000 gallons)

wine producing area for centuries, but it is only since the turn of this century that the area has expanded dramatically and production developed on a commercial basis. Before 1900 most farms and households had their own small vineyard and the wine produced was for personal consumption. There were, however, noted growers whose wines were exported and eagerly sought after. Famous growers included Georgi Androv, Zakhari Syoyanov, Vassil Patvanov, Dano Yonchev, Tsvetko Tsvetkov and Vassil Krustenyakov. They produced wine in the traditional way in small cellars and wine made in this way is still popular in Germany. At an exhibition in London in the nineteenth century the wine merchants of Europe were amazed at the quality of wine

offered by Vassil Krustenyakov. He had taken a small barrel to the exhibition to prove to the rest of Europe "that the Bulgarians produce good wine too". His family carried on the tradition and their wines from Vratsa region won the gold medal at the Plovdiv Exhibition in 1882 and a bronze medal in the Bordeaux exhibition the same year. The Vratchabski Misket still has an international reputation.

After the end of the Turkish rule the amount of vineyards expanded dramatically, despite the phylloxera outbreak, and although still small and privately owned, they covered more than 1,200 hectares (2,965 acres) in 1940. The Veslets wine cooperative, the first in the region, was founded in Vratsa in 1921. In 1933 the first cooperative winery opened, built with funds from the state agricultural bank, and the following year the first industrial vineyards were planted. The cellar had three properties with 8,000 litre (1,760 gallon) casks and a total capacity of 400,000 litres (88,000 gallons). The cellar also had its own distillery and grapes were brought in on ox carts. The processing of the grapes was primitive. They were emptied into transportable crushers placed over the vats and the juice allowed to run straight in. The must for the white wine was racked before fermentation, but red wines were fermented with grapes, stems and all.

After nationalization vast new areas of vineyards were planted after careful surveying to find the best soils and locations. The vineyards were planted with wide spaces between the lines so that machinery could be used. The area under vines increased nine fold and the region specialized in red and white table wines made from both local and imported varieties.

The region also played a major role in developing new varieties for dessert wines for the developing export market. These included development of early ripening varieties like Cardinal and Tsaritsa na lozjata (Queen of Vines) and, more recently, Trakijski Misket and Dunavski Misket. Between 1947-78 16 concrete tanks, with a total capacity of 500,000 litres (110,000 gallons) were added to the Veslets cellars. In 1952 Vinprom Vratsa was established to run the 1,000 hectares (2,471 acres) of vineyards and process the grapes and since then there has been a continuing programme of building and modernization.

Because the vineyards were expanding so fast – 5,600 hectares (13,837 acres) by 1953 – the wineries could not cope and the harvest used to start at the end of August and continue until the snow prevented picking. Young wines had to be distilled into spirits because they could not be stored in the cellars. It was because of this that the cellar in Krivodolo was built in 1956 and designated to concentrate on the production of quality dessert wines for ageing and export.

There were 2,000 hectares (4,942 acres) of vineyards around Vratsa, 626 hectares (1,546 acres) around Mezdra, 1,235 hectares (3,051 acres) around Biala Slatina, and 1,600 hectares (3,953 acres) around Oriahovo. The average yield was 5 tonnes a hectare (4.92 tons an acre). In 1962 new plants were built together with a spirits bottling line. In 1965 the enterprise had to cope with a harvest of 29,000 tonnes (28,536 tons) of grapes and every available container was commandeered. Even the swimming pools in the local sports stadiums were used to store must. The must was then used to produce grape honey for export or grape concentrate for liqueur.

The main expansion in Vratsa took place between 1968 and 1970. New cellars were built and the capacity doubled to 5,500,000 litres (1,210,000 gallons). New cellars had already been completed in Biala Slatina and Oriahovo with a capacity of six million and five million litres (1.3 million and 1.1 million gallons) respectively. By 1976 total capacity had increased to 20 million litres (4.4 million gallons) in anticipation of a future need to process up to 20,000 tonnes (19,680 tons) of grapes.

The Vratsa viticulture region in the northwestern part of Bulgaria is divided into three sub-regions: the plain and foothills where production is divided into four distinct areas, two producing dessert wine varieties, one grapes for red wine, and the other grapes for white. Main dessert wine varieties grown on the plains are Bulgar, Tsaritsa na Lozjata, Shalsa Dorei, Misketova, Tshaush, Hamburg Misket and Italia. Dessert varieties grown on the hills are Tamjanka, Vratshanski Misket and Harsh Lavelju. Red varieties are Gamza, Cabernet Sauvignon and Barbera, and

| | Vratsa: area under production | | |
| | area | established vineyards | new vineyards |
	hectare/acre	hectare/acre	hectare/acre
Gabare	473.6/1,170	466.1/1,151	7.5/18.5
Vratsa East	271.1/669.8	232.8/575.2	38.0/93.8
Borovan	40.0/98.8	40.0/98.8	
Bjaia Slatina	50.9/125.7	50.9/125.7	
Krivodol	73.6/181.8	37.6/92.9	36.0/88.9
Vratsa west	132.8/328.1	116.8/288.6	16.0/39.5
Orjachovo	738.2/1,824	688.4/1,701	50.0/123.5

Of the 1,780 hectares (4,398 acres) planted with vines, 1,633 hectares (4,035 acres) bear fruit and 147.5 hectares (364.4 acres) are new vineyards. Grapes for wine cover 1,665.3 hectares (4,114 acres) and dessert grapes cover 114.9 hectares (283.9 acres). The average yields is two tonnes a hectare (1.9 tons an acre), 1.7 tonnes (1.6 tons) for wine grapes, and up to 4.9 tonnes (4.8 tons) for table grapes. Production averages 3,135,000 litres (689,700 gallons) – 2,678,000 litres (827,167 gallons) for table wines and 457,000 litres (100,540 gallons) for dessert wines.

A traditional Bulgarian house, rendered and then painted in bright colours.

for the whites, Rkatziteli; the hills and semi-mountainous region where Zartshin, Gamza, Cabernet Sauvignon and Merlot are grown for red wines, Italian Riesling and Aligoté for white and sparkling wines, and Bulgar, Tsaritsa, Shasla, Hamburg Misket and Perla Djoksaba for dessert wines; and the semi-mountainous and mountainous zone, where there are still many small private vineyards growing mostly Pamid, Senzo and Hamburg Misket.

There are now 1,780 hectares (4,398 acres) of vineyards in Vinprom Vratsa in seven agro-industrial complexes. The workers are organized into specialized brigades for working in the vineyards, although a great deal of the work is now mechanized.

Other agriculture in the region includes cereals, sunflower, sugar beet, beans, soya beans, fodder crops, fruit and vegetables and livestock.

The vineyards can be divided into the following soil and climatic zones: Vratsa East – the soils are mostly strongly eroded black earth, grey woodland and alluvial meadow with a high percentage of sandy clay over loamy clay, marl and limestone. In places thin layers of sandstone have been exposed. The zone has a moderate continental climate with January temperatures averaging 3.2°C (37°F) and July 22.7°C (72.8°F). The average annual temperature is 10.6°C (51°F) and the annual average rainfall 57 centimetres (22 inches) unevenly distributed throughout the year, the maximum rainfall is in June and the least in February. Vratza West – mostly grey woodland and alluvial meadow soil over limestone, marl and sandstone. The zone has a mountain climate with the highest temperatures in July and August which are also the months of lowest rainfall. The earliest autumn frost recorded was October 10 and the latest spring frost April 22. Krivodol – the zone is divided by the river Botunja and the soils

The main grape varieties and wine styles and their production		
Variety style	**hectare/acre**	**total production**
Pamid	63.0/110.8	287,000 litres (63,140 gallons)
Senzo	16.0/39.5	13,000 litres (2,860 gallons)
Cabernet Sauvignon	426.8/1,054	668,000 litres (146,960 gallons)
Merlot	574.6/1,419	777,000 litres (170,940 gallons)
White wine	584.9/1,445	316,000 litres (69,520 gallons)
Vratsanski Misket	165.4/408.7	82,000 litres (18,040 gallons)
Dunavski Lazur	14.0/34.5	30,000 litres (6,600 gallons)
Rkatziteli	163.8/404.7	44,000 litres (9,680 gallons)
Ugni Blanc	12.0/29.6	27,000 litres (5,940 gallons)
Riesling	37.6/92.9	133,000 litres (29,260 gallons)
Furmint	18.0/44.4	new plantings
Mixed	174.1/430.2	617,000 litres (135,740 gallons)
Dessert	114.9/283.9	457,000 litres (100,540 gallons)
Bulgar	114.9/283.9	457,000 litres (100,540 gallons)

are mainly black earth and grey woodland on sandstone, clay, limestone and gravel. The zone has a moderate continental climate with clearly pronouced seasonal variations. Maximum temperatures are in June and the minimum in January. The maximum annual rainfall is 955 millimetres (37 inches). Gabare, Oriahovo, Borovan and Biala Slatina – deep black earth, grey woodland and alluvial meadow on limestone, sandstone and clay. The zone has a continental climate with cold winters and hot summers. The maximum rainfall is in May and June and the minimum in August. Total annual rainfall is about 153 millimetres (6 inches).

The soil and climate in the different zones are well suited to vines and the local varieties produce high quality grapes, which ripen well and produce good sugar levels. The vintages of 1985 and 1986 were hit by drought and very hot weather.

Annual production
1980 3,602 tonnes
  (3,544 tons)
1981 8,759 tonnes
  (8,618 tons)
1983 8,664 tonnes
  (8,525 tons)
1984 6,002 tonnes
  (5,905 tons)
1985 2,566 tonnes
  (2,524 tons)
1986 2,385 tonnes
  (2,346 tons)

In the last few years, wines produced in Vratsa have won 17 gold, 27 silver and four bronze medals at international exhibitions. The winery still concentrates on producing table wines, brandies and liqueurs. The dessert wine Vratsa temenuga, with 23 per cent sugar and 13 per cent alcohol, has won international acclaim.

The region has a number of Designated Geographical Regions, but no Controliran Region wines and there are no plans to introduce any at present. The DGRs are Veslets from Biala Slatina, the village of Burkatshevo and the Oriahovo region, and the village of Gorni Vadin. In these regions the variety Vratchanski Misket is produced from which the DGR Veslets dessert wine Vratchanski Misket and sweet-scented brandy Vratchanska temenuga is made.

FOLKLORE   Work in the vineyards begins in the early spring each year, after the celebration of the Holiday of the Vine Grower, the feast of Trifon Zarezan on February 14. In this region, the festivities start at midday when all the people assemble dressed in national costume. Visitors are welcomed with gifts of bread, salt and sparkling wine. To music, everybody makes their way to the vineyards where the oldest grower, festooned with garlands, ritually prunes the vines. He then pours wine from a special wooden vessel (a baklitsa) over the vines and says "let the vintage be profitable and rich". The people then return to the settlement for feasting, singing and dancing which lasts for the rest of the day and well into the night.

Vines and wine have always played an important part in the lives of the people of the region and there are many songs and dances associated with them. There are traditional picking songs that they used to sing during the vintage.

VIDIN   The viti-vinicultural complex of Vinprom Vidin takes in the sub-regions of Novoselski, Vidinski, Dunavski and Rabishki. The region consists of mainly leached black earth in Novoselski, dark-grey woodland soil in Dunavski and Vidinski and light-grey woodland soil in Ribiski.

The total temperature during the growing season varies between 3,600 and 3,700°C (6,512-6,692°F), at about 200 metres (656 feet) above sea level, and between 3,000 and 3,200°C (5,432-5,792°F) at higher altitudes. There are an average 217 days without frost. Autumn months, especially October and November, have low rainfall which helps the grapes ripen and builds up sugar levels.

There are 136,400 hectares (337,044 acres) of cultivated land in the region, of which just over 3 per cent are planted with vines. About half the vineyards are privately owned and they are planted mainly on the northern slopes of the hills which vary between 80 and 550 metres (262.4-1,804 feet) above sea level. The Rabishki sub-region rises in places to 550 metres (1,804 feet) but most of the vineyards in the Novoselski, Vidinski and Dunavski sub-regions are at a height of 200 metres (656 feet). The Vinprom vineyards have 400 hectares (988 acres) of dessert varieties and 1,600 hectares (3,953 acres) for wine. Other agriculture in the region is mainly cereals (wheat, maize and barley) apples, tobacco and livestock.

There are four wineries in the region. Novo Selo produces only high quality red wines, Rubtsi specializes in the production of high quality white wines from Rkatziteli, Furmint and Aligoté. In Rabisha sparkling wines are made including the famous *méthode champenoise* Magura. At Vidin wine for distillation and vinegar is produced, and there are also distilleries.

Four-fifths of grape production is for wine of which 64 per cent is for red and 36 per cent white. Gamza accounts for 50 per cent of the wine grape varieties, Cabernet Sauvignon and Merlot 30 per cent with Rkatziteli, Aligoté, Furmint, Saperavi and others making up the remainder.

Pruning starts after the harvest and continues over winter until April 15 or 20. The vines are trained using the high stem system and workers prune manually or use pneumatic cutters. Spraying takes place between the second half of May until the middle of July and tractor-drawn sprayers and helicopters are used to combat insects and diseases, especially mildew and oidium. The vintage starts at the end of September and the grapes are picked by hand and put into plastic pails and containers and then transported in larger containers on lorries to the wineries.

The vineyards concentrate on producing high quality grapes to produce high quality wines and the vintages for the past ten years or so have been good, apart from those of 1981 and 1982 when the density of vines was so high that it reduced sugar accumulation in the grapes. Stocking rates have been reduced and pruning methods adapted to prevent this happening again. The wineries produce between seven and eight million litres (1.5 million and 1.7 million gallons) of wine a year.

A great deal of experimental work has been conducted in the vineyards especially to improve pruning techniques and planting methods. The vines are now planting with wide rows between the lines. An experimental wine station was founded in Novo Selo in 1953.

The region has one AOC wine at present, Gamza from Novo Selo which has been produced since 1979 from grapes grown on southern facing vineyards around the village of Vinarovo. Yields are restricted to between five and six tonnes a hectare (4.92 and 5.9 tons an acre) and the grapes are not gathered until they have a minimum sugar content of 21 per cent. The grapes are picked manually and selectively to ensure only the best reach the winery.

FOLKLORE   The region's main wine celebration is on February 14, when all the villagers take part in the Holiday of the Vine Grower.

RUSSE   The district of Russe has boundaries with the Danube, the plain of Predludogorie and the foothills of the Danube Plain. The landscape is varied from plain, to hills and mountains. Vines have been grown here since the time of the Thracians. Even under the Turkish occupation when the amount of vineyards declined, the vineyards and wines of Pirgos and Pirgovo were famous. Russe has always been the centre of the winemaking activities of the region, and an experimental station was founded there in the mid-Nineteenth Century by the Turkish regional governor Mithad Pasha. It developed many new varieties and introduced new equipment for the vineyards and wineries.

Varietal production at Vidin	
Gamza	2,500,000 litres (550,000 gallons)
Cabernet	1,500,000 litres (330,000 gallons)
Merlot	300,000 litres (66,000 gallons)
Saperavi	150,000 litres (33,000 gallons)
Rkatziteli	1,000,000 litres (220,000 gallons)
Bouquet	200,000 litres (44,000 gallons)
Aligoté	150,000 litres (33,000 gallons)

The variety Bolgar-Affuzali-Datje de Beirut was first planted around Russe and spread to virtually every other part of the country after 1864. In 1944 dessert varieties dominated, and there were four private wine companies handling between them between 500-600 tonnes (492-590 tons) of grapes. Wine production was primitive and it was not until 1940 that the first cooperative was founded to produce wines following French winemaking methods. The cellar had a capacity of two million litres (440,000 gallons) but produced only red and white table wines for sale locally.

After nationalization in 1947 there were about 4,500 hectares (111,195 acres) of vineyards. That year the cellars in Dve Mogilli and Bjala were built, followed by the first part of the No. 4 cellar in Russe in 1959. There was also an extensive planting programme to increase the area under varieties such as Harsh, Lavelju, Rkatziteli, Cabernet Sauvignon and Fetjaska Alba, and new varieties such as Pirgovo, Lud Gidija and others were created. The No. 4 cellar was extended in 1964 and a new cellar built in Bjala in 1970 to cope with the increased volume of grapes. At the same time a modernization programme was under way to improve winemaking and create high quality wines. In 1967 a modern

A vineyard of Riesling grapes growing near the village of Trastenik in the Russe region.

plant, built by the French company Sifel, was opened for stabilizing and bottling the wines with an annual capacity of 28 million litres (6.1 million gallons), and in 1974 a cold sterile bottling line was introduced.

The area is divided into sub-regions which, because of the soils, local micro-climates and altitude are especially suitable for grape production. The hilly zone along the Danube Collar is particularly well suited to the production of white and dessert grapes. The hilly land around the town of Bjala, because of its heavier black soil and hotter climate, is favourable for the production of red grapes, while at an ever higher altitude around the villages of Borovo, Ekzarh Josif and Obretenik, quality white grapes are grown. Most of the region has chernozem, grey woodland or black earth soils on loess, in some places 40 metres (131 feet) deep. In the eastern part of the region the underlying rock is limestone and in the west, limestone and marls. Subterranean water is usually found between 10 and 15 metres (32-49 feet) throughout the region. The chernozem soils are mostly alkaline with poor nitrogen, average phosphorus and high calcium content. The grey woodland soils are mostly acid, high in carbonates but low in organic matter and minerals. This soil type on the more southern slopes is most suited to the production of grapes for high quality white table wines. The carbonated black earth soils on a deep loess bed allow the vine roots to penetrate very deep to locate water, essential because drought is often a feature of the very hot summer months. The soil is weak alkaline, with low levels of nitrogen, poor phosphorus but high calcium contents. Vineyards on these soils are planted between 80 and 300 metres (282 and 984 feet) above sea level.

In the district there are 147,000 hectares (363,237 acres) of cultivated land, of which 3,000 hectares (7,413 acres) are vineyards. The villages of Ivanovo and Slivo Pole concentrate on vine growing and wine production. There are 3,200 hectares (7,907 acres) of fruit and vegetables and the rest of the farm land is for cereals, fodder crops and livestock. The area is noted for its apples grown on 2,000 hectares (4,942 acres) followed by pears, apricots and peaches. Peppers grown around the villages of Pirgovo and Trastenik are also famous.

Of the 3,000 hectares (7,413 acres) of vineyards, 2,500 hectares (6,177 acres) are planted with wine varieties and 500 hectares (1,235 acres) with dessert grapes. The main wine varieties are Cabernet Sauvignon 650 hectares (1,606 acres), Rkatziteli 800 hectares (1,976 acres), Merlot 260 hectares (642 acres), Muscat Ottonel 260 hectares (642 acres) and Riesling 120 hectares (296 acres). Other varieties such as Dimiat, Harsh Lavelju, Fetiaska Alba, Pinot Chardonnay, Pamid, Saperavi and Gamza occupy the rest. The dessert varieties are mainly Plevn, Muscat d'Ada and Alfonce Lavelle. Production of the grapes is carried out by 23 brigades and collectives formed into ten agro-industrial complexes.

Winemaking is carried out in four cellars, one each in Russe and Dve Mogilli, and two in Bjala. The cellars in Bjala and Dve Mogilli specialize in the production of red wines.

The average annual temperature for the year is about 4,000°C (7,232°F) and the average annual rainfall is about 570 litres a square metre (125 gallons a square foot). The average temperature of the hottest month is about 23.7°C (74.6°F) and most of the rain falls during the spring and autumn. It is a typical continental climate – the summers are hot and dry and the autumns long, warm and dry. The summer temperatures enable the grapes to ripen comparatively early before the late autumn rains, which can cause rotting. Early autumn and late spring frosts occur about every eight years and can do immense damage to the vines. In some years, between 80 and 100 per cent of the vines in the high altitude vineyards have frozen.

The vines are trained using the high stem Umbrella and Improved Moser systems. Different pruning techniques are used depending on variety, but they are generally based on producing shorter fruit rods and knots of two eyes. Sprays are applied regularly to control disease and insects. The main chemicals used are copper sulphate, sulphur dust and thyosol.

The vintage starts in the second half of September with Muscat Ottonel the earliest ripening variety. The grapes are picked by hand and, for special wines, they are picked selectively. The grapes are transported in tubs and the lorries do not have to travel more than 15 kilometres (nine miles) to a winery. The main harvest starts between October 1 and 10 when the major varieties – Cabernet Sauvignon, Rkatziteli and Riesling – ripen. Technologists monitor the ripening of the grapes from the end of August to ensure they are collected exactly at the right stage of ripeness. There are a number of meetings between the brigades, wineries and technologists before the vintage starts to establish in what order the vineyards are to be tackled.

The enterprise has seven lines for processing the grapes for white wine. Three have a capacity of handling up to 20 tonnes (19 tons) of grapes an hour with crushers, static-dynamic filters and continuous presses, and two using similar equipment have a capacity of 50 tonnes (49 tons) an hour. The other two lines are used to produce must for special wines. The grapes are pressed three times. The must from the first pressing is used for the production of tables wines, juice from the second goes for dessert wines, and must from the final pressing is used for distillation into brandy. The must is sulphated and fined with bentonite. For high

Above left *The control desk in the stablization plant of the Russe winery.*

Above right *View of the bottling plant in the same winery with a labelling machine in the foreground.*

quality wines, bentonite is not used and the must is passed through a centrifuge to remove sediment.

Fermentation takes place in 30,000 litre (6,600 gallon) vinificators in the open air. Water is automatically sprayed down the outside of the tanks to control fermentation temperature, which is not allowed to exceed 22°C (71°F). Vigorous fermentation takes between seven and ten days, and the young wine is then allowed to cool down before being transferred to 25,000 litre (5,500 gallon) ferro-concrete tanks for the fermentation to be completed. Again, the higher quality wines are centrifuged before being transferred to the ferro-concrete tanks. After fermentation, the wines are filtered and stabilized. The aim is to complete this process before the end of December when the worst of the winter frosts begin.

Red wine is produced in the two cellars at Dve Mogoli and Bjala using concrete tanks, and in the new Cellar 4 in Russe where vinificators have been installed.

Winemaking using the ferro-concrete tanks follows traditional methods. The grapes are crushed and the must, skins, stems and pips piped to the fermentation tanks. There are five processing lines, three capable of handling two tonnes (1.9 tons) of grapes an hour, and two able to cope with 50 tonnes (49 tons) an hour. The must is sulphated before fermentation starts. Fermentation relies on natural yeasts and is not allowed to exceed 26°C (73°F) and, depending on the characteristics of the vintage, the must is agitated periodically to increase its contact with air. Very occasionally, if the temperature starts to rise a quantity of the fermenting must is drawn off, usually at night, until the temperature falls and then it is replaced. A greater threat comes from naturally low temperatures, especially at night. The young wine is cooled down and immediately transferred to 30,000 litre (6,600 gallon) concrete tanks for the quiet fermentation.

A new technology has been introduced for the production of red wine using the "Jambol" vinificators. The fermentation takes place under much more controlled conditions, with constant monitoring of temperature. Water is used to cool the tanks down and the marc is removed mechanically. Pure yeasts are used to start fermentation. During fermentation, which lasts between two and five days, water is poured down the outside of the tanks to reduce the temperature of the must and the young wine is then agitated for up to 20 minutes. When the temperature starts to rise again, the water cooling operating begins again.

The initial vigorous fermentation takes between two and a half to three days. When it has reached a relative weight of 1010 or 1015 it is allowed to cool down, passed through a centrifuge and transferred to ferro-concrete tanks.

The region is also noted for its dessert wines, although these are only produced in limited quantities. The must is fermented, fortified with spirit and has grape concentrate added if necessary to increase the sugar level. The wine is then aged, spending at least a year in casks in the open air exposed to the sun.

The total yield of wine produced, including dessert wines and wine distillate is between 70 and 73 per cent of the equivalent weight of grapes harvested. The yields of the table wines is between 60 and 65 per cent. The average annual production is between seven and ten million litres (1.5 and 2.2 million gallons).

There is a great deal of experimental work carried out in the region, and a new scientific station was opened in 1965.

The area has one Controliran Region wine, Bjalo ot Russenski brjag, approved in 1986, a white blended wine sold on the home market. It is produced from grapes grown round the villages of Pirgovo and Trastenik, in the areas known as Novite

Production of varieties at Russe	
Dimiat	500,000 litres (110,00 gallons)
Rkatziteli	2,000,000 litres (440,000 gallons)
Muscat Ottonel	700,000 litres (154,000 gallons)
Riesling	1,200,000 litres (264,000 gallons)
Fetijaska	100,000 litres (22,000 gallons)
Cabernet Sauvignon	3,000,000 litres (66,000 gallons)
Merlot	800,000 litres (176,000 gallons)
Aligoté, Gamza, Senso, Saperavi	500,000 litres (110,000 gallons)

losja and Vishkata. Both are in the Danube Collar in hilly terrain with a special micro-climate, virtually ruling out the risk of frosts. Summer temperatures are hot which helps the grapes ripen early.

The enterprise hopes that another micro-region around the village of Tzenovo could become another Controliran Region area within a few years. It is especially suited to producing high quality red wines. There is already a lovely, light Cabernet Sauvignon produced which has achieved the status of AO.

FOLKLORE AND CUISINE

The main wine festival celebrated is the Holiday of the Vine Grower on February 14.

The region has its own special cuisine because of its proximity to the Danube. Over the centuries Russe has developed trading links with many nations and its cuisine reflects traditional as well as European and Middle East cooking. The influence of the river is also reflected in the wide range of fish dishes. The cuisine is characterized by the use of many spices and vegetables. The specialities include fish soup, baked fish and fish glace. The Middle East influence can be seen in the great variety of cakes and grilled meats and vegetables baked in earthen pots.

SOUTHERN REGION

JAMBOL **J**ambol (spelt Yambol on some maps) is at the eastern end of the Southern Region. The River Tundja, which flows down from the Balkan range, passes through the region and on into Turkey in the south.

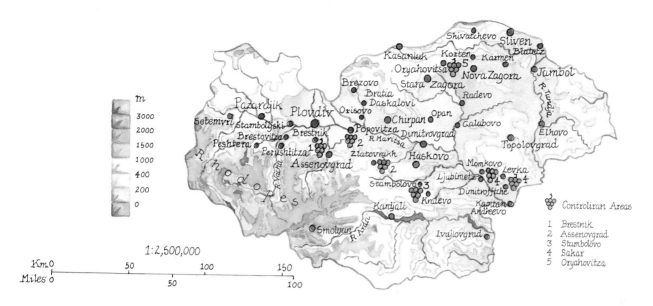

1:2,500,000

In wine terms, Jambol covers the regions of Straldzha, Jambol Elhovo and Topolovgrad; and the sub-regions of Straldzha, Zimnitza, Iretchekovo, Kaltchevo, Malak Monastir and Oreshnik. The region of Straldzha has light sandy clay soil and the flat terrain has a slightly southern exposure. Iretchekovo is hilly with black earth and leached woodland soils. Malak Monastir has a slightly sloping terrain with a southeastern exposure and woodland soils. Oreshnik is very hilly with woodland soils. The region is characterised by dry springs and hot summers. The average temperatures in Jambol in July are 23.1°C (73°F) and in August 22.6°C (72°F). In Elhovo in July they are 23.5°C (74°F) and in August 22.8°C (73°F).

In 1924 the Misket wine cooperative was established, the first joint effort in the area to grow grapes and produce wine. In 1943 three families – the Hatchevi, Valtchanovi and Sheitanov – founded the Loztzentral enterprise and after nationalization in 1947 it became part of the newly created State Monopoly. Because of the increased production a new cellar was built in Jambol in 1947 together with a new bottling line for wines, brandies and sugar drinks. In 1965 a further cellar was constructed in Straldzha with a capacity of processing 6,000 tonnes (5,904 tons) of grapes. The four cellars (Jambol, No 1 and 2; Straldzha, Elhove) now process at least 16,000 tonnes (15,744 tons) of grapes for wines and the well-known Straldzha muskat brandy. The area is noted for its Jambol misket wine. There are eight agro-industrial complexes in the Jambol organization and an experimental agricultural irrigation station.

Approximately 224,000 hectares (553,504 acres) of land in the area are cultivated, the main agricultural produce being cereals, vegetables and fruit growing, however only 4,600 hectares

(11,366 acres) are planted with vines. The main vine varieties are Cabernet Sauvignon, Merlot, Red Misket, Rkatziteli, Muskat Ottonel and Pamid. They are planted in equal proportions of red to white. Cultivation follows the standard pattern, with the vintage normally starting around September 25 when the grapes are gathered for transport to the wine cellars.

Sugar content is determined by sampling at the weighing reception area and the grapes are then crushed. The juice for red wines is pumped with the skins still intact to fermentation tanks for the initial vigorous fermentation and then to ferrous–concrete tanks when fermentation is completed. The wine is racked several times and pumped into steel concrete storage tanks where it is kept until bottling.

After crushing, the juice for the white wines is filtered and fermentation is controlled by cooling the tanks with water. Bentonite is usually used during the fermentation to preserve the aromas. After fermentation, the wine is racked, treated with sulphur and then filtered again. Finally it is pumped into ferrous concrete tanks for storage.

The aims of the winery are intense colour and bouquet and strong varietal characteristics. No sugar is added and the grapes for the white wines have a natural sugar content of between 18 and 20 per cent, the reds 20-24 per cent. Total acidity for the whites varies between 6 and 8 grams per litre and for the reds between 6 and 7 grams per litre.

For the last five years Jambol has been working closely with the Japanese company Sanraku, developing styles of wine suitable for the Japanese market. A variety of Cabernet Sauvignon has been produced under controlled irrigation to extract the maximum level of colour and aroma. Manol Borganov, the group master and technologist in the cellar at Straldzha, has been honoured with the Gold Medal of Labour for his work as a wine producer in the Vinprom Jambol enterprise. He has worked there since leaving school.

At Jambol, wine statistics are given in tonnes, which allows comparison of the contributions made by the various varieties: between 8,000 and 10,000 tonnes (7,872 and 9,840 tons) of wine are produced annually: Misket 2,000 tonnes (1,968 tons), Rkatziteli 1,800 tonnes (1,771 tons), Cabernet Sauvignon 3,500 tonnes (3,444 tons), Merlot 1,500 tonnes (1,476 tons), Muskat Ottonel 600 tonnes (590 tons) and Pamid 600 tonnes (590 tons).

FOLKLORE The main folk holiday celebrated is Triffon Zarezan, the festival of the vine grower in early spring, to celebrate the fertility of the earth which bears the grapes.

HASKOVO The Haskovo (sometimes written Khaskovo) Combine covers the central part of the southern region and takes in the sub-regions of Strandzha Sakar, Dimitrofftche 11, Stambolovo, and I. Momkovo. The soils are eroded woodland, carbonate black earth and sandy clay humus. Most of the vineyards are in the hills at an average altitude of 250 metres (800 feet) above sea level. This area is close to the frontiers with Greece and Turkey, in the very south of Bulgaria.

Vines have been grown in the region for thousands of years and it was one of the centres for the worship of the wine god Dionysus. Evidence supporting this has been found in excavations near the village of Voivodovo where wine artefacts from the fourth century BC have been found. There have also been similar finds in the village of Jabulkovo and near the villages of Brjastovo-Harmanli and Kralevo. Amphorae in a tomb in the village of Mezek, decorated with the head of a maenad (female follower of Dionysus) and a satyr, show that wine played an import role throughout this period. Vine sickles from the Middle Ages have been discovered in the village of Ljubenovo.

Since 1944 the district of Haskovo has developed as a large new viticultural region. The first wine cellar was built at Haskovo and was followed by those at Ljubimetz and Stambolovo.

Farming land in the region covers 223,000 hectares (551,033 acres) of which 130,000 hectares (321,230 acres) are planted with crops and 5,500 hectares (13,590 acres) with vines – 600 hectares (1,482 acres) of dessert varieties and 4,900 hectares (12,103 acres) of wine varieties. Other agricultural produce includes cereals, fodder crops, cotton, fruit and nuts. The region is noted for melons, sesame, monkey nuts and silk production.

The wine varieties grown are nine times more popular than the dessert grapes grown and five times more red grape varieties are grown as white. Merlot is the most common, followed by

Cabernet Sauvignon, Pamid and Pinot Gris. The main white varieties are Dimiat followed by Rkatziteli, Red Misket, Ugni Blanc, Muskat Ottonel and Tamjanka.

There are ten agro-industrial complexes producing grapes – Haskovo south, Haskovo north, Stambolovo, Mineralni bani, Dimitrovgrad, Harmanli north, Harmanli south, Svilengrad, Ljubimetz and Levka. The complexes with the largest vineyards have organized special viticulture brigades and have introduced industrial technologies for the growing and production of grapes using the very latest techniques. Vinprom Haskovo has three wine cellars for handling grapes – at Haskovo, Ljubimetz and Stambolovo.

The climate of the region is suitable for the normal development of the vine, so the grapes are used for the production of high quality white and red table wines. The climate is moderate continental and in the more southern part of the region the influence of the Mediterranean is felt (the sea is not far away beyond Greece). The winters are mild and humid, the summers dry and hot. The average monthly temperature during the hottest month is 23-25°C (73-77°F). The total annual rainfall is between 550 and 700 millimetres (21 and 27 inches) and is evenly distributed during the course of the vine's growing period.

The great variety of soil types and the favourable climatic conditions has led to selective planting of varieties to give optimum results. The pruning starts after the celebration of the traditional Triffon Zarezan holiday and is done according to a carefully worked out schedule aimed at programming the vintage. The vines are grown in wide-set rows and are trained tall, then in the Umbrella system.

The vintage usually starts in the middle of September and the grapes are picked by hand. They are then transferred to metal tubs or "ships" for transport by truck to the wine cellars. After automated unloading, the grapes for red wines are crushed and transferred with the skins to metal fermentation tanks. The most modern equipment is used during fermentation to extract the intensity of colour and flavour required. The fermentation temperature is automatically controlled and the juice still on the lees regularly and evenly agitated. The automated lines can handle up to 50 tonnes (49 tons) of grapes an hour, and after fermentation the wine is stored in metal tanks of either 200, 400 or 600 cubic metres (261, 523 or 784 cubic yards).

Each variety is received at the cellars separately where it is weighed and analysed for quality and sugar content. After crushing, the must is treated with a solution of sulphur dioxide depending on its condition and temperature. In the case of white wines yeast is added immediately after crushing when the juice

arrives in the fermentation tank, for red wines, the yeast is added two hours after the sulphation.

When the wine reaches a relative density of between 1020 and 1040 it is pumped out and filtered, and the marc is then removed from the tanks. The wines from the vinificators are filtered again after about five days and then returned until fermentation is complete.

After crushing, the juice of the white grapes is filtrated in the filtering-press system. The must is pumped to the fermentation tanks where temperature is controlled by irrigation. After the initial vigorous fermentation the wine is separated from the yeast precipitate and pumped to other holding tanks where the remaining fermentation takes place. The young wines are then blended with others of the same variety from the same region. The young wine is then filtrated again and held in tanks to await bottling.

Because of the good climate and special wind conditions which prevent the development of grape diseases, the region specializes in the production of quality and high quality wines. The wines are characterised by a strong fruit scent of ripe grapes, a high alcohol content (between 12.5 and 13°) and relatively low total acidity.

Experimental work in the vineyards is conducted by the Vassil Kolarov Agricultural Institute in Plovdiv under the leadership of Professor Babrikov. New techniques include continual monitoring of the vineyards to indicate in advance when tasks should be carried out such as pruning. It also includes leaf diagnosis to determine how much manure needs to be applied. A system of droplet irrigation has also been developed which has involved a considerable amount of mechanical work in the vineyards.

Each year, just before the vintage, grapes are analysed both in

The average volume of wine produced each year is about 15 million litres (3,300,000 gallons). The following types of wine are produced: Dimiat 1,400,000 litres (308,000 gallons), Ugni Blanc 100,000 litres (22,000 gallons), Misket 300,000 litres (66,000 gallons), Rkatziteli 100,000 litres (22,000 gallons), Muskat Ottonel 60,000 litres (13,200 gallons), Pamid 300,000 litres (66,000 gallons), Pinot Gris 100,000 litres (22,000 gallons), Cabernet Sauvignon 1,500,000 litres (330,000 gallons) and Merlot 6,000,000 litres (1,320,000 gallons).

Above Trellising of vines around houses is a common practice in both villages and cities. The shade provided by the vines is very welcome in the summer.

Below left Fermentation tanks for red wine in the Sliven winery.

Below right A magnificent wooden barrel used for ageing the wine.

the wineries' own laboratories and in Sofia to give the wine makers advance information about the condition of the harvest. The grapes are tested for sugar, tartaric acid, wine and malic acids, aminonitrogen and common phenol substances.

The region includes the quality controlled areas of Stambolovo, Gledka, Haskovo, Momkovo, Levka, Mustarak and Tankovo. In 1987 production also started on the new Haskovo Dimiat, a wine of declared geographical origin. There are also the AC wines Sakar Merlot and Stambolovo Merlot. Both are noted for their ruby brilliance, noble bouquet and mild and harmonious taste. The Trakia Merlot, produced in this region, won the Gold Medal in 1982 at the International Exhibition in New York. Vinprom-Haskovo controls the vineyards and checks on the quality designations, in conjunction with Vinprom-Sofia and IVP-Sofia.

FOLKLORE AND CUISINE

The Haskovo district is an area which has remained reasonably autonomous in cultural terms. It has its own folklore and traditions reflecting that most of the people have always worked on the land. It has always been a rich area, having grown cereals and grapes since ancient times, and more recently tobacco. Stock breeding is now also important. Local crafts include ceramics, wrought iron and gold work. Copper is important in Haskovo and Harmanli, and one handicraft, Jahnadzhijstvo, found only in

Richly coloured braids from the Haskovo district.

Haskovo is dependent on the growing and processing of sesame in the area.

The local costumes are very colourful and Haskovo has the National Museum of Costumes and Fabrics. The women's costumes vary according to ornaments and style from settlement to settlement, while the men's costumes generally are characterised by full bottomed breeches and jackets, both richly braided. This is known as the Tchernodreshkovoso style.

Because it is primarily an agricultural community, there are many festivals celebrating farming, the seasons and the harvest. The main festivals are Koleduvane and Survakane, which take place dring the winter, Zagovezni, on the eve of spring, Easter, Gergjovden – the Day of George – and Bobos Harat and mummers' dances.

The region has its own cuisine, some recipes dating back to the Thracians. The food is always accompanied by wine – and nearly always by dry wine. The menu encompasses all kinds of meat – fish, chicken, lamb, mutton, veal, pork and game. Besides being boiled and stewed, meat is also served grilled. The very savoury babetzi (a meat delicacy served with red wine) are characteristic of the region. Towards the end of summer, the housewives will start to prepare Stomma sirene, a delicacy that can only be drunk with fine, light wines.

Another tradition is the baking of special breads, using a combination of different sorts of doughs with various milk products and walnuts, almonds and sesame. Other traditional local dishes include hotchpotch, Thracian pasty, fish with onion, lamb with fresh onions and almonds, fish in pumpkin leaves, bread stuffed with mince meat, milk loaf with cheese, Sirene pod kapak, Filevo sausages, stuffed spleen, dock with eggs and cheese, Christmas grilled meat, peppers stuffed with aubergine, and Kanakli chicken.

SLIVEN Sliven is in a hilly district to the north of Jambol, close to the Balkan-Stara mountain range, which rises in a protective belt to the north. Vinprom Sliven is in the east of the southern region, and includes the towns and districts of Sliven, Karmen, Nova Zagora, Tvarditza, Shivatchevo; the villages of Korten, Blatetz and Padarevo, and covers the sub-regions of the vineyards in the foothills of the Balkan-Stara Planina, from the town of Tvarditza in the west to the borders with Burgas and Jambol districts Petolatchkata and Padarevo. Also included are the vineyards in the foothills of Sredna Gora, a range of hills to the south of the River Tundja. The vineyards of Nova Zagora, and the centres of Radevo, Sokol and Elenovo are also part of the Sliven district.

The area has a moderate continental climate, with a large part of the total annual rainfall during the growing period. The area has an average altitude of 250 metres (800 feet) above sea level. The soils are mostly sandy or sandy clay with good drainage. Most of the region has a southern exposure.

The white wine varieties account for 60.52 per cent of plantings as follows: Rkatziteli 29.45 per cent; Red Misket 15.26 per cent; Muskat Ottonel 15.23 per cent; Dimiat 4.70 per cent; Pinot Chardonnay 2.03 per cent; Tamjanka 1 per cent; Sauvignon 1 per cent; Silvaner 1 per cent. Up and coming white varieties include Riesling and Traminer.

The growers are organized into 56 brigades which are self-financing economic units. All the grapes are processed at one of the six wine cellars in Padarevo, Blatetz, Sliven, Shivatchevo, Korten and Nova Zagora. The cellars at Sliven and Nova Zagora are the largest in the country.

The region's climatic conditions have a strong influence on the growing conditions. The total annual temperature during the growing period is 3,868°C (6,994°F). During the last five years, it has varied between 3,500 and 3,700°C (6,332 and 6,692°F). The growing period is 210 days and the average period between spring and autumn frosts is 234 days. The relative humidity of the air during the ripening period is July 56 per cent, August 55 per cent and September 59 per cent. From November to March there is an average rainfall of 220.6 millimetres (8 inches), from April to July 243.8 millimetres (9 inches) and from August to November 121 millimetres (4 inches).

The viticultural year starts with pruning, usually towards the middle of November and this continues until the second half of March. Spraying to combat pests and diseases starts about the middle of May and continues until the middle of August, and all the spraying is done using either light aircraft or helicopters. Applications of fertilizer are regularly made to the soil and irrigation is extensively used. A new irrigation project at Sredna Tundzha is under construction, which will make it possible to irrigate the districts of Gavrailovo, Sliven, Blatetz and parts of Nova Zagora, Mlekarovo and Kermen. The eventual plan is to have drip irrigation in all the vineyards.

The vintage usually starts about September 20 and Muscat Ottonel is the first variety to be harvested. Everyone in the region is recruited to take part in the vintage, which has to be carefully planned because of the large areas involved. Because the region specializes in quality wines, it is essential to have the grapes picked and delivered to the wineries as quickly as possible and occasionally this means drafting in people from outside the area to help. The grapes are gathered in plastic pails, each holding 10 litres (2.2

The total area covers 361,400 hectares (893,019 acres) of which 135,300 hectares (334,326 acres) is cultivated land. About 88,300 hectares (218,189 acres) is under crops and 10,576 hectares (26,133 acres) are planted with vines of which 2,500 hectares (6,177 acres) are new, as yet unproductive vines. The vineyards account for 20 per cent of all Bulgarian wine production.

The region is predominantly intensive agriculture and stock breeding. Production includes (per year) cereals 305,000 tonnes (300,120 tons – wheat 152,000 tonnes/149,568 tons, barley 50,000 tonnes/49,200 tons and maize 98,000 tonnes/96,432 tons), vegetables 50,000 tonnes (49,200 tons) and fruit 30,000 tonnes (29,520 tons).

Red wine varieties account for 39.48 per cent of plantings with Cabernet Sauvignon the most important at 20 per cent, followed by Merlot at 7.76 per cent, Pamid 6.9 per cent and Slivenska shevka 2.64 per cent. Other red varieties growing in popularity are Pinot Noir and Gamey.

Top *Trellised wines are a feature of the Sliven estate.*

Centre left *The catacomb of tunnels which was once a disused underground war shelter has been converted into cellars.*

Centre right *One of the tunnels houses the tasting room which is furnished with cushioned benches and red woven mats.*

Bottom *A typical row of vines in one of the Sliven vineyards.*

gallons). The pickers leave the full pails between the lines as they progress and the grapes are then transferred to a container with a 400 kilogrammes (882lb) capacity on a trailer towed by a tractor. The full containers are quickly delivered to a central site where the grapes are transferred into containers with a 4.064 tonne (4 ton) capacity for transport by lorry to the cellars.

The different varieties are picked separately and transferred separately to the wineries. Constant checks are made in the vineyards to ensure that picking takes place when the grapes are in their best condition. The whole vintage takes between 25 and 30 days. This is necessary not only to ensure the grapes reach the wineries quickly, but to avoid uncertain late autumn weather.

When the grapes arrive at the cellars, they are weighed, analysed for sugar content and checked for variety. Unloading is automatic with the containers being moved by electric hoists and it is at this stage that the quality of the grapes is assessed.

The grapes for the white wine are lightly pressed twice, the juice is immediately drawn off, filtered and pumped to holding tanks. The wine is then passed through static-dynamic filters where the must is separated. Sugar is extracted from the marc which is pressed again and then processed into a fodder for cattle. The must is mildly sulphated and left for at least 18 hours to precipitate out most of the coarse particles. The cleared must is then siphoned off and pumped into the fermentation tanks. The fermentation temperature is controlled, with water flow over the

tanks, at between 17 and 22°C (62 and 71°F). After the initial vigorous fermentation, the young wine is separated from the sediment and desulphated if necessary. It is then allowed to complete its fermentation before a last fining and sulphation.

The grapes for red wine are crushed and pumped together with the skin, pips and stems into their tanks. Fermentation of red wines is automatically controlled and the marc is extracted mechanically. Between 12 and 14 hours after the fermentation tanks are filled a "top" forms on the vigorously fermenting liquid. As soon as sensors detect the formation of this crust, the automatic programmer takes over. The programmes last between 36 and 48 hours depending on the style of wine being made. When the programme has finished, the young wine is filtered, the marc is removed, pressed lightly again to extract more liquid and taken to the distillery to produce alcohol by direct distillation. The final residue of marc is then used as cattle feed. The young wine is again piped to tanks for the final stage of the vigorous fermentation which lasts for about another four days. The wine is then separated from the sediment and the conditions created for the quieter malolactic acid fermentation. A chromatographic analysis is used to determine when this second fermentation is complete. The wine is then decanted, treated with sulphur and stabilized.

The young red wines are tested at this stage to decide how

The Sliven district produces between 40 and 50 million litres (8.8-11 million gallons) of wine a year, consisting of between 40 and 44 million litres (8,800,000 and 9,680,000 gallons) of dry table wine, about 3 million litres (660,000 gallons) of dessert wines and about 3 million litres (660,000 gallons) for wine distillate.

The tables wines are as follows:

White wines   (19,750,000–25,750,000 litres/4,345,000–5,665,000 gallons):

White Pamid	up to 300,000 litres (66,000 gallons)
Riesling	150,000 litres (33,000 gallons)
Rkatziteli	13-17 million litres (2,860,000–3,740,000 gallons)
Misket	5-7 million litres (1,100,000–1,540,000 gallons)
Blanc de Noir	300,000 litres (66,000 gallons)
White dessert wines	1,000,000 litres (220,000 gallons)
Rosé wines	300,000 litres (66,000 gallons)

Red wines (16,100,000 and 19,100,000 litres/3,542,000–4,202,000 gallons):

Pamid	500,000 litres (110,000 gallons)
Shevka	100,000 litres (22,000 gallons)
Cabernet Sauvignon	12-15 million litres (2,640,000–3,300,000 gallons)
Merlot	up to 2,000,000 litres (440,000 gallons)
Sliven dessert wine	1,500,000 litres (330,000 gallons)

The Sliven district produces between 40 and 50 million litres (8.8-11 million gallons) of wine a year, consisting of between 40 and 44 million litres (8,800,000 and 9,680,000 gallons) of dry table wine, about 3 million litres (660,000 gallons) of dessert wines and about 3 million litres (660,000 gallons) for wine distillate.

long they should be aged, when they should be bottled and their export potential. After storing in holding tanks, the wines are blended and only bottled after the most detailed tasting and chemical analysis.

Over the last ten years the quantity of grapes grown and processed has ranged from 33,000 to 90,000 tonnes (32,472-88,560 tons). Sugar content at the time of harvesting varies between 17 and 21 per cent for white varieties and between 19.5 and 24 per cent for red varieties. Acidity of the grapes is between 7.5 and 12 grammes per litre, with a favourable ratio of wine acid. The red wines are characterised by intense colour, good fruit scent and balance. The whites are elegant with a subtle but perceptible bouquet. In certain areas, especially Padarevo, Shivatchevo and Korten wines of outstanding qualities are produced.

A great deal of experimental work is carried out in the vineyards around Sliven in co-operation with local and national research stations. Much of this work is concerned with testing new varieties and developing new growing techniques for existing varieties. The cellars at Korten are carrying out experimental work on processing techniques and the genetic qualities of varietals.

THE VINTAGE AT THE TURN OF THE CENTURY

In the old days the vintage in the district of Sliven always started around October 10. The vintage started on the same day and at the same time throughout the area and everybody took part. Before dawn the villagers would assemble in the vineyards and bonfires would be lit to take away the early morning chill. They would all enjoy a traditional breakfast of bread and dried beef softened by soaking in wine, and at first light the vintage began. Working in lines abreast, the pickers would empty the baskets of grapes into containers on horse drawn carts. When these containers were full, the grapes were driven back to the winery.

The men crushed the grapes with their feet standing in tubs. The juice escaped along a channel and was collected in another smaller vessel. White wine was produced by immediately separating the must from the skins, stalks and pips, while the red wine remained with the crushed grapes in unsealed barrels for between 12 and 15 days. The must was then transferred to another unsealed barrel where the fermentation was allowed to continue. When this was complete, the wine was again transferred into another cask for maturing. Casks in the deep cellars had already been prepared by washing with hot water, cleaning thoroughly and then dried and fumigated with sulphur. They were washed out again to remove most of the sulphur because this retarded the fermentation. The new wine was poured into the barrels which were then sealed.

The marc from the white wine was covered with leaves and twigs from walnut and quince trees and mud (made by mixing wood ash and water) was smeared over. This sealed in the marc and prevented it going sour before it was needed for distillation to brandy.

By 1912 there were up to 15 distilleries operating in and around Sliven. The best, and also the first, was owned by Steffan Popov. Today the district has about 110 centres for the production of brandy, the best of which are in Blatetz, Korten and Sliven.

PIONEERS OF WINE QUALITY

The first "modern" winery was built in 1890 in the vineyards to the east of Sliven. It was managed by an agronomist called Zabunov but was soon abandoned. In 1904 the first viticultural syndicate was founded in Sliven to import American rootstock, vines and equipment. Two years later, the growers formed a cooperative and in 1920 the first production cooperative was formed. This Shevka cooperative recruited Steffan Popov as its first chairman.

In 1904 Steffan Popov was one of the country's leading wine specialists. He, his brother Zahari and Peter Dankov were the first three from Sliven to graduate from the Vidin viticulture school. Between 1910–13 he visited France to buy American rootstock and by 1925 he had four hectares (9.8 acres) of nursery vineyards in the district producing up to 500,000 grafted vines. Other famous wine growers at this time were Janaki Lessenov, Georgi Petkov, Neno Tzanev, Gerogi Zhetcheoolu and Steffan Pandov.

The father of Bulgarian wine production was Professor Nedeltcho Nedeltchev. He graduated from the Sliven Gymnasium

A traditional haycart is a common sight in the Bulgarian countryside.

in 1908 and enrolled as a scholarship student at the Montpelier agricultural and wine college in France. After graduating in 1912 he returned to work at the Pleven experimental station and was then recruited as the specialist at the Shevka wine cooperative in Sliven. In 1931 he was appointed professor of viticulture and viniculture at Sofia University, and from 1944–46 was the first dean of the newly founded Agronomical faculty in Plovdiv. For his services to wine he was elected to the Italian Academy of Wine Growing in 1964, and to the French Academy of Agricultural Sciences in 1965.

Since 1944 both the vineyards and wine cellars in Sliven have been transformed. Industrial techniques have been introduced for the vines, wines and brandies. In 1952 when Vinprom was created, five privately owned cellars were nationalized, and together with Shevka, merged to form the Sliven Winery. There were also cooperative cellars in Pararevo and Korten, and three private cellars in Nova Zagora. All were merged with the Sliven enterprise.

In Shivatchevo a new winery had been built in 1950. Between 1960–62 the new cellar in Nova Zagora was constructed, and between 1961–66 the new cellar in Sliven came into operation. In 1970 construction work was completed on a new cellar in the village of Blatetz. Over the last ten years there has been an intensive modernization programme carried out in all the cellars with production and storage capacity greatly increased. Total acreage topped 12,000 hectares (29,652 acres) in 1982 but has been reduced in the last few years because of a shortage of labour to maintain the vineyards.

New reception centres for the arrival of the grapes have been developed and installed, new pressing equipment and controlled fermentation tanks have been introduced as well as new bottling facilities. New brand names for the wines have been created – Slivenska Perla for natural grape brandy, and Haidushko Bile and Sliven for wines. There are wines from declared geographical regions – Pinot Noir from Slivenska Shevka, Misket and Cabernet Sauvignon from the region of Sliven, and the special Slivenska vodka. There is also a special vodka distilled from wine made from Cabernet Sauvignon grapes.

The enterprise can now process up to 4,500 tonnes (4,428 tons) of grapes a day without overloading the 31 separate processing lines. The highly automated plant has a capacity of almost 95 million litres (20,900,000 gallons) of which 81 million litres (17,820,000 gallons) is for primary wine production. New vineyards have been planted with Chardonnay, Sauvignon, Pinot Noir, Riesling and Traminer for the production of Controliran Region wines.

The mummers' dance ritual is enacted seven weeks before Easter on the feast of Bartolomeus and is thought to encourage health and prosperity for the village.

FOLKLORE AND CUISINE Zagovezni is celebrated seven weeks before Easter and everyone gathers in the centre of each village to dance. At night bonfires are lit in the village and on surrounding hills. The men of the village leap over the fires because this is supposed to ensure good health by driving away diseases. The villagers compete to see who can have the biggest bonfire because they used to believe that all the land illuminated by the flames would be protected from hail in the coming year. Villagers still take pieces of burning wood from the fire and shoot them like arrows from bows into the sky. Folklore said that if the villagers helped the sun replenish its fire, the sun would thank them with a large harvest. In the village of Mladovo, an old man, who dresses in shabby clothes and is made up to look frightening, makes the rounds of all the bonfires, waving a burning rag to drive all the evil spirits away.

After all the fires have burnt out, the tables are laid for a special meatless meal. There is always fish, pasties, khalva, other dishes and wine. In some dishes a piece of khalva is suspended on a string from the ceiling and the villagers have to try and catch it with their mouths. This is called "hamkae". In the village of Kobatchite all the villagers disguise themselves after eating and try to fool their friends.

The festival can last three days after which the villagers may go to church. The fourth day is the feast of Bartolomeus, and the excuse for more festivity with a mummers' dance. The mummers' dance and games stem from an old masquerade ritual aimed at encouraging fruitfulness and health for the villagers, crops and animals. Many villages still celebrate the mummers' dances including Padarevo, G. Aleksandrovo, Blatetz, Topoltchane and Zhelju Voivoda. The ritual garment consists of a mask of rags with two horns, plumage and a beard made from sheep's wool. The people wear white trousers, bells on a belt around their waist and carry large staffs draped with sheep skins. The disguised revellers visit every house in the village and at each they are handed a small quantity of flour from a bowl. When the bowl is empty the housewife spins it and if it comes to a rest bottom up the family will enjoy a fruitful year. The traditional dress in the Sliven district is a blouse, a special skirt called a sukman, an apron, a belta jacket and slippers.

Todorovden, or The Day of Todor, is celebrated on March 2, or on the Saturday of the week after Zagovezni. Its main feature is "kushii", or horse racing, and everyone takes part. It is especially popular in the villages where there are many horses – Konevo, Mladovo, Zheljo Voivoda and Kovatchite. The women prepare a special bread for the day, often shaped like a horse, and sometimes coated in treacle, which is given to neighbours for good luck and health. Another ancient ritual is that the women wash their hair with water in which there is a little chaff. This chaff will have been used by them to comb the horse from head to tail and it was said that in this way, their hair should grow as strong as the tail of the horse.

Triffonovden, or The Day of Triffon, is celebrated on February 14 to mark the start of the pruning of the vines. Pruning is done by each grower at his own vineyard very early in the morning. He cuts three vine rods from three vine plants which are then sprinkled with wine and woven into a wreath which he wears on his head. All the villagers then assemble for a traditional meal of warm bread, boiled chicken and wine, always served from wooden jugs. After the meal, and accompanied by bagpipes and rebecs, the growers assemble in the main square before marching in turn to all the houses. Every household is given one vine twig for fruitfulness in the coming year.

Regional specialities include Kotlen fish soup, boiled mutton Sliven style, Kavarma chicken, Windmill hotch-potch, pork steak Sliven style, fruit pies and home made strudel.

CHIRPAN The Chirpan vineyards are in gentle countryside between the River Maritsa, which flows east from the Plovdiv plain, and the low hills of the Sredna Gora. The Vinprom enterprise is centred on the town of Chirpan and takes in the sub-regions around the towns of Chirpan and Stara Zagora, and the micro-regions around Dulboki, Radnevo, Opan, Trankovo, Galabovo, Gurkovo, Mag-

lizh, Kasanluk, Br. Daskalovi and Orisovo.

Vines have always been grown in the region and before the phylloxera outbreak there were about 3,600 hectares (8,895 acres) of vineyards, largely around the town of Chirpan, and growing mainly Mavrud. Almost every family owned at least one vineyard but after the phylloxera, which arrived in 1895, the industry went into sharp decline. Work on replanting the vineyards started at the turn of the century and the dessert varieties Bolgar and Tchaush were planted, together with Dimiat, Mavrud and Pamid for table wine. The grapes were usually sent out of the region for processing.

Immediately before the Second World War the vineyards in the Chirpan district covered more than 12,000 hectares (29,652 acres), mainly owned by small growers operating independently. Since 1945 cooperatives have been established. The wineries have been modernized and expanded and the vineyards greatly extended. After rigorous trials new varieties started to be planted after 1960, particularly Riesling, Cabernet, Merlot, Aligoté, Rkatziteli and the dessert grapes Cardinal and Tzaritza na lozjata. Most of the region is between 200 and 300 metres (656-984 feet) above sea level, soils are mainly black earth, woodland and wood humus over limestone, and most of the vineyards have a southerly, southeasterly or southwesterly exposure.

The wineries use the latest automated equipment to unload the grapes and assist with the fermentation. In the Chirpan cellar alone there are now 45 fermentation tanks for red wine and ten for white. The Jordan Todorov plant, which produces sparkling wines, is the most up to date in Bulgaria and also has the greatest output at 14 million bottles a year. In Stara Zagora there is a new plant for the production of table wines, and in Dulboki vinegar is made.

The region is divided into 13 agro-industrial complexes, and these are sub-divided into vineyard farms and brigades of workers. There are 11 wineries/cellars – two in Chirpan, the others in Svoboda, Beren, Granit, Br. Daskalovi, Spasovo, Stara

There are 156,000 hectares (385,476 acres) of cultivated land, of which 6,050 hectares (14,949 acres) are planted with vines. Other agriculture in the region includes cereals, fruit (pears, peaches, cherries and plums), vegetables (tomatoes, peppers, onions, cabbage, beetroot), fodder crops, sunflowers and cotton.

Grapes Grown in Chirpan			
Red		**White**	
Cabernet Sauvignon	25.8 per cent	Rkatziteli	15.8 per cent
Merlot	33 per cent	Dimiat	3.9 per cent
Pamid	10.2 per cent	Aligoté	5.4 per cent
Red Misket	3 per cent		
Others	1.8 per cent		
Dessert grapes	1.1 per cent		

Zagora, Dalboki, Oryahovitsa and Kasanluk.

The vineyard and cellars of the winery in Stara Zagora.

The average annual temperature is 12.5°C (54.5°F) the hottest months are July (23.2°C/73.7°F) and August (23.8°C/74.8°F). The lowest temperatures are in January with an average of 1°C (33.8°F). There are on average 238 days free from frost. The earliest date for the first frost is October 19, and the latest for last frost April 27. The rainfall is evenly spread throughout the year.

Because of the climate and the siting of the vineyards there is good growth and high yields. Grapes for sparkling wine are ripe at the beginning of September and the other varieties ripen fully by the end of the month. Training is according to the umbrella system, and the vines are treated against mildew and oidium fungus.

The vintage for the sparkling wine grapes starts on September 10, and for the rest of the grapes on September 20. Fermentation is carried out in either metal or ferrous concrete tanks. The wines are then filtered, fined and stabilized with sulphur and then transferred to holding or ageing tanks before blending and bottling. The average volume of wine produced is between 16 and 20 million litres (3.5-4.4 million gallons) a year.

Experimental work is carried out at the crop research station in Chirpan. It conducts research into new varieties and tests the genetic properties of all planted varieties. The enterprise also has its own scientists who conduct field trials and develop new techniques for growing and cultivation. The enterprise produces the Controlled Origin wines Staro Tcherveno from Oryahovitsa, and the appellation wines Chirpansko tcherveno and Iskra-Chirpan. The Controlled Origin regions of Kolena and Oryahovitza are for Merlot and Cabernet Sauvignon only.

FOLKLORE
AND CUISINE

The main festival is the Day of the Vine Grower, Trifon Zarezan, celebrated on February 14.

Special dishes of the region include sausages, and yellow cheese fried in eggs and bread crumbs. There are many dishes involving beans, stews and rice. The main meat dishes are grills, meatballs, goulash and poulty, especially baked.

PERUSHTITZA

South of the city of Plovdiv, the land rises towards the Rhodope Mountains which form the frontier with Greece. The region was inhabited by the Thracians and wine has certainly been produced virtually uninterrupted since then. Plovdiv was then known as Hebros, and later, under the Greeks, became known as Philippopolis. There have been many archaeological discoveries of vessels, engravings and frescoes which illustrate the long history of winemaking.

This enterprise covers the sub-region of Plovdiv and the micro-regions of Brezov, Hisar, Assenovgrad, Brestnik, Perushten and Dragomir. Until the 1920s when the first local cooperatives were formed, all production was on a small scale with family farms tending their own vineyards and making their own wine. As the cooperative movement grew in the 1920s and 1930s, the

The main varieties for wine and their share of total production are: White – Red Misket 24.27 per cent, Ratziteli 10.09 per cent, Aligoté 0.40 per cent, Sauvignon 0.50 per cent, others 1.59 per cent; Red: Cabernet Sauvignon 37.25 per cent, Merlot 16.55 per cent, Pamid 4.41 per cent, Mavrud 2.11 per cent, others 2.82 per cent.

There have been enormous differences in the size of the Chirpan district's harvest over the last ten years:

Year	Production
1977	31,200 tonnes (30,700 tons)
1978	30,800 tonnes (30,307 tons)
1979	36,700 tonnes (36,112 tons)
1980	28,300 tonnes (27,847 tons)
1981	39,400 tonnes (38,769 tons)
1982	47,300 tonnes (46,543 tons)
1983	30,700 tonnes (30,208 tons)
1984	37,200 tonnes (36,604 tons)
1985	26,300 tonnes (25,879 tons)
1986	15,100 tonnes (14,858 tons)

The smaller harvests in 1985 and 1986 were the result of a severe drought followed by a freezing winter.

---

enterprises became larger. The biggest were Uspeh in Perushtzitza, Nov Zhivot in Brestovitza and Stanimashki Mavrud in Assenovgrad. Since 1945 there has been a rapid expansion in the number of vineyards. In August 1947 the cooperatives and private vineyards were nationalized, and state wine production enterprises were created. New plants were built at Brezovo, Banja, Assenovgrad and Stambolijski, and the existing wineries were modernized and extended.

The districts of Brezovski and Hisarski have red and grey woodland, sandy clay and less leached black earth soils. In Assenovgradski, Brestnishki, Brestovishski and Perushtinski, which includes the Rhodopa hills. The predominant soils are red, carbonated black earth, leached black earth and alluvial. The soils in the Dragomirski district are black earth and red woodland.

The vineyards are between 150 and 200 metres (492-656 feet) above sea level on slopes of between 8 and 10°. They cover 8.35 hectares (21,831 acres) out of a total 12,900 hectares (31,875 acres) of cultivated land. Other agricultural products are cereals, fruits, vegetables, tobacco, peanuts and maize.

There are 12 producer cooperatives in the enterprise, and the main wineries are in Perushtitza, Assenovgrad and Karlovo. There are 11 cellars (Brestnik, Stambolijski, Brestovitza, Perushtitza (2), Brezovo, Saedinenie, Banja, Moskovetz and Zlatovrah) for processing the grapes and three plants (Assenovgrad, Banja and Perushtitza) for processing, stabilizing and bottling the wine and spirits.

The average annual temperature is between 12.5 and 13.5°C (54.5-56.3°F) and the total temperature between April and October is between 4,100 and 4,500°C (7,412-8,132°F), more than enough to ripen the grapes. The autumns are warm and dry and ideal for building up sugar content in the grapes.

The various micro-regions have been chosen because of their suitability of soil and climate, and especially because of their low incidence of frosts which can harm the high stem vine growing system used. The soils are generally deep, well aerated and warm.

The vines are planted in well spaced lines to allow mechanized spraying, ground clearance and the movement of vehicles to collect the gathered grapes during the vintage. Pruning starts during the second half of February and the soil in the vineyards is ploughed and fertilized. The lines between the vines are kept clear of weeds by using cultivators about every six weeks during the growing period. Fertilizers, phosphorus, nitrogen and nitrates are added at the rate of 250-300 kilogrammes a hectare (551-661lb per acre). Minimum irrigation is carried out if necessary. The vines are sprayed to prevent the spread of wild yeasts, insect attack, mildew and other fungal diseases.

The vintage usually begins in the second half of September, starting with the white varieties. The last variety gathered is Mavrud which is usually collected during the first half of November. The grapes are picked by hand. At the winery the grapes are weighed and tested for quality and then automatically unloaded into the crushers.

The grapes for white wine are gently crushed without separating them from their bunches. The must is passed through static-dynamic filters and treated with sulphur dioxide, and then allowed to cool, often with the aid of bentonite, before being transferred to the metal fermentation tanks. Pure yeast cultures are added and the fermentation is kept between 18 and 22°C (64-71°F) by allowing cold water to run down the outsides of the tanks. After the initial vigorous fermentation, the young wine is separated from the marc and transferred to ferro-concrete tanks, where additional sulphation may be carried out. When fermentation is over the young wine is cleared, filtered and moved to holding tanks. Great care is taken to ensure the wines stay in optimum condition during this stage by regular controls and analyses.

Grapes for red wines are crushed more vigorously and while the must is still with the marc it is sulphated, up to 7 grammes a thousand litres (0.24oz per 220 gallons) and then piped to fermentation tanks where selected yeast cultures are introduced. A variety of fermentation tanks are used including ferro-concrete tanks. Other systems include Blasher, Universal and Rottowinificators. Fermentation is carried out between 28 and 30°C (82-86°F), and water is automatically poured down the outside of the tanks, or heat exchangers are used to control the temperature. After the initial vigorous fermentation the young wine is separated from the marc and then left for several days before being filtered. The aim is to break down both the sugar and fruit acid as much as possible and this can be achieved by desulphating the red wine and gelatining if necessary. The wines are then stored in ferro-contrete or metal tanks.

The vintages between 1978 and 1987, with the exception of 1982, have been good, and those for the last five years very good because of the autumn droughts. The droughts led to lower yields but much higher quality.

There is a great deal of experimental work carried out in the region and this includes different pruning techniques, especially for Mavrud and Cabernet Sauvignon, to produce maximum yields. There are also studies into differences in yields and qualities of varieties according to rootstock, soil fertilization and prevention of pests and diseases. Research into winemaking techniques includes work on different processes for sulphating the must, speeding the maturation of red wines, implementation of new types of yeast, and investigation of the fruit-acid bacteria to see if it can be applied to produce fruit-acid fermentation. There are two colleges in Plovdiv both offering specialist courses in vine growing and wine production. These are the High School for the Food Processing Industry, and the Vassil Kolarov Higher Agricultural Institute.

About 60 per cent of the white production and 65 per cent of the red is for quality wines. Blended branded wines include Vecheren Zvan, Zagore, Starijagrad, Assenitza, Trakia and Ognen Tantz. The following are the average volumes of quality varietal wines produced:

Misket Karlovoand Brezovo Misket	8-9 million litres	(14-15.8 million gallons)
Aligoté	200,000-400,000 litres	(352,000-70,400 gallons)
Cabernet Sauvignon	13-15 million litres	(22.8-26.4 million gallons)
Merlot	5-7 million litres	(8.8-12 million gallons)
Mavrud	500,000-800,000 litres	(880,000-1,408,000 gallons)
Pamid	1-1.5 million litres	(1.7-2.6 million gallons)

The region was among the first to have Controliran Region wines designated. The Controliran Region vineyards are monitored both locally, by an expert panel in Plovdiv, and by the state organizations in Sofia. Yields are restricted to 6000 kilogrammes per hectare (13,230lb per acre) and controls are laid down for pruning, sugar content, processing and ageing. A Central Tasting Commission has to approve all new wines before a certificate can be issued. This follows extensive chemical testing, and tastings. The wines include the well-known red Mavrud of Asasenovgrad, the wine of Brestnik, and the white Misket of the Rose Valley. The Brestnik wine is blended and the rest are pure varietals.

FOLKLORE AND CUISINE   At Easter the villagers in the Brestnik area paint chicken eggs red and bury them in the vineyards. According to an old tradition this protects the vines from damage by hail. Women were not allowed to take part in the pruning of the vines because this was considered man's work and women might bring bad luck.

The area is rich in agriculture, especially fruit, vegetables and livestock. The local cuisine includes many different mixed salads and a number of vegetable dishes which incorporate eggs, cheese and milk. The main dishes are kavarma, grilled meats and Plovdiv hotch-potch.

A stringful of bright red and yellow chillies.

SOUTHWEST REGION

KJUSTENDIL

The Vinprom Enterprise Kjustendil is southwest of Sofia and includes the sub-regions of Kjustendil, Stanke Dimitroff, Boboshevo, Kotcherinovo, Rila and Dragovishtitza. Vines have been grown since Thracian times but until nationalization, the vineyards were fragmented and privately owned. Production methods were primitive and most of the wine was for home or local consumption. Vinprom Kjustendil was founded in 1947. The new reception area at the Boboshevo wine cellar was built in 1974 and in 1985 the Pirin Vinificators were introduced.

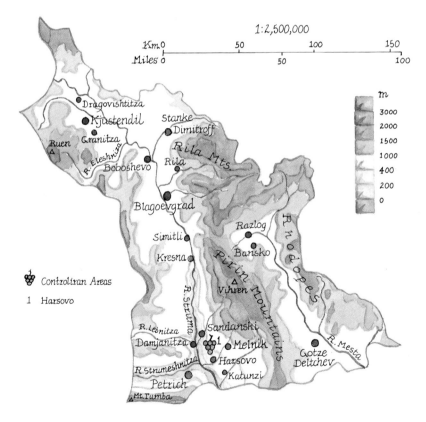

The soils in the region are mostly leached woodland, composed of sandy clay, low in organic matter and slightly acidic. The altitude of the region varies between 500 and 550 metres (1,640 and 1,804 feet) above sea level, the average annual temperature varies between 3,650° and 4,200°C (6,602-7,592 feet), and the average annual rainfall varies between 40 and 60 litres a square metre (8.8-13 gallons a square foot).

The enterprise is divided into four agro-industrial complexes – AIC "Ossogovo" Kjustendil; AIC "Dupnishka komuna" Stanke Dimitroff; AIC "Septemvrijtzi" Boboshevo; and AIC "Xth Congress" Kotcherinovo. There are two wine cellars – one in the town of Boboshevo and the other in the village of Granitza.

The region has a transitional continental climate. One of the main features is an even distribution of rainfall in every month, between six and eight per cent of the annual total. Winters are relatively mild and the summers warm for the altitude. The soils of the area are on sandy clay, limestone and granite, but there has been heavy erosion.

The vines are planted close together because of the terrain and the vineyards are not suitable for mechanization. The soil between the vines is broken up to prevent weeds and there is a regular programme of spraying to control insects and disease.

The vintage starts towards the end of September and the grapes are gathered by hand in plastic pails and containers. The grapes are then emptied into tubs for transport to the cellars for processing. Grapes for white wine are received at the cellars,

---

There are 6,000 hectares (14,826 acres) of cultivated land in the region, of which 420 hectares (1,037 acres) are planted with vineyards.

Sub-regions are:

Kjustendil	42 hectares	(103 acres)
Stanke Dimitroff	95.5 hectares	(235 acres)
Boboshevo	89.3 hectares	(220 acres)
Kotcherinovski	161.4 hectares	(398 acres)
Rilski	10 hectares	(24 acres)
Dragovishtenski	23 hectares	(56 acres)

Other agricultural products in the area mostly involve fruit growing (cherries 260 hectares/642 acres, apples and pears 280 hectares/691 acres).

The main wine varieties and their total vineyard percentage

Rkatziteli	43.98 per cent
Riesling	7.76 per cent
Aligoté	0.3 per cent
Pamid	27.32 per cent
Cabernet Sauvignon	13.78 per cent
Others	7.16 per cent

weighed and checked for quality and sugar content. The pressure exerted on the grapes during crushing depends on the quality of the wine to be made. The must is then filtered and pressed, filtered again and passed to the fermentation tanks where yeast is added. The young wine is drawn off the sediment after the vigorous fermentation, transferred to new tanks where the fermentation is completed.

Grapes for red wines are received in the same way and checked, crushed and the must, skins, stems and so on passed to Pirin vinificators where yeast is added. After vigorous fermentation the young wine is drawn off the marc, and fermenation continues in other tanks. The marc is removed and KOK presses are used to provide wine for distillation.

Vintages have varied in the last few years from the disasterous one of 1985 when just 592 tonnes (582 tons) of grapes were harvested, to 1980 when 2,778 tonnes (2,733 tons) were gathered. In 1986 the harvest was 1,530 tonnes (1,505 tons) and in 1987 1,500 tonnes (1,476 tons).

FOLKLORE AND CUISINE

The region celebrates the Holiday of the Vine Grower as its main wine festival on February 14.

The most famous regional speciality is Kjustendil cabbage pastry.

BLAGOEVGRAD

This Vinprom enterprise south of Sofia includes the sub-regions of Blagoevgrad, Gotze Deltchev and Sandansko-Petritchki. The area has been famous for wines since ancient times, especially the exported Melnishko vino. The wine was kept in the Melnik cellars, a network of tunnels carved into the ground with a constant temperature of between 10 and 12°C (50-53°F) throughout the year. The wine was transported abroad in huge caravans and carried in goat skin wine bags.

It is still possible to visit the winery under the merchant's house in the beautifully preserved village of Melnik, which with its 400 inhabitants, is Bulgaria's smallest city. There is also a fascinating museum in the village which is surrounded by the remarkable sandstone pyramids, a natural feature caused by erosion over tens of thousands of years. After nationalization in 1947 the vineyards were re-organized, machinery was introduced where possible and the wineries were modernized. Because the area is suitable for producing high quality red wines, traditional varieties started to be replaced with Cabernet Sauvignon and Merlot.

Processing and production was concentrated in four cellars – Damjanitza, Harsovo, Blagoevgrad and Gotze Deltchev. In the last ten years the capacity of the cellars has doubled, and French Gaske thermo-vinification equipment introduced for the production of quality red wines, the only such equipment in Bulgaria. Last year it processed 12,000 tonnes (1,476 tons) of grapes and produced 8.5 million litres (1.8 million gallons) of a new light style Cabernet Sauvignon. Apart from producing this highly attractive and commercial wine, the process is much more efficient. The normal wine yield from more traditional methods would be about 50 per cent of the grape weight.

Each of the processing lines can handle 100 tonnes (98 tons) of grapes a day and the cellars now have a combined processing capacity of 1,300 tonnes (159 tons) a day which means the entire vintage can be processed within 20-25 days, a prerequisite for high quality wines. In 1985 a new bottling line was installed in Damjanitza capable of cold, sterile bottling and with an annual capacity of 2.5 million bottles.

The first cooperative was founded in the region in Harsovo in 1933 by Professor Nedeltchev, Andon Shalamanov and others.

Today the soils of the area are mostly leached woodland soils,

The beautiful 14th century monastery of Rozhen, south of Melnik, is surrounded by vines.

and in the Melnishki region they are strongly eroded. The Petritchki micro-region is between 150 and 250 metres (492–820 feet) above sea level, the Sandanski and Melnishki micro-regions about 250 metres (820 feet), and the Blagoevgradski and Gotze Deltchev sub-regions are between 400 and 600 metres (1,312–1,968 feet) above sea level. The vineyards are planted on hill slopes and terraces unsuitable for other crops. The main agricultural enterprise in the region is tobacco, followed by fruit and vegetables.

There are 5,267 hectares (13,014 acres) planted with vineyards, about 8.15 per cent of the total cultivated land in the region. Of the vineyard area 4,600 hectares (11,366 acres) are for wine, of

Above left *Distinctive buildings in the Blagoevgrad region.*

Above right *The underground network of tunnels which comprise the Melnik cellars and allow the wine to be kept at a constant temperature.*

Below *Orderly rows of vines spread across the foothills of the Vlahina mountains.*

which 4,200 hectares (10,378 acres) are fruit bearing and 645 hectares (1,593 acres) are dessert varieties, of which 537 hectares (1,326 acres) bear grapes. The highest vineyards are at 1,000 metres (3,280 feet) and thanks to their sheltered position, produce fine quality Cabernet Sauvignon.

The vineyards are controlled by ten AIC's: Blagoevgrad, Simitli, Kresna, Strumjani, Sandanski, Katunzi, Petritch, Gotze Deltchev, Fadzhidimovo and Garmen. There are three wineries – Damjanitza with a capacity of 25 million litres (5.5 million gallons), Blagoevgrad three million litres (660,000 gallons) and Gotze Deltchev two million litres (44,000 gallons). Almost 85 per cent of the vineyards are situated in the most southern part of Bulgaria in the Sandanski-Petritchki micro-regions. The vineyards are exposed to warm air streams following the valley of the River Struma. The climate is transitional continental with a pronounced Mediterranean character. The total annual temperature, averaging 5,073°C (9,163°F) over the last 40 years, is the highest in the country. The active temperature for the Sandanski-Petritchki sub-region is 4,500°C (8,132°F), Blagoevgradski 3,600°C (6,512°F) and Gotze Deltchevski 3,200°C (5,792°F). In Sandanski-Petritchki there are an average 238 days free from frost, and it is very rare for the vines to be damaged by very low temperatures. The total annual rainfall averages 534 litres a square metre (117 gallons a square foot).

The Blagoevgradski sub-region is situated in the foothills of the Rila and Vlahina mountains. In Gotze Deltchevski the vineyards are on the northern slopes of the Pirin mountain and the southern slopes of the Rhodopes. Because of the relatively high altitude, 600 metres (1,968 feet) above sea level, the region suffers from very low temperatures, down to -30°C (-22°F), which freezes the vines.

The Sandanski–Petritchki sub-regions lie between the southern slopes of the Pirin mountain, Ograzhden, Belassitza and Slavjanka. It is an extinct volcanic area cut by many picturesque valleys.

The main wine varieties and their total production

Shiroka Melnishka	225.7 hectares (557 acres)
Cabernet Sauvignon	105.5 hectares (260 acres)
Rkatziteli	149.5 hectares (369 acres)
Merlot	116.5 hectares (287 acres)
Muscat Ottonel	116.5 hectares (287 acres)
Aligoté	76 hectares (187 acres)
Sandanski Misket	34 hectares (84 acres)
Others	80 hectares (197 acres)

Rivers intersecting the area include the Struma, Sandanska Bistritza, Pirinska Bistritza and Strumeshnitza. In Sandansko-Petritchki the viticultural year starts with pruning which begins in March. There are usually four spraying sessions against insects and disease. The rows between the vines are usually ploughed in the spring to keep weeds down, and this is repeated two or three times during the early growing season. Herbicides are used against perennial weeds.

The grapes start to ripen after August 15 and regular field meetings are held to determine the order of picking. The first grapes to be gathered are usually Muscat Ottonel, Tamjanka and Sandanski Misket, usually in the first week of September when they have a sugar content of between 18 and 20 per cent.

After the September 15 Cabernet Sauvignon, Merlot, Rkatziteli and Aligoté is harvested – the first two varieties usually maintaining a sugar content of between 22 and 25 per cent until the end of the month. The Shiroka Melnik variety, which is only found in the Sandanski–Petritchki sub-region, has a long growing period, and harvesting for it starts at the beginning of October and continues until the end of the month. The grapes are gathered by hand in plastic pails and emptied into tubs on trailers which take them to containers on lorries for transport to the wineries. The variety has masses of natural tannin and tremendous ageing potential.

The vintages of 1977, 1980-84 and 1986 were similar in having very warm and dry months of September and October which led to relatively high sugar contents. All the grapes could be collected and there were no losses due to botrytis. In 1978 a cold and late spring and rainy autumn meant the harvest started 15 days late and there were losses because of botrytis. In 1979 very high October temperatures and humidity were ideal conditions for rot which hit yields, and in 1985 severe winter temperatures in the Gotze Deltchev sub-region, and very high summer temperatures hit production. Between 1983 and 1985 the region was hit by very low winter temperatures and hail storms, with total losses amounting to more than 22,000 tonnes (21,648 tons).

Experimental work in the region includes pruning and growing techniques to improve yields, tests to boost sugar accumulation, and irrigation systems. The latter has become more important because of the very high summer temperatures experienced in the last few years. Drip irrigation has been introduced in many areas. The experimental station at Sandanski has introduced many new varieties including Melnik 55, Melnishki rubin (ruby), Melnik 82, Melnik Jubilee 1300 and Sandanski Misket. All the varieties have been developed to produce grapes in a 15–20 day shorter growing period and thus avoid the autumn

The 10th century monastery of Rila lies tucked away high up in the mountains protected by stone walls. As well as icons and parchments, it contains more than 20,000 volumes. The building is one of Bulgaria's key architectural monuments.

rains which lead to botrytis. The varieties also produce grapes of higher quality.

The Melnishki Controliran Region was designated in 1979 for the production of Melnik wine from Harsovo. The Melnik wine was a great favourite of the late Sir Winston Churchill and for many years he had three barrels, each containing 500 litres (110 gallons), delivered annually to his home in the south of England.

FOLKLORE AND CUISINE

The Holiday of the Vine Grower is the main wine festival, celebrated in mid-February. The region has many speciality dishes, many of them based on lamb. Roasted lamb and dried and smoked meats are traditional dishes.

SUB-BALKAN REGION

SLAVJANIZI   The Vinprom Slavjantzi includes the Sungurlarska valley, where the famous red Misket variety is grown. The valley boundaries are the Rishki Pass in the east, the Avramov Pass in the west, by Stidivo (an arm of the Balkan Mountains) in the north and by Grebenetz (another arm) in the south.

Controliran Areas

1   Rozova Dolina
2   Sungulare

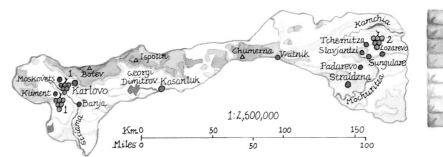

1:2,500,000

The region has an average height of 200 metres (656 feet) above sea level. The height rises to 504 metres (1,653 feet) towards Grebenetz, and 1010 metres (3,313 feet) near Stidivo. The winters are mild and the summers cool. There is rainfall spread throughout the year, which increases with altitude. The soils are mainly sandy or woodland types.

Wine has been produced in the area for centuries but the area did not really expand until after the end of the Turkish occupation. The region's most famous wine, Red Misket, won gold medals at international exhibitions and the district developed a flourishing export trade in both wines and brandies.

Wine production received a further boost after the end of the First World War and local consumer cooperatives constructed new wine cellars in the villages of Sungurlare in 1929, and the following year in Slavjantzi, Grozden, Tchernitza, Padarevo and Lozarevo. The cellars in the villages of Padarevo, Slavjantzi, Grozden and Sungurlare then broke away from the consumer cooperatives and formed independent viti-vinicultural coops, the last three uniting between 1938–42. The cellars continued their independent activities until April 1950 when they became part of the state monopoly. Slavjantzi became the centre of the new enterprise in 1951 with a total vessel capacity of 6.3 million litres (1.3 million gallons). By 1951 smaller cellars like Avramov, Padarevo, Tchernitza, Essen, Velislav, Vezenkovo, Beronovo and

Sungurlare had joined the enterprise raising its total capacity to 9,552,000 litres (1,103,440 gallons). The Vinprom enterprise Slavjantzi was formed in 1954 and by 1959, after various re-organizations it had a total capacity of 23,650,000 litres (5,203,000 gallons).

Vineyard expansion and larger harvests meant the cellars had to be extended, and in 1962 the production of vermouth was started. A flourishing export market in Poland quickly developed and in 1969 a middle bottling line for the vermouth plant was installed in Lozarevo. In 1976 a line for bottling thermo-stabilized wines was commissioned in Sungurlare and an expansion programme, in anticipation of increased grape production, was started to boost the cellar capacity to 36,736,000 litres (8,081,920 gallons), of which 25,303,000 litres (5,126,660 gallons) were for table wines.

Today, there are 3,390 hectares (8,376 acres) planted with vines, of which 14 per cent are young and as yet unproductive. All the vineyards are larger than 40 hectares (98 acres) and the vines are trained according to high and semi-high system. In 1987 about 24.2 hectares (60 acres) of the vineyards will be drip irrigated. Other agriculture in the region is mainly cereals, fodder crops, fruit, vegetables and livestock. The main fruits are cherries, peaches, pears, apples and apricots, and the main vegetables are tomatoes and cucumbers. The enterprise has its own canning factory, producing tinned goods for export.

There are four agro-complexes in the region, divided into 13 brigades responsible for the vineyards, and five wineries/cellars. Four cellars specialize in the production of white wines, although a little red is produced – Slavjantzi, Sungurlare, Tchernitza and Karnobat. The fifth cellar at Lozarevo is the only winery in the country producing and bottling vermouth.

The major wine varieties and their share of production are: Red Misket 33 per cent, Rkatziteli 31 per cent, Muscat Ottonel 13 per cent, Pamid 7 per cent, Chardonnay 3 per cent, Cabernet Sauvignon 2 per cent and other varieties such as Ugni Blanc, Karatza and Riesling 11 per cent.

Pruning starts immediately after the harvest and the vineyards are ploughed in the early spring to impede weed growth. Cultivation of the soil continues at intervals into the summer. Herbicide applications are sprayed during the autumn and over winter, and there are regular sprayings until the middle of summer to combat pests and diseases. Pruning is carried out mainly by hand but pneumatic shears have been introduced.

The vintage normally starts between September 15-20. The grapes are picked by hand and put into plastic pails which are emptied into self-unloading trailers pulled by tractors between the lines. The trailer unloads the grapes into tubs on lorries for transport to the wineries. About 96 per cent of production is white wine, the remainder being red Cabernet Sauvignon.

The wineries are fully automated and the crushers can cope with between 25 and 50 tonnes (24 and 49 tons) of grapes an hour. The filtration and pressing is done using Vilmes presses in the Slavjantzi cellar, Winematics and Vilmes presses in the Sungurlare cellar, and VSSS presses with a 20 tonnes (19 tons) an hour capacity in the Tchernitza cellar, and 50 tonnes (49 tons) an hour in the Karnobat cellar. The filtrated marc is passed to continuous presses and the juice sent for distillation. The must for the wine is sulphured in a free-flow chamber, filtered and transferred to water cooled fermentation tanks. Fermentation generally takes place between 18 and 22°C (64-71°F), but a refrigeration plant has been installed in the Slavjantzi cellar to control fermentation between 14 and 16°C (57-60°F). The must is brought into contact with five per cent yeast of the strain Montranie and the first stage of fermentation takes place between five and seven days. The wine is drawn off when it reaches a density of between 1000 and 1010, and transferred to ferro-concrete tanks for the quiet second stage of the fermentation to take place. After four to six days the wine is racked and a second sulphation made. The young wine is then transferred to holding tanks, constantly topped up, ready for blending at about the end of February. The region produces between 13 and 22,000 tonnes (12,792-21,648 tons) of grapes annually.

The wines are blended in shipments of 200,000 litres (4,400 gallons) but kept apart as varietals until this stage. Since 1977 there have been big fluctuations in the harvest because of bad weather.

Experimental work at the enterprise's own research station includes testing, selecting and introducing new varieties (wine and

Harvest production

1977	17,984 tonnes (17,696 tons)
1978	23,733 tonnes (23,353 tons)
1979	22,412 tonnes (22,053 tons)
1980	29,983 tonnes (29,505 tons)
1981	21,981 tonnes (21,629 tons)
1982	31,906 tonnes (31,395 tons)
1983	26,985 tonnes (26,985 tons)
1984	28,366 tonnes (27,912 tons)
1985	26,648 tonnes (26,221 tons)
1986	24,299 tonnes (23,910 tons)

dessert). There is also a great deal of research into mechanisation both in the vineyards and the wineries. The enterprise has won 85 gold medals, 104 silver medals and four bronze medals for its wines and vermouths.

The area is noted for its Controliran Region designation "Misket of Sungurlare", approved in 1979. The grapes come from a small region around Sungurlare, Ichernitza and Lozarevo. The terrain is slightly sloping with a southern exposure. The total temperature during the growing period is on average 3,600°C (6,512°F). The wine is produced from Red Misket and aged in oak casks in the underground cellars at Slavjantzi at a temperature of about 14°C (57°F). In 1986 the AOC wine "Bjalo from Slavjantzi" was also approved. It is a blend of 70 per cent Red Misket and 30 per cent Rkatziteli.

FOLKLORE   The region celebrates the Holiday of the Vine Maker on February 14.

RECIPES

SALADS

SHOPSKA SALAD	1lb 1oz/500g	peppers
	10oz/300g	tomatoes
	4oz/150g	cucumber
	4oz/150g	ewe's milk cheese (or Greek Feta)
	1	onion
	4 tablespoons	olive or vegetable oil
		salt
	1/2oz/15g	parsley
	1 teaspoon	vinegar
	1	small hot pepper

Roast and skin the peppers, remove the seeds and cut into small pieces. Peel and dice the tomatoes and cucumber, and cut the onion into thin slices and crush by hand. Mix the peppers, tomatoes, cucumber and onion together and salt to taste. Add the oil and parsley and mix thoroughly. Serve in a bowl or in individual portions and grate the cheese over the salad. Cut the hot pepper into small pieces and add to the top of the salad.

KYOPOOLOU (Aubergine purée)	1lb 5oz/600g	aubergines
	6 tablespoons	vegetable oil
	2 tablespoons	vinegar
	1/2oz/15g	parsley (chopped)
	4oz/150g	tomatoes or two hard boiled eggs (sliced)
		salt
	1	clove garlic

Bake the aubergines on a very hot plate so that the inside remains light in colour. While still hot, skin the aubergines carefully and purée. Stirring continuously, add the oil gradually, then the crushed garlic, salt, vinegar and chopped parsley. Stir vigorously for 10 to 15 minutes until the purée becomes lighter in colour. Garnish with slices of tomato or hard boiled egg and parsley, and serve.

HARICOT BEAN SALAD		
	8oz/250g	*haricot beans*
	3oz/100g	*spring onions (finely chopped)*
	½oz/15g	*parsley*
		salt
	3 tablespoons	*vegetable oil*
	2-3 tablespoons	*vinegar*
		paprika
	7oz/200g	*olives*
		Lemon (sliced)

Boil the beans and strain. Add the finely cut onions, add salt, oil, vinegar and parsley to taste and paprika if desired. Mix the salad and serve garnished with olives and slices of lemon.

LYUTIKA SALAD		
	1lb 10oz/750g	*red peppers*
	3oz/100g	*tomatoes*
	1	*onion*
	4-5	*cloves garlic*
	4 tablespoons	*vegetable oil*
	½oz/15g	*parsley (finely chopped)*
		salt
	1 teaspoon	*vinegar*
	2-3	*small hot peppers*

Roast and skin the peppers, remove the seeds and cut into small pieces. Peel the tomatoes, de-seed and cut into small pieces. Crush the tomatoes and peppers together in a wooden mortar. Clean, chop and crush the onion with the garlic and add to the peppers and tomatoes, together with the finely chopped parsley, salt and vinegar. Mix thoroughly and serve garnished with roasted small, hot peppers.

MONASTERY	1lb 1oz/500g	peppers
SALAD	14oz/400g	aubergines
	14oz/400g	cucumber
	4 tablespoons	vegetable oil
	½oz/15g	parsley (finely chopped)
	1	clove garlic
	1 teaspoon	vinegar
	2 tablespoons	walnut kernels.

Roast and skin the peppers, de-seed and remove the stalks, and sprinkle with salt, teaspoon vegetable oil and vinegar. Peel and finely chop the cucumber, mix with the finely cut parsley and stuff into the peppers. Roast the aubergines, skin them and purée. Add the rest of the vegetable oil and crushed garlic to taste, then the crushed walnut kernels, salt to taste and mix thoroughly. Place the purée in the centre of a serving dish with the stuffed peppers around it. Slices of tomato and/or hard boiled eggs can be used to garnish.

PORK	2-4	pork trotters
TROTTERS	5-6	cloves garlic
SALAD	3 tablespoons	vinegar
	3 tablespoons	vegetable oil
		salt and black pepper
		paprika
	7oz/200g	olives
		pickled gherkins

Rinse the pork trotters, put into cold water and bring to the boil. When the water starts to boil add salt. When the meat is well cooked and can be easily separated from the bones, remove from the heat and allow to cool. Remove the meat from the bone and cut into strips. Crush the garlic and mix with the vinegar and oil. Arrange the meat on a serving dish, pour the mixture over it, add black pepper and garnish with olives and/or pickled gherkins.

ONION AND	14oz/400g	onions
OLIVES SALAD	7oz/200g	olives
	2 tablespoons	vegetable oil
	1 tablespoon	vinegar

Peel several medium-sized onions, cut into thin slices and crush with a little salt. Add the oil, vinegar and olives and mix well.
Leeks can be used to prepare the same salad.

HORS D'OEUVRES

YOGHURT DRESSING

2 fl oz/60ml	live yoghurt
2	egg yolks
5 fl oz/150ml	olive oil
2 tablespoons	vinegar (tarragon ideally)
1 tablespoon	flour
1	clove garlic (crushed)
½ teaspoon	of sugar
½ teaspoon	French mustard
3 tablespoons	chopped dill or watercress

Place the flour, crushed garlic, sugar, mustard and 5 fl oz/150ml of water in a saucepan and simmer over a very low flame, stirring continuously for five minutes until you have a very thick sauce base. Simmer for a further three minutes and remove from heat.

Allow to cool for three minutes then whisk in the egg yolks. Continue whisking with one hand while very slowly pouring in the oil. Place in the fridge for two to three hours until thoroughly chilled, mix in the yoghurt and watercress and whisk vigorously for at least three minutes, until smooth and fluffy. Chill again for 30 minutes and serve on its own or with a summer green salad, or mixed with peeled and diced cucumbers.

SCRAMBLED EGG WITH ROAST PEPPERS

2lb/1kg	peppers
3oz/100g	butter
4-5	eggs
7oz/200g	ewe's milk cheese
½oz/15g	parsley (finely chopped)

Roast and skin the peppers, de-seed, cube and fry in the butter. Beat the eggs, add the grated cheese and fry to taste. Serve hot with finely chopped parsley on top.

AUBERGINE PASTIES	

1lb 12oz/800g	*aubergines*
4oz/150g	*ewe's milk cheese (grated)*
4	*eggs*
4 fl oz	*vegetable oil*
1oz/50g	*flour*
1oz/50g	*bread crumbs*
1lb 1oz/500g	*yoghurt*
	salt and black pepper
½oz/15g	*parsley (finely chopped)*
1	*clove garlic*

Clean the aubergines and cut in slices about ½in (1cm) thick. Salt them and leave to stand for about 15 minutes. Squeeze the water from them and fry until golden. Make a stuffing using the cheese, two eggs and finely chopped parsley and put one tablespoon measure between two fried slices of aubergine. Press the "pasties" together, dip in flour, beaten eggs and then the breadcrumbs. Give a final coating of egg and fry in very hot oil until golden.

   The pasties must not be put on top of each other after being taken out of the oil. Serve with yoghurt seasoned with crushed garlic, or with a salad according to the season.

DRY TARATOR	

1lb 1oz/500g	*yoghurt*
4oz/150g	*cucumber (finely chopped)*
2oz/60g	*walnut kernels (crushed)*
1 teaspoon	*vegetable oil*
½oz/15g	*parsley*
	dill
	salt
1	*clove garlic*

Strain the yoghurt and add the finely chopped cucumber, crushed walnuts, garlic, oil, dill and salt to taste. Mix thoroughly and serve with finely chopped parsley and dill on top.

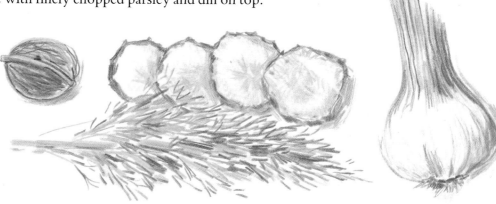

VEGETABLE MARROW PASTIES

1lb 12oz/800g	vegetable marrow
4oz/150g	ewe's milk cheese (grated)
4oz/150g	butter
5	eggs
½pint/300ml	milk
1oz/30g	flour
	salt and black pepper
	dill

Cut the marrow into thick slices, scrape off the rind, clean and cut into strips, salt a little and fry until golden brown. Arrange one half of the fried slices in a suitable pan and cover each slice with a stuffing made of grated cheese, two eggs, dill and black pepper. Put the remaining slices on as lids and bake for 15-20 minutes. Beat the rest of the eggs and mix with the flour and milk, then pour this mixture over the "pasties" and bake for a further 10-15 minutes until a pleasant brown colour. Serve with salad.

The pasties can be prepared in the same way as the aubergine pasties, but the marrow does not need to be left in salt first.

CHEESE SOUFFLÉ

8oz/250g	fetta OR salty ewe milk cheese
6	eggs
4oz/125g	butter
3oz/90g	flour
1oz/30g	breadcrumbs
10 fl oz/300ml	milk
2oz/60g	grated parmesan cheese
	salt
	black pepper
	cream of tartar to taste

Melt the butter and slowly stir in the milk and flour to make a white sauce. Allow to cool a little before adding three egg yolks. Crumble the fetta cheese into the mixture and add a touch of pepper.

Whisk six egg whites with a touch of salt and cream of tartar until stiff and standing in peaks, then fold into the soufflé base. Butter a soufflé dish well, sprinkle with breadcrumbs add the mixture and sprinkle with the grated parmesan. Bake in a pre-heated oven 190°C/375°F, gas mark 5, for about 20 minutes until fully risen and brown on top.

SOUPS

**TOMATO
SOUP**

1lb 5oz/600g	tomatoes (peeled and grated)
2oz/50g	butter
2	onions
2 pints/1 litre	hot water
4oz/125g	vermicelli (crushed)
3	eggs
	salt
1/2oz/15g	parsley
	black pepper

Finely chop the onions and fry in butter until brown, add salt to taste, then add the peeled and grated tomatoes and hot water. Boil for 8-10 minutes and then add the crushed vermicelli. When the soup is ready, beat the eggs and add through a strainer, stirring to avoid them curdling into strips. Serve with finely chopped parsley and black pepper.

**NETTLE SOUP
WITH
WALNUTS**

1lb 1oz/500g	nettle leaves
1	onion (finely chopped)
2 tablespoons	vegetable oil
5oz/175g	walnut kernels (crushed)
	salt

Clean and rinse the nettles thoroughly and put into boiling, salted water. When the nettles become soft, remove, strain and chop finely. Lightly fry the finely chopped onions in the oil and add the flour (stirring continuously). Add the nettles and dilute with the water they were boiled in. Boil for another 5-6 minutes, remove from the heat and add the crushed walnut kernels. (The walnuts can be substituted by 2 eggs and a half a cup of yoghurt, mixed well and then added to the soup.) The flavour of the soup is enhanced by serving with crushed garlic or with ground savoury or mint.

CHEESE SOUP
(the gardeners'
way)

8oz/250g	string beans
1	cabbage (finely chopped)
10oz/300g	peppers (finely chopped)
10oz/300g	tomatoes (peeled and grated)
1lb/450g	potatoes (diced)
1	carrot (finely chopped)
1½oz/35g	butter OR
3 tablespoons	vegetable oil
1 tablespoon	flour
8 fl oz/250ml	milk
3oz/90g	grated cheese
	salt
½oz/15g	parsley

Clean the beans and boil in salted water with the cabbage, carrots and peppers for ten minutes then add the diced potatoes. Brown the flour with the butter or oil then add the peeled and grated tomatoes. Stir the flour and tomatoes and pour into the soup. Remove from the heat. Boil the milk and melt the grated cheese in it. Add this, together with the parsley, to the soup and stir.

HARICOT
BEAN SOUP

10oz/300g	haricot beans (sliced)
3oz/100g	tomatoes (peeled and finely sliced)
1-2	carrots
1	stick celery
1	onion
3 tablespoons	vegetable oil
2 pints/1 litre	water
4oz/125g	rice
1lb 1oz/500g	yoghurt
1 tablespoon	flour
	salt
1 teaspoon	paprika
½oz/15g	parsley (finely chopped)
	dill (finely chopped)

Finely chop the onions, grate the carrots and celery and stew them all together with the oil and 4 fl oz/125ml water. When the water has evaporated, add the haricot beans, salt to taste and a teaspoon of paprika. Boil the rest of the water, add to the haricot beans and simmer. When the beans are about half cooked, add the rice, peeled and finely sliced tomatoes and the flour diluted with water. Continue to simmer until the beans are cooked and before removing from the heat add the finely chopped parsley and dill. Serve with yoghurt or crushed garlic diluted with vinegar.

HARICOT BEAN SOUP 2

8oz/250g	haricot beans
4 tablespoons	vegetable oil
1	onion
1 tablespoon	of flour
2	tomatoes OR
1 tablespoon	tomato purée
	salt
1 tablespoon	paprika
	mint
½oz/15g	parsley (finely chopped)
2-3	small hot peppers

Clean the beans, cover with cold water and leave overnight or for 5-6 hours. Strain the water, add fresh cold water and boil. When the beans are soft, add the paprika, tomatoes or tomato purée, and the flour which has been lightly fried until brown and then diluted with the oil. Also add the small hot peppers, mint and salt to taste and simmer for 10-15 minutes. Serve with finely chopped parsley and vinegar to taste.

LAMB SOUP

1lb 1oz/500g	lamb
1	onion (chopped)
2 pints/1 litre	water
1oz/25g	rice
1½oz/35g	butter
1 tablespoon	flour
2	eggs
	salt
	vinegar
½oz/15g	parsley
1 tablespoon	paprika

Cut the meat into cubes and brown in the oil, then brown the flour and chopped onion. Add a teaspoon of paprika and hot water and bring to the boil. When the soup begins to boil, add the rice and the rest of the paprika. Before removing from the heat add the parsley. Remove from the heat and stir the eggs into the soup and add vinegar to taste. (The vinegar can be substituted with yoghurt or lemon juice.)

LAMBS LIVER
SOUP

1lb 5oz/600g	lambs liver
2oz/60g	spring onions (finely chopped)
2oz/60g	butter
1oz/25g	rice
2	eggs
2-3 tablespoons	vinegar
1 tablespoon	paprika
	salt and black pepper
	mint
½oz/15g	parsley (chopped)

Boil the liver for 15-20 minutes in salted water, strain and dice. Filter the broth. Brown the finely chopped onions in the butter, add paprika and pour into the broth. When the soup comes to the boil, add the rice, salt and black pepper. Boil until the rice becomes soft, add the diced liver and mint, and boil for a further 3-4 minutes. Immediately after removing the soup from the heat, stir in the eggs and add 2-3 tablespoons of vinegar. Serve with chopped parsley.

FISH SOUP

1lb 1oz/500g	small fry
2-3	onions
3 tablespoons	vegetable oil
2 tablespoons	flour
2-3	eggs
½	carrot
	stick of celery
1	parsnip
	salt and black pepper
½oz/15g	parsley (chopped)
1 tablespoon	paprika
	savoury

Clean and dice the vegetables and place in salted water. When the water is almost boiling add the cleaned fish. Brown the flour in the oil, add the paprika and dilute with the soup. Boil over a moderate heat for about half an hour, add salt to taste, black pepper, parsley and savoury. After removing from the heat, stir in the eggs and add lemon juice to taste.

CALVES' TROTTERS JELLY

2.2lb/1kg	*calves trotters*
2	*eggs*
4 fl oz/125ml	*milk*
	salt
1 teaspoon	*vinegar*
1	*clove garlic*

Rinse the calves trotters in cold water, then place in fresh cold water and boil. Add salt when the soup comes to the boil and leave it boiling until the meat starts to come off the bones. Take out the trotters and strain the broth to remove the small bones. Dice the meat and return to the broth. Beat the eggs in the milk and stir into the soup, taking care to avoid curdling. Crush the garlic with a little salt diluted in the vinegar and add to the soup. Serve hot.

HOT BEAN SOUP

1lb 1oz/500g	*haricot beans*
2oz/60g	*dried cabanos or other spicy sausage*
5oz/180g	*belly of pork or smoked bacon*
2	*carrots*
2	*parsnips*
2	*onions*
64 fl oz/2 litres	*beef stock*
2	*small dried chilli peppers*
2 tablespoons	*tomatoe purée*
	salt and pepper

Soak the beans overnight then drain, cover with cold water and bring to the boil. When they start foaming, drain again and cover with the beef stock. Add quartered carrots, onions, parsnips and salt, peppers and chillis, together with thinly sliced sausage and large cubes of pork or bacon. Simmer over a low flame for about 1½ hours. Add tomoto purée and simmer for a further 10 minutes. The liquid will reduce by about half, strain off the remainder and put to one side, together with the meat, sausage, boiled onions and beans.

Take about three-quarters of the beans and blend with the onions to obtain a thick paste. Skim the fat off the liquid and use the liquid to thin the paste, then add the meat, sausage and remainder of the beans. Reheat gently and serve.

MEATLESS DISHES

SHOPSKI CHEESE

14oz/400g	ewe's milk cheese
7oz/200g	tomatoes (chopped)
8	eggs
1oz/50g	butter
4	small hot peppers
	salt
1 tablespoon	paprika

Grease four earthenware bowls with some of the butter and divide the cheese equally between them. Place the chopped tomatoes on top and coat with half the butter. Roast in a moderately hot oven (180°C/350°F, gas mark 4) for 10–12 minutes. Use two eggs per bowl, beat and pour over the roasted cheese, then add one small pepper, the remaining butter, salt and paprika to taste and roast again until a pleasant reddish colour. Serve hot.

EGGS PEASANT STYLE

8	eggs
1lb 9oz/750g	yoghurt
3oz/100g	butter
2-3 tablespoons	vinegar
1	clove garlic
	salt
1 tablespoon	paprika

Boil 16 fl oz/500ml of water in a shallow saucepan with the vinegar and salt to taste. Carefully break the eggs over the boiling water and leave until the yolk disappears within the egg white. Boil to the desired hardness. Beat the yoghurt with the crushed garlic and divide equally among four plates. Carefully remove the eggs with a draining spoon and put two on each plate. Melt the butter in a pan, add the paprika, brown and pour over the eggs.

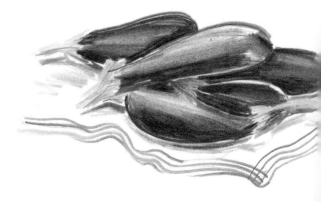

SPRING BEANS
(monastery fashion)

2.2lb/1kg	spring beans
10oz/300g	tomatoes (sliced)
2-3	carrots (sliced)
2	sticks celery (sliced)
1	clove garlic (finely chopped)
1-2	onions (finely chopped)
4 fl oz/125ml	vegetable oil
3oz/90g	sour plums
	salt
½oz/15g	parsley
	mint

Clean the beans, cut into small pieces and put in a saucepan with the sliced tomatoes, carrots and celery, finely chopped onions, garlic, vegetable oil, parsley and 3 or 4 leaves of mint. Stir the ingredients together and just cover with hot water. Place a tight fitting lid over the saucepan and simmer until the vegetables have softened and there is almost no water left.

AUBERGINE HASH

1lb 9oz/750g	aubergines
8oz/250g	tomatoes
2	onions
8oz/225g	rice
2 tablespoons	vegetable oil
3	eggs (beaten)
12 fl oz/375ml	milk
1 tablespoon	flour
	salt and black pepper
½oz/15g	parsley

Wash the aubergines, cut crosswise into circles, salt them and leave for 10-15 minutes. Squeeze the water out and fry in a little vegetable oil until golden brown. Using the same oil, slice the onion and brown. Add 1-2 tomatoes, 8 fl oz/250ml of water and the rice. Boil until the rice is cooked. Add salt to taste and season with black pepper and parsley.

Slice the remaining tomatoes in circles and arrange half in a pan. Put half of the fried aubergines over them and cover with the rice. Arrange the remaining aubergines and tomatoes in a layer on top, pour 2-3 tablespoons of vegetable oil over the hash and cook for 25-30 minutes in a hot oven (210-220°C/425°F, gas mark 7).

To make a sauce, thin the oil with the milk and eggs, add the flour and brown. Pour the sauce over the hash and return to the oven until it acquires a reddish-brown crust.

IMAM BAYALDU

1lb 12oz/800g	*aubergines*
6 fl oz/175ml	*vegetable oil*
8oz/250g	*tomatoes*
8oz/250g	*onions*
3oz/100g	*carrots (grated)*
	stick celery (grated)
5-6	*cloves garlic*
½oz/15g	*parsley*
	salt

Use aubergines of similar size and shape, wash and de-stalk them. Peel off a strip of skin lengthwise on opposite sides of the aubergine and make slits. Salt and leave for about half an hour, then rinse thoroughly in cold water, squeeze dry and fry in a little oil uniformly on all sides.

Slice the onions and fry with the grated carrots and celery in the remaining fat. Peel and grate the tomatoes, cut the garlic cut into strips and add to the onions, carrots and celery. Add the parsley when the liquid has boiled away. Stuff the aubergines with the fried vegetables and arrange in a pan with two or three slices of tomato on top of each on. Add a little warm water and cook in a moderately hot (180°C/350°F, gas mark 4) oven for 15-20 minutes. Any stuffing left over can be spread under the aubergines. When cooked, remove and allow to cool and serve cold.

MUSHROOM MESS

11oz/350g	*mushrooms*
3oz/100g	*butter*
4 tablespoons	*flour*
	salt and black pepper

Clean the mushrooms and soak for several minutes in cold water. Wash thoroughly, cut into slices and drop into boiling water. When they are soft, add salt to taste. Strain the broth off the cooked mushrooms and filter through a dense strain. Brown the flour in the melted butter, add finely ground black pepper and add the broth until a moderately thick sauce is obtained. Return the mushrooms to the pan and bring to the boil until the sauce thickens. Serve hot.

BAKED HARICOT BEANS

1lb 1oz/500g	*haricot beans*
5-6	*onions*
8 fl oz/250ml	*vegetable oil*
1 tablespoon	*tomato purée*
3-4	*small hot peppers*
	salt
1 tablespoon	*paprika*
½oz/15g	*parsley (chopped)*
	mint

Soak the beans overnight and then boil in salted water. Cut four of the onions into slices and arrange a third in the bottom of a shallow baking pan. Cover with half of the beans, then another third of the onions, then the remaining beans and finally the last of the onions. Chop the remaining onions very finely and brown in the oil, then add the paprika and thinned tomato purée, mint and chopped parsley. Pour this brown sauce over the beans, put three or four small peppers on top, and cook in a moderately hot (180°C/350°F, gas mark 4) oven for 15-20 minutes. Can be served hot or cold.

HOTCH POTCH WITH RICE

8oz/250g	*rice*
10oz/300g	*onions (finely chopped)*
1lb 12oz/800g	*tomatoes*
2	*peppers (chopped)*
6 fl oz/175ml	*vegetable oil*
4	*eggs*
1lb 1oz/500g	*yoghurt*
	salt and black pepper
½oz/15g	*paprika*

Brown the onions in the oil, add the rice and the chopped peppers, brown a little, add salt and a little paprika and black pepper. Slice the tomatoes and arrange on top. Pour 3-4 tablespoons of oil and half a cup of water over the hotch potch and put in a moderately hot (180°C/350°F, gas mark 4) oven. When the vegetables are well cooked, beat the eggs, mix with the yoghurt and pour over the vegetables. Replace in the oven until a fine brown crust is obtained.

BULGARIAN AUBERGINES

3	aubergines
8oz/250g	mushrooms
3	cloves garlic
1	large red pepper
4oz/125g	butter
½ teaspoon	salt
1 teaspoon	freshly ground black pepper
1 tablespoon	breadcrumbs
1 tablespoon	grated parmesan cheese
8 fl oz/300ml	live yoghurt

Prick the aubergines with a fork in several places then place under a hot grill and cook on all sides until the skin turns black and soft to touch. Do not allow the aubergines to burst. Slice them in two using a sharp knife and remove the flesh which should be placed on a tilted chopping board to allow as much liquid as possible to drain away.

Chop the mushrooms and peppers finely and slice the garlic into slivers. Heat the butter in a pan and sauté the garlic for a couple of minutes, add the mushrooms, red pepper and seasoning and cook gently for 7-10 minutes.

Mash the drained aubergine flesh with a fork in a bowl and add the contents of the pan having drained off the excess liquid and mix. Fill the aubergine skins with the mixture, sprinkle with the cheese and breadcrumbs and grill for up to 10 minutes or until nicely browned. Serve with the yoghurt.

GREEN BEANS PLAKIA

1lb 9oz/750g	young green beans
2	onions
3	large green peppers
2	tomatoes
2	cloves garlic
3 fl oz/90ml	olive oil
1 teaspoon	paprika
1 teaspoon	salt
3 fl oz/90ml	milk
½ tablespoon	dill (chopped)
½ tablespoon	parsley (chopped)

Chop the beans in two and remove the stringy pieces, chop the onions and garlic finely and dice the peppers after de-seeding. Heat half the oil in a pan and gently fry the onion and garlic until soft. Add the peppers and cook for another 10 minutes until soft then add to the beans, remaining oil, seasoning and 3 fl oz/90ml of water and boil. After about 10 minutes, when the beans start to soften, add the milk, lower the heat and simmer for a further 10 minutes. Dice the tomatoes finely and add to the beans, then add the chopped herbs and simmer for a further 5 minutes stirring occasionally and serve immediately.

GARDENER'S MOUSSAKA

2	*large onions*
1	*carrot*
1	*head of celery*
¼	*cabbage*
2	*courgettes*
3	*potatoes*
1lb 1oz/500g	*tomatoes*
4oz/125g	*green beans*
4oz/125g	*rice*
3	*eggs*
7 fl oz/210ml	*milk*
1oz/45g	*flour*
3 fl oz/90ml	*olive oil*
1 tablespoon	*chopped parsley*
	salt

Preheat the oven to 200°C/400°F, gas mark 6. Clean all the vegetables and grate or chop them finely. Heat the oil in a frying pan and lightly fry the vegetables for 10-15 minutes, stirring constantly until soft. Add 3 fl oz/90ml of water and simmer for a further 5 minutes. Boil the rice separately in 4 fl oz/125ml of water and add to the vegetables when soft together with the salt, pepper and half the chopped parsley.

Grease a cake tin well and add the mixture. Mix the flour, eggs and milk into a thin batter and pour over the vegetables and rice. Sprinkle the remaining parsley over the batter and bake in the pre-heated oven for 30 minutes or until nicely browned all over. Allow to cool a little, cut in slices and serve.

GRILLED MUSHROOMS

14oz/400g	*mushrooms*
1oz/50g	*butter*
	salt and black pepper
	lemon juice

Wash and de-stalk the mushrooms and leave to dry on a towel. When they are dry, salt them, place on a hot grill and roast for about 15 minutes. Brown the butter, pour over the mushrooms and serve with a seasoning of black pepper and lemon juice.

MEAT DISHES

PEPPERS STUFFED WITH VEAL

2.2lb/1kg	peppers
1lb 9oz/750g	minced meat
4oz/150g	butter OR other fat
4oz/150g	rice
7oz/200g	tomatoes (peeled and chopped)
2	onions
8oz/225g	yoghurt
3	eggs
1 tablespoon	flour
1 tablespoon	paprika
	black pepper
½oz/15g	parsley
16 fl oz/500ml	water

Wash the peppers and remove the stalks and seeds, and salt lightly on the inside. Finely chop the onions and lightly brown in the fat. Add the paprika and rice, stir and add 4 fl oz/125ml of hot water. Stir in the meat, peeled and chopped tomatoes, some chopped red pepper and parsley. Remove from the heat when it begins to boil. Fill the peppers with this stuffing, dip them in flour and arrange in a deep saucepan. Add the rest of hot water and cook in a moderately hot (180°C/350°F, gas mark 4) oven for about 40 minutes.

Beat the yoghurt with the flour and eggs, add some of the sauce from the pan, pour over the peppers and replace in the oven for a further ten minutes.

The stuffed peppers can also be cooked on a hot plate. The sauce is prepared by mixing the milk, eggs and broth without flour. Bring to the boil stirring continuously to prevent the eggs curdling. Pour over the peppers and shake a little to allow the sauce to spread uniformly.

PARSON'S
STEW

1lb 8oz/750g	*lean pork*
1lb 9oz/750g	*small onions*
4oz/150g	*butter OR other fat*
2	*cloves garlic*
3-4	*tomatoes (or 1 tablespoon tomato purée)*
1 tablespoon	*flour*
6 fl oz/175ml	*white wine*
	salt and black pepper
1 tablespoon	*paprika*
2-3	*bay leaves*

Skin the onions, peel the garlic and brown them both in the fat without salt. Remove the onions and garlic and put the diced meat into the fat, add salt and brown slightly. Add enough hot water to cover the meat and cook over a low heat for a further 15-20 minutes. Add the onions, garlic, bay leaves and black pepper and continue to simmer for 1½ hours.

Mix the tomatoes (or purée) and the flour with the wine and pour over the meat. Add more hot water if necessary but do not thin the sauce too much. Cook until the meat is tender.

WRAPPED
ROAST LAMB

2lb 2oz/1kg	*boned leg lamb*
10oz/300g	*tripe*
3	*bunches spring onions (chopped)*
2-3	*small hot peppers*
3oz/120g	*butter*
	salt and black pepper
½oz/15g	*parsley (chopped)*
4-5	*blades mint (chopped)*
1 tablespoon	*paprika*
8oz/250g	*yoghurt*

Cut the meat into cubes and brown in the oil. Add the chopped onions, parsley, mint and salt and cook until the onions become soft. Add the paprika and black pepper, stir well, remove from the heat and divide into six portions. Cut the tripe into six parts, soak in cold water then wrap around the stuffing. Arrange on a buttered dish, add a little hot water and 2-3 tablespoons of butter and cook in a moderately hot (180°C/350°F, gas mark 4) oven for 1¼-1½ hours.

The dish is served either with a thick yoghurt or a sauce made of 3 eggs beaten together and mixed with one cup of yoghurt. Put in the oven or under a grill until a brown crust is formed on top.

ROAST MEAT
SHOPSKI
FASHION

2lb 2oz/1kg	*veal, mutton or pork*
11oz/350g	*tomatoes (sliced)*
7oz/200g	*onions (finely chopped)*
7oz/200g	*peppers (cubed)*
3	*whole small peppers*
4oz/150g	*butter*
½oz/250g	*yoghurt*
3	*eggs*
½oz/15g	*flour*
	salt and black pepper
½oz/15g	*parsley*
1 tablespoon	*paprika*
	savoury
8 fl oz/250ml	*hot water*

For the best results cook in an earthenware pot with a tight fitting lid.

Bone the meat, cut into cubes and lay in the bottom of the pot. In layers, add the finely chopped onions, sliced tomatoes and cubed peppers, then the whole small peppers, salt, black pepper, paprika, savoury and parsley. Stir together and add the fat and hot water. Cover tightly and simmer for about 2½ hours on top of the oven. Transfer to an oven dish, cover with the yoghurt mixed with the flour and beaten eggs, and place in a hot (210°C/425°F, gas mark 7) oven for about 15 minutes.

ROAST VEAL
WRAPPED IN
PAPER

2lb 2oz/1kg	*veal (from the leg)*
1-2	*onions (finely chopped)*
4oz/150g	*butter*
	black pepper
½oz/15g	*parsley (finely chopped)*
2-3	*leaves mint (finely chopped)*

Cut the meat into cubes, add salt, black pepper, butter, finely chopped onions, mint and parsley. Mix well and transfer to a sheet of greased paper. Wrap carefully into a packet with the ends bent inside and put into a well buttered pan. Coat the outside of the packet with butter, add a little water and cook in a moderately hot (180°C/350°F, gas mark 4) oven, turning carefully 2-3 times to ensure uniform cooking. Serve the whole packet at the table, cut with a knife and take out the meat with a tablespoon. Serve with salad.

STUFFED VINE LEAVES

8oz/250g	vine leaves
1lb 1oz/500g	lean lamb OR veal
1	slice white bread
1	onion
4oz/125g	rice
1 teaspoon	ground cinnamon
1 teaspoon	salt
½ teaspoon	black pepper
2 tablespoons	chopped dill
1	small sprig rosemary
2 tablespoons	olive oil
2 tablespoons	tomato purée OR 6 very ripe tomatoes
3 fl oz/90ml	lemon juice
5 fl oz/150ml	sour cream

Blanch the vine leaves in boiling water for five minutes until they start to change colour. Place spine upwards on a board ready for stuffing.

Soak the crustless bread in water for a few minutes, squeeze out as much liquid as possible and mince with the meat. Chop the onion finely and fry until soft. Add the rice and fry gently for two or three minutes then cover with 2 fl oz/60ml of water. Reduce heat and simmer for about five minutes.

Mix the rice and onion with the minced meat, add the chopped herbs, salt and pepper. Mix well and add 3 fl oz/90ml water. Fill the leaves with the mixture and fold to make a neat parcel. Pack closely together in the bottom of a pan and place a lid or plate on top to press them down even tighter. Make a sauce out of the blanched and blended tomatoes or purée, diluted in enough water to just cover the leaves. Salt to taste, add 1 tablespoon of olive oil, the sprig of rosemary and simmer for an hour on a low heat.

Remove from the heat, add the lemon juice, cover and put in a moderate (180°C/350°F, gas mark 4) oven for another 30 minutes. Allow to cool a little, add the soured cream or yoghurt to the sauce and serve with red cabbage and apple salad. This is a traditional Christmas supper dish.

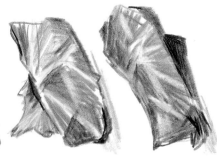

ROAST FISH

2lb 2oz/1kg	*fish*
3 tablespoons	*vegetable oil*
3	*onions (sliced)*
2-3	*peppers*
1-2	*tomatoes (peeled and finely chopped)*
	salt and black pepper
1 tablespoon	*paprika*
½oz/15g	*parsley.*
12 fl oz/375ml	*water*

Cut the peppers into large slices and fry with the onions until they become soft, add the tomatoes, salt, paprika, black pepper and parsley. Cut the fish into strips and add to the ingredients, stir and transfer to a sheet of greased paper. Fold the paper into an envelope, place in a pan, smear liberally with oil, add the water and cook in a moderately hot (180°C/350°F, gas mark 4) oven. Serve with salad.

DOBRUDJA
KEBABS

2lb 2oz/1kg	*leg of mutton*
4	*cloves garlic*
8oz/250g	*tomatoes*
12	*bay leaves*
1 fl oz/30ml	*olive oil*
2	*onions*
2	*green peppers*
1 teaspoon	*salt*
3	*sprigs thyme*
½ teaspoon	*pepper*

Dice the meat into small cubes and discard all fat. Sprinkle with salt, pepper and thyme and slice the garlic into slivers and place a piece into a cut in each of the cubes. Slice the tomatoes, onions and peppers in large rings.

On six long skewers, place the meat cubes, separated by alternate rings of tomatoes, onions, peppers and bay leaves. Brush the skewers with oil and grill, rotating constantly and brushing occasionally with oil. Serve with red cabbage and apple relish.

FISH IN A
JACKET

1lb 15oz/900g	*fish (chub is ideal)*
4oz/130g	*vegetable oil*
8oz/250g	*flour*
1	*egg*
3oz/10g	*yeast*
10fl oz/315ml	*water*
	salt

Clean the fish, rinse and salt. Prepare a soft dough from the flour, yeast, egg, water and salt and let it rise. Divide the dough in two and roll out. Grease a sheet of paper and place one of the pieces of dough on it. Cover the dough with the fish and place the second piece of dough and a second sheet of greased paper on top of the fish. Fold the ends of the paper to form a packet. Cook very slowly in a moderate (180°C/350°F, gas mark 4) oven.

GRILLED MEAT

Grilled kebapches (oblong rissoles), meatballs on small skewers, chops and so on is the typical cuisine of Bulgaria. Grilling the meat at high temperatures forms a thin crust sealing in the meat's juices and goodness.

KEBAPCHES

The most delicious kebapches are prepared from minced lamb or from equal parts of minced lamb and veal. The meat normally used comes from the ribs, shoulder or neck.

1lb 9oz/750g	*minced meat*
1	*onion (very finely chopped)*
1 teaspoon	*ground or crushed cinnamon*
	salt
8 fl oz/250ml	*water*

Mix the meat, onion and cinammon together and salt to taste. Knead the meat by adding a little water until it acquires the necessary elasticity to form the kebapches. Put the kebapches on an oiled hot plate, or grill, and turn frequently to avoid becoming overdone. Do not prick the kebapches while turning.

Serve immediately with finely chopped and mixed onions, parsley, small hot peppers, tomatoes, haricot beans and pepper relish.

Grilled meatballs are prepared in much the same way as kebapches. Finely chopped small hot peppers are sometimes added to the minced meat with the chopped onions.

GRILLED LAMB

1lb/450g	*lamb*
2	*onions (finely chopped)*
1	*clove garlic (finely chopped)*

Bone the meat and cut into cubes. Salt, add the finely chopped onions, a little garlic and mix, and leave covered for up to 3 hours. Remove the onions and stick the pieces of meat on small skewers. Cook on a hot grill until the meat becomes dark red and soft.

BAKED TOMATOES WITH MEAT

1lb 5oz/600g	*veal or mutton*
1lb 15oz/900g	*tomatoes*
4oz/120g	*fat*
3oz/100g	*onions*
3oz/100g	*rice*
3oz/100g	*pepper*
6 fl oz/175ml	*milk*
2	*eggs*
	salt
½oz/15g	*parsley (finely chopped)*
	pepper
1 tablespoon	*paprika*
4 fl oz/125ml	*hot water*

Slice off the top of the tomatoes and hollow out with a spoon (put the "lids" and pulp to one side). Chop the onions and peppers very finely and fry until soft in two-thirds of the fat. Then add the rice, salt, pepper, paprika and hot water. Once the water has been absorbed, add the meat, about one-third of the tomato pulp and the parsley. Stir well and then stuff the hollowed-out tomatoes with the mixture and cover with the tomato lids. Arrange the tomatoes in a row on a baking dish, pour on the remaining fat and strained tomato pulp and bake in a moderately hot (180°C/350°F, gas mark 4) oven for 20-25 minutes. Beat the eggs, mix with the milk and salt to taste. When the tomatoes are ready, pour the eggs and milk over them and bake for another few minutes in a hot oven.

KAPAMA (lamb with spring onions)	

1lb 8oz/750g	*meat*
14oz/400g	*spring onions (finely chopped)*
8-10	*cloves garlic (finely chopped)*
3oz/100g	*butter*
1 tablespoon	*flour*
	salt
	pepper
½oz/15g	*parsley (finely chopped)*
5-6	*leaves mint*
8 fl oz/250ml	*water*
2	*eggs*
4oz/125g	*yoghurt*

Slice the meat into cubes, place in a saucepan and add the onions, garlic, parsley, mint, the fat and water (add pepper, paprika and salt to taste). Put a tight lid on the pan and cook over a moderate heat until the meat is very tender. Just a few minutes before removing from the heat, add the flour diluted with some cold water. Serve with yoghurt.

JERKED KEBAP (lamb kebap with spring onions)

1lb 9oz/750g	*leg lamb*
6-7	*spring onions (finely chopped)*
3oz/100g	*butter*
	salt and pepper
½oz/15g	*parsley (finely chopped)*
8 fl oz/250ml	*hot water*

Cut the meat into large cubes and fry in the fat. Add salt, pepper and 4 fl oz/125ml hot water and bring to the boil. When the water has nearly evaporated add the rest of the water. When the meat is very tender, add the onions, parsley and stir until heated through and serve immediately. Serve hot with fried potatoes, onions, gherkins and green salad.

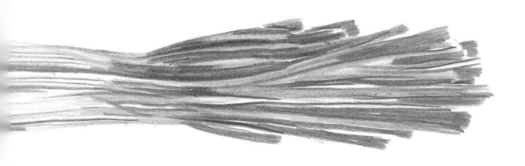

ROAST VEAL IN AUBERGINES

2lb 2oz/1kg	veal
7oz/200g	onions (finely chopped)
8oz/250g	tomatoes (peeled and finely chopped)
1lb 15oz/900g	aubergines
3oz/150g	butter
3-4	eggs
6 fl oz/175ml	white wine
1 teaspoon	flour
½oz/15g	parsley
1 tablespoon	paprika.
12 fl oz/375ml	water

Bone and dice the meat, add a teaspoonful of flour and fry with half the butter. Wash the aubergines, scoop out the insides and brown them uniformly. Use the remaining butter to brown the onions and the inside flesh of the aubergines, then add the tomatoes. Boil until the liquid from the tomatoes has evaporated then add the water and wine, the meat, blackpepper, paprika and parsley and leave simmering until the meat becomes soft. Stuff the semi-browned aubergines with the meat, arrange in a pan, pour over the sauce left after stuffing and place in a moderately hot (180°C/350°F, gas mark 4) oven for 45 minutes. When done, beat the eggs and pour over the aubergines and return to the oven until browned.

SEASONED FRIED MEAT WITH LEEKS

1lb 9oz/750g	pork
15 oz/400g	leeks (finely chopped)
10oz/300g	pickled peppers
14oz/150g	butter
4-5	eggs
1 tablespoon	paprika

Cut the pork into cubes and fry in the butter, remove and keep warm. Fry the diced peppers in the remaining butter, add the finely chopped leeks and meat, sprinkle with paprika and salt. Beat the eggs and pour over the mixture. Cook by stirring until the eggs have curdled to the desired hardness. Serve hot.

GRILLED VEAL OR PORK CHOPS

Tenderize the chops with a meat hammer, lay them on a bed of finely chopped onions and leave for 1-2 hours. Remove the onions and grill the meat, adding salt at the end. One sign that the meat is cooked right through is the appearance of juice droplets on the upper surface. Serve hot, with fried potatoes, roast and skinned peppers, relish and pickles.

PHEASANT WITH CHERRIES

1	pheasant
5 fl oz/150ml	sour cream
1lb 1oz/500g	Morello or red cherries
2 fl oz/60ml	dry white wine
3oz/90g	butter
2 tablespoons	dessert wine
2	onions
½ teaspoon	paprika
	salt and pepper

Soak the cherries in the dessert wine for 2–3 hours. Remove the stones carefully. Sprinkle or brush the pheasant with the dry white wine. Chop the onions finely and fry in the melted butter until soft but not brown. Add the pheasant, increase the heat to moderate and fry on all sides for about 15 minutes shaking the pan frequently to avoid sticking. When the bird is browned on all sides, add the cream by pouring slowly all around the pheasant. Lower the heat and braise for a further 15 minutes basting continuously. Add salt and pepper to taste.

Arrange on a large dish, pour the sauce over the bird and arrange the soaked cherries around it. Sprinkle the bird and cream with a light dusting of paprika and serve. This is a Bulgarian adaptation of a traditional turkish dish.

STUFFED
CABBAGE
LEAVES

1lb 9oz/750g	*pork fillet*
1	*cabbage pickled in brine*
6	*onions*
4oz/125g	*lard*
24	*peppercorns*
4oz/125g	*smoked bacon*

Chop the onion finely and fry in the lard until soft but not brown, then add the peppercorns and salt. Slice the pork into thin rectangles about one inch (25mm) long. Cut the cabbage stalk off and undo the leaves, choosing the thinner, inner ones. Wrap a piece of meat and one tablespoon of onion with two or three peppercorns in each leaf. Chop the rest of the cabbage into thin strips and use to line the bottom of a saucepan. Place the stuffed cabbage leaves on top using slices of smoked bacon between the layers.

Dilute 8 fl oz (300ml) of the pickling brine from the cabbage with enough water to cover the cabbage leaves and boil uncovered on a moderate heat until all the liquid has evaporated and the meat inside the leaves is soft. Serve on a bed of rice or Polenta.

HOTCH
POTCH WITH
MUTTON

2lb/900g	*meat*
8oz/250g	*spring beans*
10oz/300g	*potatoes*
8oz/250g	*tomatoes*
7oz/200g	*peppers*
4oz/150g	*onions (finely chopped)*
4oz/150g	*aubergines*
3oz/100g	*okra*
7oz/200g	*cabbage*
4oz/150g	*butter*
1-2	*carrots (finely chopped)*
	sour grapes
1 tablespoon	*paprika*
½oz/15g	*parsley*
3-4	*eggs*

Dice the meat and place in an earthenware pan, add salt, paprika, butter and the onions and carrots. Cover the meat with hot water and place in the oven. Slice the potatoes, cut the tomatoes and peppers into large pieces and, with the spring beans, stew in a little salted water. When the meat is tender, add the vegetables, salt and sour grapes and return to a hot (210-220°C/425°F, gas mark 7) oven for 1½-2 hours. When there is almost no water left in the sauce remove the pan from the oven. Beat the eggs and pour oven then return to the oven until the eggs brown.

DESSERTS

SEMOLINA KHALVA

8oz/225g	*melted butter*
11oz/350g	*sugar*
1lb/450g	*semolina*
32 fl oz/1 litre	*water*

To make the syrup, add the sugar to the water and bring to the boil stirring continuously. Brown the semolina in the butter again stirring continuously. When the syrup has turned yellow, pour over the semolina and stir until all the syrup has been absorbed. Remove from the heat, cover with a cloth and lid for about 20 minutes. Remove the lid and cloth and stir with a fork, then replace the lid until the khalva has cooled. Serve with crushed walnut kernels and cinnamon.

WALNUT CAKE IN SYRUP

8oz/250g	*caster sugar*
10oz/300g	*raisins*
1 teaspoon	*baking soda*
1 teaspoon	*cinnamon*
7oz/200g	*marmalade*
8 fl oz/250ml	*water*
6oz/175g	*walnut kernels (crushed)*
1oz/30g	*lemon rind*
7oz/200g	*flour*

Dilute the marmalade with the water, add the walnut kernels, a little grated lemon rind and then gradually add the flour until a soft dough is obtained. Spread the dough in a buttered dish and bake in a moderately hot (180°C/350°F, gas mark 4) oven for 1¼-1½ hours.

When the cake has cooled off, cut into pieces and cover with a syrup made by melting the sugar in 16 fl oz/500ml water.

WHITE
COOKIES

8oz/250g	*butter*
4oz/150g	*powdered sugar*
12oz/370g	*flour*
3oz/100g	*sugar (sprinkling on top of cookies)*

Melt the butter, cool and allow to set, then beat with a wooden spoon until it turns white. Add the sugar and beat for another 10-15 minutes, then add the flour and make a plain dough from which the cookies can be formed. Arrange them on a slightly greased baking tray and cook at a low temperature (150°C/300°F, gas mark 2) so that the cookies stay almost white. Powder liberally with sugar when cold.

WALNUT
BISCUITS

9oz/260g	*butter OR vegetable oil*
7oz/200g	*sugar*
8oz/250g	*walnut kernels (ground)*
1lb 1oz/500g	*flour*
	rind from half a lemon
1	*eggwhite*

Melt the butter and add the sugar, ground walnuts, grated lemon rind and the flour. Knead the dough, divide into five pieces and roll each one to a depth of about ½cm. Cut out biscuit shapes using a tumbler, dip one side only into beaten eggwhite, then into crushed walnuts mixed with sugar and lay in a lightly buttered baking tray. Bake until golden in a moderately hot (180°C/350°F, gas mark 4) oven. The biscuits can then be eaten as they are or joined using a marmalade filling.

PRUNES WITH
WALNUT
KERNELS

1lb 1oz/500g	*dry prunes*
4oz/115g	*sugar*
4 fl oz/125ml	*red wine*
1lb 1oz/500g	*walnut kernels*

Soak the prunes in water until they are soft, then strain and carefully remove the stones. Stuff the prunes with the walnut kernels, put them onto a baking tray, sprinkle with powdered sugar, pour the wine over them and bake in a moderately hot (180°C/350°F, gas mark 4) oven for about half an hour, until the syrup has thickened considerably. Serve cold.

SESAME RINGS

8oz/250g	*butter OR fresh lard*
8oz/250g	*sugar*
4	*eggs*
1 teaspoon	*hartshorn*
	juice from one lemon
	sesame
7oz/200g	*flour*

Melt the butter, add the sugar and beat thoroughly. Then add the eggs one by one, continuing to beat vigorously. Add the hartshorn and lemon juice and finally the amount of flour necessary to obtain a dough which can be rolled.

Roll the dough into a sheet about ½cm thick and cut rings out of the dough using a tumbler and a smaller glass. Dip them in milk, roll in sesame (enough to cover the rings) and bake in a moderately hot (180°C/350°F, gas mark 4) oven until golden. The sesame rings remain tender for a long time if kept in airtight tins or glass jars.

2lb 2oz/1kg	*ripe plums*
4oz/125g	*brown sugar*
1	*stick cinnamon*
	rind of 1 lemon
4 fl oz/120ml	*dessert wine or Madeira*
2 fl oz/60ml	*Bulgarian plum brandy*
2oz/60g	*sultanas*

PLUMS IN BULGARIAN BRANDY

Preheat the oven to 155°C/300°F, gas mark 2. Cut the plums in half and remove the stones. Place in a casserole, sprinkle the sugar over them and add the cinnamon and lemon peel. Pour the wine over, cover and stew for between 40 and 60 minutes or until the plums are soft.

In the meantime soak the sultanas in the brandy. When the plums are ready, remove a little juice if necessary, add the sultanas and brandy and serve immediately.

BULGARIAN
BITTER
CHERRY
SHERBET

2lb 2oz/1kg	*bitter cooking cherries*
2lb 2oz/1kg	*sugar*
1 teaspoon	*lemon juice*
6 drops	*vanilla essence*

Wash the cherries, remove stalks and boil in a saucepan with 4 fl oz/120ml of water for about 5 minutes. Allow to cool then strain through a very fine muslin. Allow the liquid to stand until clear with any residue settled at the bottom.

Measure out 8 fl oz/300ml of the liquid and pour over the sugar in the bottom of a copper pan. Bring to the boil over a very low heat until the sugar is completely dissolved. Increase the heat, skim off any scum rising to the top and wipe the sides with a clean cloth to remove all traces of scum.

Test to see if the syrup is ready by dripping a few drops into a glass of cold water. If the sugar dissolves immediately, return to the heat and keep boiling fast. If the sugar crystalizes on contact with the cold water the sherbet is ready.

Remove from the heat, cover with a wet cloth and allow to cool until you can touch it with your hand without discomfort. Wedge the pot firmly, then mix the sherbet vigorously with a large wooden spoon or rolling pin, turning in one direction only. When the sherbet starts to change its colour, add the lemon juice and continue stirring for a further 5 minutes.

Scoop the sherbet out of the pot and into a jar. Seal with greaseproof paper and a lid and store in a cool, dry place, but not in the fridge.

The sherbet can be added to ice cold water for a refreshing, tangy drink on a hot summers day, or added to stewed fruits.

APPLE CAKE

4	*eggs*
12oz/340g	*sugar*
4-5	*apples (grated)*
7oz/200g	*flour*
2 teaspoons	*cinnamon*
2 teaspoons	*hartshorn*

Beat the eggs thoroughly with the sugar, add the hartshorn, cinnamon and the grated apples. Gradually add the flour until workable dough is obtained (the dough should not be more than about 3cm (1inch) deep). Transfer to a baking dish and bake in a moderately hot (180°C/350°F, gas mark 4) oven for 20-30 minutes. When cooked, allow to cool, cut into pieces and powder

HELIX PASTRIES

FOR THE DOUGH –

½oz/15g	*yeast*
4 fl oz/125ml	*warm milk*
7oz/200g	*flour*
2 teaspoons	*sugar*
3 teaspoons	*melted butter*
1	*egg*
	salt

FOR THE STUFFING –

4oz/150g	*walnut kernels (crushed)*
1	*eggwhite*
1 teaspoon	*cinnamon*

THE SYRUP –

1lb 1oz/500g	*sugar*
1 pint/625m	*water*

Thin the yeast to a paste with the milk and mix with the sugar, pinch of salt and a little flour. Leave to rise then add the butter, egg and the necessary amount of flour to obtain a soft dough. Knead thoroughly and roll into a shape about 30cm² (five sq in). Smear the dough with a beaten eggwhite, sprinkle with walnut kernels mixed with cinnamon and make a compact roll. Cut the roll into 15-16 pieces and lay them on their flat side, not touching one another, in a buttered baking tray. Brush them with melted butter to prevent sticking and bake until golden in a moderately hot (180°C/350°F, gas mark 4) oven and leave to cool. Mix the sugar and water to make a syrup, and when heat. Remove from the heat as soon as it starts to boil, leave for 10-15 minutes, then pour over the helices.

BULGARIA A-Z
GAZETEER OF BULGARIAN TOWNS AND CITIES

BLAGOEVGRAD

Blagoevgrad is a district town in the southwest, 101 kilometres (63 miles) south of Sofia and re-named in this century after Dimiter Blagoev, founder of the Bulgarian Workers' Marxist Party. It is situated in the eastern part of the Blagoevgrad Valley at an altitude of 410 metres (1,312 feet) above sea level. The river Bistritsa, a tributary of the Struma, flows through the town. Blagoevgrad is noted for its thermal springs and in 1963 was declared a spa town. In ancient times it was the site of a Thracian settlement called Skaptopara, founded because of the mineral springs. During Ottoman rule it became an important market town. In the sixteenth century a monastery was founded, and in the eighteenth and early nineteenth centuries the town became a major crafts and trade centre. Until 1912 the town was under Ottoman rule, but it became a revolutionary centre during the 1923 uprising.

Today, the town is a leading industrial centre with food, tobacco and engineering factories, breweries and an agro-engineering estate. It has a teachers' training college, technical high schools, a hospital, sports and spa facilities, a theatre, a museum and a broadcasting station. Buildings of interest are the Church of the Holy Virgin (1844), famous for its wood carvings; the houses of the Varosha district; and the G. Izmirliev Museum House.

BURGAS

Burgas is 385 kilometres (240 miles) east of Sofia and the administrative, political and cultural centre of the district on the Black Sea coast of the same name. It is a spa town, an international seaside resort and stands on the site of many former settlements which can be traced back through Bronze Age, Thracian and Roman times. It has always had strategic importance and gets its name from the Greek word "pyrgos" which means "tower".

Freed from Ottoman rule in 1878, Burgas rapidly developed into an important sea port, commercial and industrial centre. Today, it is the country's biggest seaport with rail links to Sofia and the interior. There are petro-chemical plants, oil refineries, shipyards, fish factories and timber mills. The surrounding agricultural area supplies mainly grain, poultry, cattle and vegetables, but there are also vineyards and many of the grapes are processed in the town. The town has many colleges, a hospital, a theatre, an opera house, an art gallery and a museum. Of architectural interest is the Church of Saints Cyril and Methodius, built in 1894 of andesite and marble, and monuments to political and cultural leaders. The town hosts the annual Sunny Beach Music Festival, a ten day music and international folklore festival.

GABROVO

Gabrovo is a district town near the centre of Bulgaria, 220 kilometres (136 miles) northeast of Sofia, on the northern slopes of the Shipka Mountain on the river Yantra, at an altitude of 390 metres (1,248 feet). Remains of late Stone Age and Copper Age settlements have been found, as well as Thracian tumuli and roads, and Roman and Medieval fortresses and churches. The town began to develop in the fourteenth century because of its position on the trade route between the Carpathians and Constantinople and it figured prominently in the struggle for freedom against the Turks. Famous as both a crafts and industrial centre, crafts included iron work, cutlery, gun, clock and shoemaking, as well as lace work, leather and woollen goods, which were exported to Russia and throughout Europe. The town was the cradle of Bulgarian education, the first monastery school opening here in 1625, and the country's first secondary school in 1872.

Today, Gabrovo is a major industrial town and the main industries are textiles, machine building, metal working, leather and fur, shoemaking, and food. There are theatres, and the museums include the National Museum of Public Education, the Museum of Architecture and Construction, and the Museum of Humour and Satire. The oldest part of the town is around the clock tower (1833), but the Aprilov water fountain built in 1762 survives. Also of interest is the Church of the Holy Virgin (1865), famous for its wood carvings and icons, and on a rock in the middle of the Yantra river is a monument to Racho the Blacksmith, the legendary founder of the town. Nearby is the historic village of Bozhentsi, an architectural preserve, and the Shipka-Buzludje National Museum Park.

HASKOVO

Haskovo is situated in the south by the river Haskovo, 234 kilometres (145 miles) southeast of Sofia. To the west of the town are mineral springs. Remains of Neolithic and Thracian settlements have been found and in the Middle Ages it was a trading and military centre. By the ninth century it had become a fortified town with a garrison permanently stationed behind the 2.3 metres (8 feet) thick walls.

The main industries are chemical and mechanical engineering, food and drink, and textiles, but there are also wineries, breweries and meat processing plants. The town is the centre for the region's wine industry and has theatres, museums and art galleries. Of architectural importance are the Churches of the Virgin Mary (1857) and the Archangel Michael (1861), and the Kirkov School (1882). There are also a number of Revival Period houses and the remains of a Medieval fortress.

KARDJALI

This is a district town in the south, 262 kilometres (162 miles) from Sofia, on the river Arda at an altitude of 240 metres (768 feet) above sea level, and near the Kardjali and Studen Kladenets reservoirs.

A Neolithic settlement and Thracian burial mounds have been excavated and to the north stands the Muniak Fortress, the stronghold of a medieval Bulgarian settlement. The town was under Ottoman rule until 1913. It developed as a crafts centre and was famous for the Rhodope tobaccos. Today mining is the main industry, followed by tobacco and textiles. There is a teachers' training college, full sports and tourist facilities, as well as a theatre, an art gallery and museums. The town has its own symphony orchestra and hosts many cultural events throughout the year. The oldest part of the town, at the foot of Borovets Hill, has narrow winding lanes and low houses.

KJUSTENDIL

Kjustendil is a district centre in the southwest, 90 kilometres (55 miles) southwest of Sofia, near the river Banshtitsa at an altitude of 500 metres (1,600 feet) above sea level. It is a spa town, and its waters, at 23°C (73°F) are rich in mineral salts.

A reference to a Thracian settlement was made in the fourth century BC by the Greek writer Theopompus, and another reference to the town was made by Pliny the Elder in the first century AD. Its ancient Thracian name was Pautalia, from the word "pote" for "spring". The fortress on the Hissarluka Hill was built in the fourth century AD and reinforced during the reign of the Byzantine Emperor Justinian I (AD 527-565) to protect the town against attack by the Barbarians and other tribes. Under Byzantine rule, the town became a major religious and education centre. A monastery school was built in the town in 1821, and a school built on the site in 1849 can still be seen. The town was liberated in 1878

Engineering, metal working, textiles, food and drink, and wood processing are the main industries and the surrounding countryside specializes in fruit growing, tobacco and market gardening. The town is a resort with many springs and open air pools and the Dervish Banya spring dates back to 1566. There is a theatre, an art gallery and a museum, and many fine buildings including Saint George's Church in the Kolusha quarter, the

Pirkova Tower (sixteenth and seventeenth centuries), the Fetih Sultan Mehmed (1531), Ahmed Bey Mosques (1575), a wall still remaining from the Devehani Caravanserai (1606), and the Churches of the Virgin Mary (1816) and Saint Demetrius (1866). The remains of the ancient town of Pautalia, in the centre of the town, have been excavated as an archaeological reserve.

LOVECH

A district town in the north, 270 kilometres (167 miles) northeast of Sofia, on both banks of the river Ossam, at 190 metres (608 feet) above sea level. Traces of settlements dating back to the Paleolithic Age have been found in the caves surrounding the town, and there are also the remains of a fortress wall, the foundations of churches and other buildings on Hissarya Hill. The town itself stands on the site of the Thracian town of Melta, later to become Presidium Melta under the Romans, and a staging post on the road between the Danube and the Aegean. At the end of Byzantine rule in the twelfth century, its name was changed to Lovuts, later to become Lovech. The town has always been an important military base, and the stronghold resisted Byzantine attack for so long in the 1185-87 uprising that the Turks had to sign the Treaty of Lovech which formally recognized the Second Bulgarian State. The nearby monastery of the Holy Virgin was a major literary centre in the sixteenth century.

Tanning was the town's main industry and is still important together with engineering, furniture making and knitwear. The town has theatres, museums, art galleries and a zoo, and is famous for its architectural treasures including the houses and cobbled alleys of the National Revival Period in the Varosha quarter. There are a number of fine churches and the country's only covered bridge was built here between 1872 and 1874. Made of wood on stone foundations, it burnt down in 1925 and has been rebuilt using the original plans.

MIHAILOVGRAD

A wine growing town in the northwest, 114 kilometres (70 miles) north of Sofia. It is named after Hristo Mihailov, leader of the September 1923 Uprising. Remains of a Thracian settlement have been found on the Kaleto Hill and the Roman town of Montana was located at the bottom of the hill. Near the town's large spring was a shrine and temple to Diana and Apollo, and in the third century a fort was built on the hill. The ruins of many Roman villas have been discovered around the town. Under the Slavs the town was known as Kutlovitsa but it ceased to exist for a time under Ottoman rule because the population either fled or was massacred. The population gradually drifted back and the town was liberated during the Russo-Turkish war in 1877.

Today, apart from wine, the main industries are engineering, metal working, food and drink, building materials, textiles, tailoring and wood working. It is an education centre with high schools, sports facilities, theatres, museums and an art gallery. There is a museum to the 1923 Uprising incorporating Mihailov's house.

PAZARDJIK

This is a district town in the south, 120 kilometres (74 miles) southeast of Sofia. It is on the River Maritsa in the Upper Thracian Plain at an altitude of 205 metres (656 feet). The town was founded in 1485 although traces of Thracian and medieval settlements have been found. In the seventeenth and eighteenth centuries the town flourished as a port on the river Maritsa and produce from the surrounding district was stored there before being rafted on to Adrianople and Constantinople. Agriculture has always been important and the town became the venue of one of the country's largest fairs, the annual Marashki Fair. The town also produced saltpetre, and its craftsmen exhibited at the 1855 Paris Exhibition. The town was liberated from the Turks in 1878 and today is a major agricultural, food and industrial centre. It has the largest hothouse complexes in the country, vineyards and an experimental agriculture station. It has a medical school, and a number of colleges and institutes of higher education, as well as sports and tourist facilities, theatres, a museum and art galleries. Of architectural interest are the buildings of the National Revival Period, the eighteenth century Metropolitan Church of the Virgin Mary, famous for its icons, the Chapels of Saint Petka (1856), the Holy Archangel (1860), and Saints Constantine and Helena (1868-70).

PERNIK

Pernik is a district centre in the west, 31 kilometres (18 miles) southwest of Sofia. It is in the Pernik valley of the River Struma at 700 metres (2,240 feet) above sea level that Early Stone Age settlements have been found, each on the site of a previous one. Settlements were also built close by through the Bronze and Copper Ages to Thracian times and the ruins of many Roman, Slav and Byzantine settlements have also been found. In the fourth century BC it became a fortress but was destroyed by the invading Celts 100 years later.

The area was always famous for its agriculture, but in 1876 the first coal was extracted for the Turkish army. In 1890 the Pernik coalfields were declared state property and are still a major centre of coalmining and heavy industry with iron and steel works. There are libraries, theatres, art galleries and museums, including the Museum of Mining.

PLEVEN

A district centre in the central part of north Bulgaria, 174 kilometres (107 miles) northeast of Sofia, on the river Tuchenitsa, west of the Pleven Heights. Remains of settlements dating back to Neolithic times have been found and the Romans built a staging post here, and later a fort to protect it. A fourth century Christian necropolis has been excavated, one of the largest found in Bulgaria. In the Middle Ages the town was a crafts and commercial centre, and had a large cattle market, but in the late fourteenth century it was captured and destroyed by the Turks. To meet the needs of the garrisoned Turkish troops, the town was re-populated and local trades established to cater for the soldiers – including winemaking and brandy distillation.

Bulgaria's first secular girls' school was founded here in 1840, and in 1890 the country's first viticulture and viniculture college opened. After liberation from the Turks in 1878 the wine industry flourished and the town had the best equipped and most extensive wine cellars in the Balkans. The country's collection of old wines has been kept there since 1893.

Along with food processing and winemaking, other industries include building materials, textiles, knitwear, mechanical engineering, and chemicals and electrical goods. There is a wine institute, a medical school and several colleges and institutes of higher education. There are theatres, an opera house, museums, a symphony orchestra and art galleries. Many houses from the National Revival Period have been preserved and other interesting architecture includes the old bridge over the river Vit, built between 1865-66, and the Church of Saint Nicholas (1834) famous for its icons. The Churches of Sveta Parashkeva (1862) and the Holy Trinity (1893) have been declared national monuments of culture.

PLOVDIV

Plovdiv, the country's second largest city, is a district capital in the south, 156 kilometres (96 miles) southeast of Sofia. It is on the river Maritsa in the Plovdiv Hills. It is one of the oldest settlements in Bulgaria with traces of Neolithic, Chalcolithic, Bronze and Early Iron Age communities. In 342 BC the settlement on Trimontium Hill was conquered by Philip II of Macedon and turned into a city with the new name of Philippopolis. Parts of the stone wall still stand today. In AD 45 it was captured by the Romans and over the next 200 years expanded until the fourth century when it played a leading role in the administration of the province of Thrace. Coins were minted from AD 88 and under the Romans the population grew. Aqueducts linked the three hills on which the town stood, bringing in the water supply. Many mosaics and remains from this period have been excavated. The Roman town was known as Trimontium. Under the Byzantines and the Slavs the town expanded and the fortifications were improved. Pupildin, as the town was known, was a scene of many battles and was destroyed completely during the Second Crusade (1189-92). The Bulgarians wrested it back from the Crusaders and over the next 100 years extensive building work took place. For the next two centuries it became a centre for religion, education and culture until it was recaptured by the Turks in 1364, when it became the centre of a region supplying produce and goods for the Turkish army.

During the eighteenth and nineteenth centuries many industries developed, including textiles, and the traders built large houses in the surrounding hills. Because of the town's cosmopolitan nature, many foreign schools, including Greek, Armenian, Turkish and Jewish, were established. It became an international centre of learning. Today food and drink are the main industries, together with mechanical engineering, electronics and metallurgy. It is the centre of a rich agricultural region, especially vines, fruit, vegetables and tobacco.

There are many fine buildings and cobbled streets, as well as numerous churches. The city has many theatres, museums and art galleries, a state philharmonic orchestra, the Trakia Folk Song and Dance Ensemble and many other choirs and cultural groups.

RAZGRAD

A district town in the northeast, 375 kilometres (232 miles) northwest of Sofia, on the banks of the river Beli Lom which crosses the Ludogoric Plateau between 150 and 200 metres (480-640 feet) above sea level. Remains of a Paleolithic settlement, one of the largest excavated in southeast Europe, have been found. Remains from Chalcolithic, Bronze Age and Thracian settlements have also been discovered and it was here that excavations unearthed Bulgaria's largest collection of ancient coins. On the ruins of the Thracian settlement of Abritus a Bulgarian town developed, which flourished until the tenth century. The town was captured by the Turks in 1388 and it became a centre for craftsmen, especially wheelwrights, potters, tanners, cutlers and furriers. The town was liberated in 1878 and its leading industries today are food, porcelain, pharmaceuticals and mechanical engineering.

The town has sports and tourist facilities, museums, theatres and an art gallery. Of architectural interest are the buildings from the National Revival Period and those remaining from the Turkish rule. The Church of Saint Nicholas (1860) is a national monument, as are the clock tower (1764), the Ibrahim Pasha Mosque (1614), and the 1885 High School.

RUSSE

Russe is a district town in the northeast, 331 kilometres (205 miles) northeast of Sofia, high on the terraced bank of the Danube. Wine production is particularly important and has been for centuries. Many settlements dating back to the Upper Paleolithic period have been found, including fortified Thracian villages. During the first century AD a Roman castle was built, known as Sexaginta Prista ("sixty ships") because it was the base for the Lower Danube fleet. In 1388 the town fell to the Turks but because of its position so close to the Danube, it continued to be an important trading centre having links with many towns. Industries today are mechanical engineering, food, textiles and chemicals. There are also shipyards and a number of research institutes. Agriculture is important, especially vines, fruit and livestock. The port of Russe is still a major freight centre.

There are many theatres, museums, art galleries and exhibition halls, a symphony orchestra and dance groups. Of interest architecturally are the old buildings including the Lom public baths, the Church of the Holy Trinity (1632), and many of the old buildings noted for their wood carvings. It was the first place in Bulgaria to have European-style public houses and restaurants and Viennese street lamps, and there are many fine examples of neo-Baroque and neo-Renaissance architecture.

SHUMEN

Shumen is a district town in the northeast, 381 kilometres (236 miles) northeast of Sofia. It is in the eastern foothills of the Shumen Plateau 180 metres (576 feet) above sea level, and the centre of a wine growing region. The plateau has traces of settlements dating back to 5,000 BC and a Roman town surrounded by high walls was built on the site of a Thracian settlement. The town has always been fortified because of its strategic importance. In the eleventh and twelfth centuries the town was known as Misionis and in 1388 was captured by the Turks. In the middle of the last century it was the centre of Bulgarian culture. The country's first orchestra was founded here in 1851, and the Bulgarian National Theatre made its debut in 1856. It was also the home of the country's first brewery.

Leading industries today are food and drink, tailoring, engineering and woodworking. Wine production plays a major role in the local agriculture, together with pigs, fodder crops and vegetables. There is a teachers' training college, several colleges and institutes of higher education, theatres, museums, art galleries and an opera house. Of archaeological interest is the Shumen fortress to the west of the town, and architectural treasures include the Tombul Mosque (1744), the old bazaar and clock tower (1740), and many buildings from the National Revival Period.

SILISTRA

Silistra is a district town in the northeast, 443 kilometres (274 miles) northeast of Sofia. It is situated on the right bank of the Danube, bordering Romania, at an altitude of 30 metres (96 feet) above sea level. There are remains of Thracian settlements nearby, one of which was the site of the ancient town of Durostorum, a fortified town of great importance for many centuries because of its strategic position on the river. From the eighth to tenth centuries is had the Slav name of Druster, and when Bulgaria was converted to Christianity in AD 864, it became the seat of the Patriarch. It fell to the Turks in 1413 but by then had already acquired its present name of Silistra. Between 1413 and 1940 the town was part of Romania and was not returned to Bulgaria until after the signing of the Treaty of Craiova.

Today, the major industries are food, engineering, metal working, computer technology and woodworking. Viticulture is important and other agriculture includes fruit, vegetables, livestock and fish farming. The town has a busy port, a theatre, an art gallery and museums, and there are many archaeological sites of interest, including the remains of a late-Classical tomb, the ancient medieval fortress and settlement, and a necropolis.

SLIVEN

A district town in the east, 279 kilometres (173 miles) east of Sofia. It is in the centre of a wine growing region, in the southern foothills of the eastern part of the Balkan Range at an altitude of 260 metres (832 feet) above sea level. The nearby mineral springs were declared a national spa in 1967. The town developed as a fortified trading post during Roman times and remains of the walls and fortifications have been found as well as traces of a Roman basilica and necropolis. In the twelfth century the town was known as Istilifunus and was a religious centre – more than 20 monasteries were built during this time. The ruins survive of a medieval castle overlooking the town, destroyed together with the monasteries when the Turks invaded. The town specialized in armaments, ironmongery and agricultural machinery. At one stage 100,000 rifle barrels a year were being made, and the town had 70 textile mills, 66 water mills, 984 workshops and 35 inns, but almost all were destroyed by the Turks during the Russo-Turkish war (1877-78). After the town was liberated in 1878, it became one of the country's main textile centres and the first Bulgarian textile trade union was established there in 1892.

Today, its industries include food, textiles, glass and mechanical engineering. The town is the centre for the wine growing region, but fruit and livestock are also important. There are theatres, museums and an art gallery and many interesting buildings, including the Church of Saint Sophia (1808), and the Churches of Saint Demetrios (1831) and Saint Nicholas (1834).

SMOLYAN

This is a district centre in the south, 258 kilometres (159 miles) southeast of Sofia. It is on the river Cherna, in the Western Rhodopes, at an altitude of 900 metres (2,880 feet) above sea level. In 1963 the town and its surroundings were declared a national mountain health resort. The ancient Thracian tribe of Koilaleti inhabited the area but were conquered by the Romans in 11 BC. In the seventh century Slavs populated the area, and at the beginning of the eleventh century the region was captured by the Turks. During the Ottoman rule the entire population was converted to Islam, and the region re-named Aha Chelebi after the court doctor to Sultan Selim 1. Although liberated from the Turks in 1878, the town was returned to the Sultanate as part of the Treaty of Berlin, and was not finally restored to Bulgaria until October 1912.

Leading industries today are food processing, mechanical engineering, mining and woodworking. The area's agriculture includes potatoes, fodder crops, fruit, tobacco and perennial plants. A lot of livestock is also kept. The town has theatres, a museum, an art gallery and a planetarium, and many well preserved old buildings dating back to the sixteenth century. Also of interest are Saint George's Church (1858), with its murals and wood carvings (the spire was added in 1904), the Church of the Holy Spirit (1891), and the Brahom Bey's Konak (Town Hall). There are many other fine churches and historic buildings.

SOFIA

This is the capital of the People's Republic of Bulgaria. It is the country's largest city, a spa, resort and tourist centre, as well as the political and administrative heart of the country. It is the centre of the Greater Sofia Settlement System, which incorporates 12 municipalities in the city, as well as three towns and 34 villages in the surrounding district.

The town is situated in the west, in the southern part of the Sofia valley and at the foot of the Vitosha and Lyulin Mountains, at an altitude of 550 metres (1,760 feet). After Madrid, it is the highest European capital and is also one of the oldest cities in Europe with traces of Neolithic and Chalcolithic settlements. A Thracian town is known to have existed from the eighth century, near the thermal springs in the centre of the present day city. In the fifth century BC it was part of the Kingdom of Odrisae, and a Thracian settlement grew up in the first century BC which was taken over by the Romans in 29 BC. They called it Serdica, after the Serdi, the Thracian tribe. It was later re-named Ulpia Serdica and the city quickly grew in importance because it was on the crossroads of the trading routes both between the Danube and the Aegean, and central Europe and Byzantium. The town was fortified even after being absorbed into the Eastern Roman Empire in the fourth century. In AD 809 it was captured by Khan Krum and absorbed into the Bulgarian state with the new name of Sredets, before being recaptured by the Turks in 1018, and again in 1382. It was declared Bulgaria's capital on April 3 1879 and its population grew rapidly, as did its industrial base, helped by the introduction of electricity in 1900.

In 1944 more than a third of the country's industrial capacity was concentrated in Sofia but much of this was destroyed in an Allied bombing raid of that year. Today it is again the country's main industrial centre producing and manufacturing a wide range of products from construction materials to medical equipment, food to plastic, tyres to books. Agriculture in the surrounding countryside includes a pedigree cattle breeding station and farms producing meat, dairy products and vegetables.

The city boasts many fine buildings and cultural centres. The first monastery school opened in the fifteenth century, the Sofia School of Literature was founded in the sixteenth century and the Bulgarian Literary Society (later to become the Bulgarian Academy of Sciences) was established in 1869. The Sofia University was founded in 1888. Today, Sofia has many of the country's leading higher education colleges, research centres, institutes and medical complexes. It houses the National Library, National Theatre and Opera Houses, and scores of professional and amateur dramatic, operatic and dance companies. There are seven art galleries, a botanical garden, a zoo and 34 museums. Sofia is also the venue for many national and international cultural festivals each year. More than 700 buildings in the capital have been declared of national architectural importance, and the areas of ancient Serdica and medieval Sredets have been declared archaeological reserves.

STARA ZAGORA

Stara Zagora is a district town in southern Bulgaria, 231 kilometres (142 miles) southwest of Sofia. It is the centre of a wine growing region in the southeast foothills of the Surnena Gora Mountains at an altitude of 200 metres (640 feet) above sea level. Near the town is the Bereket Mound, which was inhabited by Neolithic, Chalcolithic and Bronze Age tribes, and later a Thracian fortress was built there. The Thracians built the settlement of Berbe on the site of the present town in the fifth century BC which was replaced by the Roman town of Augusta Trajana built in the second century AD. In the fifth and sixth centuries it was attacked by Huns, Avars and Slavs and repeatedly razed to the ground. Rebuilt by the Turks in the eighth century it was named Irinopolis, after the Byzantine Empress Irina, but its name was changed several times afterwards. It was burnt to the ground again during the nineteenth-century Russo-Turkish war and had to be completely rebuilt.

Today industries include food, fertilizers, textiles, mechanical and chemical engineering, brewing and tobacco. Viticulture, cereals, livestock and vegetables are the main agricultural sectors. The town has theatres, an opera house, a museum, an art gallery, an observatory and symphony orchestra. There are traces of Roman mosaics, buildings and baths to be seen, as well as the remains of a fifteenth century Eskai Mosque.

TOLBUHIN

This is a district town in the northeast, 512 kilometres (317 miles) northeast of Sofia, on the Dobrudja Plateau, about 200 metres (640 feet) above sea level. Traces of Roman settlements have been found and in the fifteenth century, a settlement called Hadjioglu-Pazardjik developed as a trading centre. After the Treaty of Berlin it was ceded to Romania and was not returned to Bulgaria until 1940.

Today the main industries are food and drink, engineering, textiles, footwear and furniture. The region specializes in cereals and livestock, especially pigs and poultry. The town has theatres, a museum and an art gallery, and has a celebrated brass band and choir. There are many well preserved buildings from the National Revival Period.

TARGOVISHTE

A district town in the northeast, 340 kilometres (211 miles) northeast of Sofia, it stands on the banks of the River Vrana in the northern foothills of the Preslav Mountains, 150 metres (480 feet) above sea level and is the centre of a wine growing region. There are traces of a Chalcolithic settlement and a Byzantine fortress was built there in the fifth or sixth century. The town was founded in the sixteenth century and became a major crafts centre over the next 300 years. Today it is an industrial and agricultural centre. Industries include food and drink, mechanical engineering and wood processing. Main agricultural sectors are vines, market gardening, fruit and livestock. There is a theatre and museums, and Torgovishte is the home of the Mizia Folk Song and Dance Ensemble. Notable buildings include the church built in 1851 by masters of the Tryvana School and houses from the National Revival Period.

VARNA

Varna is a district city in the northeast, by the Bay of Varna on the Black Sea, 469 kilometres (290 miles) northeast of Sofia. It is the centre of a wine growing region, and was declared a national seaside resort in 1950. One of the oldest settlements in Bulgaria, artefacts dating back to the middle and late Paleolithic periods have been found. There have been settlements and towns on the site ever since. Roman villas and baths have been excavated, also fourth century Christian basilica, as well as churches and other buildings from the nineth and tenth centuries. In the eighth century, the town was fortified and traces of the wall remain. Under the Greeks, the town was called Odessos, but became Varna in the seventh century when it came under Slav control. It was constantly attacked by the Turks and came under Byzantine rule in 1389 when it was made the strongest fortress on the west

Black Sea coast. It was liberated in 1878.

Today industry, tourism and vines are all important and the main industries are shipyards, cotton and textile mills, canneries, breweries and fish processing plants. The surrounding countryside is devoted to vineyards, orchards, poultry and dairy farms. There is an airport and a busy harbour plus many colleges, theatres, an opera house, museums, an aquarium, a planetarium, a symphony orchestra and sports facilities. Buildings of interest are the Church of the Holy Virgin (1883), which dominates the skyline, the Euxinograd Palace (1886), the Renaissance-style High School (1901), and the port constructed in 1906. The Golden Sands and Druzhba resorts are to the north of the town.

VELIKO TARNOVO

This is a district town in the central part of the north. It is in the centre of a wine growing region 241 kilometres (149 miles) northeast of Sofia, built up on the steep sides of the Tarnovo Gorge on the River Yantra. It is an ancient town and remains of settlements have been found dating back to the late Paleolithic period. The surrounding hills still have remains of fortress walls, gates and towers dating back to the early Byzantine period. The town became the capital of the Second Bulgarian State. Access to the heavily fortified town was through three gateways and a drawbridge, and it became famous for its crafts and architecture. Medieval coins of many nations have been found in excavations confirming the town's importance as an international trading centre. Many of the palaces and churches still remain. In 1393 the Turks captured the city and destroyed it. It was not until the seventeenth century that people returned and its reputation as a crafts centre grew again. After liberation from the Turks in 1877, the National Assembly met here, and the country's constitution was proclaimed in Tarnovo.

Today the main industries are food, machinery and textiles. Winemaking is the most important agricultural activity, together with dairy cattle, fruit and vegetables. It has theatres, a museum and an art gallery and many buildings of architectural importance. The Church of Saint Dimiter dates back to 1115, the Church of the Holy Martyrs was built in 1230. Many buildings survive from the National Revival Period, and there are the spectacular remains of the fortress on Tsarevets Hill.

VIDIN

A district town in the far northwest, 199 kilometres (123 miles) northwest of Sofia. It is in a wine growing area on the right bank of the Danube in the Vidin Plain. Prehistoric settlements have been found and Vidin was founded more than 2,000 years ago as the Roman fortress of Bononia, built on the site of a Thracian settlement. It became Vidin in the First Bulgarian State (681-1018) and was captured by the Turks in 1396. It remained a major economic centre famous for its iron, gold and silver smiths. It was liberated in 1878 and remained a crafts centre, the first factory not opening until the 1920s. The main industry today is chemicals, but there is a tyre plant, tobacco factory, cannery and clothing works. Grapes, vines, cereals, cattle and pigs are the main agricultural products and there is a viniculture and viticulture research station.

There is a busy port and marina, theatres, museums and art galleries. Much of the old city and its sixteenth and seventeenth century buildings remain. The Church of Saint Petka has paintings dating from 1633. Other buildings of interest are the Turkish Town Hall, mosque and Pazvantoglu's Library, Saint Demetrius' Cathedral and Baba Vida Fortress, now a museum.

VRATSA

Vratsa is a district centre in the northwest, 116 kilometres (61 miles) northeast of Sofia. It is in the centre of a winemaking region by the Vratsa Gorge on the River Reka at 370 metres (1,184 feet) above sea level. Remains of late Paleolithic settlements have been found and Thracian rulers were buried here in the fourth century BC. Many other relics from the twelfth to fourteenth centuries have also been discovered.

The town started as a fortified trading post in the Second Bulgarian State and became a crafts centre under Ottoman rule. The Bulgarian Cavalry was founded here in 1877, the year the town was liberated. Today, its leading industries are chemicals, mechanial engineering, metal working, food, textiles and wood working. Wine and livestock are the main agricultural products.

The town has a local history museum, a theatre, an art gallery and philharmonic orchestra. Of architectural interest are two defence towers (late seventeenth century), and the Churches of the Ascension and Saint Nicholas, which have remained virtually unchanged since the 1840s.

YAMBOL

Yambol, or Jambol, is in the southeast, 304 kilometres (188 miles) from Sofia. It is the centre of a wine growing region on the Tundja river, about 100 metres (320 feet) above sea level. There are remains of settlements dating back to Neolithic times and ruins of a Roman and Medieval fortress. From the eleventh century, it was a heavily fortified town but was captured by the Turks in 1373 after a long siege. Today its main industries are textiles, mechanical engineering, food, construction and wood crafts. There is a large winery and the surrounding fertile land supports vineyards, cereals, fruit, sugar beet and market gardening.

It is an education centre with technical high schools, museums, an opera house, a theatre, an orchestra and a Thracian folk and dance ensemble. Of interest architecturally is the covered sixteenth century bazaar in the centre of the town, the fifteenth century Eski Mosque and Saint George's Church (1737) with its wooden iconostasis. Near the town are the remains of the Roman fortress and the Monastery of Saint Spass.

WINE
STATISTICS

Purchased raw materials (grapes in tonnes) and production of table wines (in thousands of litres)

Regions	1960	1965	1970	1975	1980	1985	1986	1987
Northern								
grapes	81,398	216,344	96,849	76,594	51,414	71,173	88,608	82,805
wine	52,094	138,460	61,014	48,254	32,390	44,838	55,823	52,995
Eastern								
grapes	42,495	112,430	154,312	157,007	204,037	161,339	154,516	141,049
wine	28,046	75,328	95,673	102,054	132,624	104,870	100,435	93,897
Sub-Balkan								
grapes	15,013	32,815	32,067	22,589	43,206	38,883	38,640	39,596
wine	9,908	21,657	19,881	14,231	27,651	24,885	24,729	25,341
Southern								
grapes	49,239	131,214	137,909	126,301	183,070	156,573	126,035	175,667
wine	30,528	78,728	84,124	78,306	115,334	90,075	78,141	108.913
Southwestern								
grapes	5,710	6,981	9,748	18,155	28,445	17,456	31,240	21,655
wine	3,597	4,258	5,848	11,437	17,960	10,997	19,681	13,642
Total								
grapes	193,855	499,784	430,885	400,646	510,172	445,424	439,039	460,768
wine	124,173	318,431	266,540	254,282	325,959	275,663	278,809	294,787

Exports

Sweden

Exports to Sweden started in 1969 with traditional Bulgarian varieties – Misket from the Sungurlare region and Mavrud from the Plovdiv region. In the early 1980s, Cabernet Sauvignon from the Souhindol-Pavlikeni micro-region, Merlot from around Haskovo and Gamza from Pleven were successfully introduced. Sales of Bulgarian wines to Sweden topped 8,500,000 bottles in 1987.

Annual exports figures are (in bottles):

1975	2,447,000
1980	2,747,000
1981	2,700,000
1982	2,941,000
1983	4,443,000
1984	2,445,000
1985	2,649,000
1986	7,100,000
1987	8,500,000

Finland

Exports to Finland started in 1970. Initially only the traditional Bulgarian varieties were exported for this market – Melnik from Blagoevgrad and Mavrud from Plovdiv. In the mid-1980s, Haskavo Merlot and Shumen Chardonnay were successfully introduced.

Annual export figures are (in bottles):

1975	643,000
1980	1,639,000
1981	1,403,000
1982	1,623,000
1983	1,400,000
1984	1,008,000
1985	647,000
1986	975,000
1987	1,081,000

Belgium

Exports started in 1965 and only bottled wines were sold. The main varieties are Trakia, Mavrud, Cabernet Sauvignon, Gamza and Tamjanka. At the beginning of 1988 varietal wines were introduced – Merlot, Cabernet, Chardonnay and Riesling, as well as the Reserve wines from Cabernet, Chardonnay and Melnik.

Annual exports figures are (in bottles):

1975	92,000
1980	none
1981	4,000
1982	14,000
1983	none
1984	1,000
1985	39,000
1986	67,000
1987	76,000

Holland

Vinimpex entered the Dutch market in the early 1970s. Only bottled wines were exported, the main varieties being Misket, Tamjanka, Riesling, Cabernet, Mavrud, Trakia, Mecha Kruv and Gamza. At the start of 1988 Haskovo Merlot, Cabernet from Souhindol and Shumen Riesling were introduced together with Bourgas Aligoté, Preslav Chardonnay and the Reserve wines of Cabernet, Chardonnay and Melnik.

Annual export figures are (in bottles):

1975	18,000
1980	38,000
1981	105,000
1982	293,000
1983	227,000
1984	109,000
1985	81,000
1986	174,000
1987	203,000

Canada

Exports of Bulgarian bottled wines to Canada started in 1968 and were soon included in the lists of all the ten Provincial Liquor Boards. Initially 90 per cent of sales came from only two wines – the local Gamza and Hemus, a medium dry wine based on the Misket grape variety. These wines now account for about 50 per cent of sales having lost ground to the noble varieties like Cabernet and Chardonnay.

Annual export figures are (in bottles):

1975	600,000
1980	620,000
1981	370,000
1982	220,000
1983	320,000
1984	240,000
1985	170,000
1986	290,000
1987	660,000

In 1987 the exports to the different provinces were: British Columbia 290,000 bottles, Alberta 190,000 bottles, Quebec 40,000 bottles, Ontario 40,000 bottles and others 40,000 bottles. About two-thirds of all the exports go to Western Canada. The proportion of white and red wines is 60/40. White wines include Hemus (180,000 bottles in 1987) and Chardonnay (130,000 bottles). Reds are represented by three varieties, Gamza (130,000 bottles), Merlot (80,000 bottles) and Cabernet (60,000 bottles). There are also some exports of AOC wines (about 20,000 bottles a year), as well as Pliska wine brandy (about 20,000 bottles in 1987). All the wines exported to Canada are sold under the Sophia label and are all from Declared Geographical Regions.

United States

Since 1979 Bulgarian bottled wines have been exported to the United States through Pepsico Wines and Spirits International (Monsieur Henri Wines). As part of the exchange agreement of pepsi-concentrate is imported into Bulgaria. Bulgarian bottled wines are sold under the Trakia brand name, developed especially for the United States market. Originally the range consisted of just two varietal wines, now it contains seven.

Annual export figures are (in bottles):

1979	20,400
1980	1,538,400
1981	1,354,800
1982	1,138,800
1983	2,184,000
1984	2,232,000
1985	1,956,000
1986	2,112,000
1987	1,946,400

Sales of wines have dropped over the last three years to around 160,000-170,000 cases a year because of the fall in the exchange rate of the dollar. Work has now started on the importation and distribution of high quality Bulgarian wines – the second Trakia line.

INDEX

The following recipes are from *The Balkan Cookbook* by Vladamir Mirodan: Cucumbers in buttermilk dressing, Cheese soufflé, Yoghurt dressing, Potato charba with whey, Hot bean soup, Pheasant with cherries, Dobrudja kebabs, Stuffed vine leaves, Stuffed cabbage leaves Bulgarian aubergines, Green beans Plakia, Gardener's Moussaka, Plums in Bulgarian brandy and Bulgarian bitter cherry sherbert.